Motivating Teen and Preteen Readers

How Teachers and Parents Can Lead the Way

Jeffrey Pflaum

ROWMAN & LITTLEFIELD EDUCATION
A division of
ROWMAN & LITTLEFIELD PUBLISHERS, INC.
Lanham • New York • Toronto • Plymouth, UK

Published by Rowman & Littlefield Education
A division of Rowman & Littlefield Publishers, Inc.
A wholly owned subsidiary of The Rowman & Littlefield Publishing Group, Inc.
4501 Forbes Boulevard, Suite 200, Lanham, Maryland 20706
www.rowmaneducation.com

Estover Road, Plymouth PL6 7PY, United Kingdom

British Library Cataloguing in Publication Information Available

Library of Congress Cataloging-in-Publication Data

Pflaum, Jeffrey, 1945–
  Motivating teen and preteen readers : how teachers and parents can lead the way /
Jeffrey Pflaum.
      p. cm.
  Includes bibliographical references.
  ISBN 978-1-61048-032-1 (cloth : alk. paper)—ISBN 978-1-61048-033-8 (pbk. : alk.
paper)—ISBN 978-1-61048-034-5 (electronic)
  1. Teenagers—Books and reading. 2. Preteens—Books and reading. 3. Teenagers—
Education—United States. 4. Preteens—Education—United States. 5. Reading—United
States. 6. Parent-teacher relationships—United States. I. Title.
  Z1037.A1P48 2011
  028.5'5—dc23   2011016173

∞™ The paper used in this publication meets the minimum requirements of
American National Standard for Information Sciences—Permanence of Paper
for Printed Library Materials, ANSI/NISO Z39.48-1992.

Printed in the United States of America

We are now in want of an art to teach how books are to be read rather than to read them.

—Benjamin Disraeli

Contents

Preface for Educators, Parents, and Readers of All Ages

HELLO READING LIFE, WHEREVER YOU ARE

Do you read to your children? Did your parents read to you as a child? Do you read before going to bed at night? When is your time to read? Where do you like to read? What are your favorite books?

Is reading an illuminating solitude? How is reading an escape from everyday life? Does the outside world fade away after reading the first word of a book? Has a book ever been your mentor or coach? Do you think of books as loyal friends living inside your mind?

Does reading life affect real life? Has reading changed your awareness? Is reading about open-mindedness? Do you experience freedom while reading? Do you feel like you're inside an imaginary reading bubble when reading? How can reading be a return to your self?

Are sad and depressing books worth reading? Do you read poetry for enlightenment, pleasure, and to your kids? Do you read fantasies just to trigger your imagination? Do you remember reading boring textbooks in school? Can you recall taking standardized reading tests? What early reading experiences are fondly remembered?

Is reflection part of your daily reading-life experiences? Do you contemplate thoughts and ideas while reading? Can reading also be described as an entertainment center in the mind? How is reading all about self-communication? Why is reading a magical, mysterious process?

How important are words to you? Do you ever ponder or meditate on a word? Are words your friends or enemies? What do words trigger in the mind? Can you recall the last time a word took you on an adventure ride through your imagination?

Can reading and books inspire and change lives? Can reading bring peace? What are reading's "lonely pleasures"? How much energy and passion do you bring to reading? What attitude is communicated to your kids about reading, books, and words? Are you a lifelong reader? Is reading fun for you?

So, discussion leaders, where are you? What responses ran through your mind as you read this laundry list of questions on reading life? Did you, while reading the questions, take a moment or a side trip to: *stop, recall, reflect, and think* about answers? This is what *Motivating Teen and Preteen Readers* is about: jumpstarting the brain with diverse, mindful, challenging questions that need answers to reconnect readers of all kinds—the struggling, reluctant, and outstanding—to a new vision that reenergizes reading life and creates a passion for reading.

The list of questions touches upon some key topics and ideas featured in *Motivating Teen and Preteen Readers*. Examples are:

- reading as an enlightening solitude;
- reading as a counselor and friend;
- connections between reading and real life;
- reading books and changing awareness;
- reading and the feeling of freedom;
- reading as a return to the self;
- the effects of early reading experiences on reading life;
- the reflection-contemplation connection to reading;
- reading and intrapersonal communication;
- reading as a magical, mystery voyage through the mind;
- the significance of and creativity in words; and
- passion as an attitude toward lifelong reading.

By asking diverse questions and receiving many different written responses, and then continuing the dialogue with expansive, follow-up questions into reading life, you develop in adolescents, as discussion leaders, an intrinsic motivation to read. Kids will read because they want to read.

The four books of questions in *Motivating Teen and Preteen Readers* will:

- make young people aware of their reading lives;
- help them reflect on their reading experiences and worlds;
- generate inner or self-motivation to read *and* write;
- impact reading and reading life in meaningful ways; and
- empower adolescents to take responsibility for their reading.

Preface for Students
Dazzling Your Mind with Reading

From the first moment you hear a new CD or song, or see the awesome image on the latest DVD you bought, or the videogame that pops up in front of your eyes on the monitor, you get hooked, all lit up, ready to rock 'n' roll. The mind and body tune into sights, sounds, and blazing action—whether it's a great song, an amazing movie, or your best game, you're coming home, rambling down the road of chills, thrills, and spills, reveling in that instant lightning flash of excitement. Everything's buzzing, and yes, you're definitely going to fry those brains tonight and have a lot of fun doing it. Yeah, yeah, yeah, you're far into that dream world, the wonder-world that keeps you feeling good, going faster, faster, zoom, zoom, zoom—and why shouldn't you feel good?

But what about reading and books—where do they fit in this sweet picture of fun and games? How do they connect with the speeding electronic, technological, and outrageous visual world that's firing up your brains right now? Do they belong to the same universe and operate on the same channel?

Think about it: the second you open up a book and your fingers touch its pages, a feeling triggers your inner life as you beam down on the first word, and then it's blast off, or really, blast in, to your reading world. Almost magically, you leave the outside world behind and you're off to another reality, the virtual reality of reading.

Your reading self takes over quickly: it has been waiting along with an imaginary inner or mind's eye to help scan, find, and create pictures from words. And don't forget the imaginary narrator who tells or reads the story as images dart across an imaginary TV screen in the mind's magic reading theater, where shows, plays, dramas, and documentaries take place.

Characters, settings, conversations, and facts (data, knowledge, and news) bombard your imagination. This visualized, make-believe, invisible dream world is made visible through the enchantment, mystery, and hypnotic experience of reading.

And so there you are, inside your reading world, thinking thoughts, feeling feelings, seeing mind-pictures, off on a pleasure cruise that begins with a touch, making contact with a book, a piece of paper. After reading that very first word, boom, bang, bam, you slide into one of the millions of galaxies of writers' imaginations, where you meet, energize, challenge, and re-create your own imagination. You are wherever you read: you are in that world, in your world, in that moment, present inside your head, and psyched up because you experience the peaceful solitude of reading, a place where stories, histories, and fantasies illuminate and intrigue your mind.

Welcome to true reading.

Welcome to an honest and loyal friend.

Welcome to your reading.

Acknowledgments

I want to thank everyone who gave their time to review and help put together *Motivating Teen and Preteen Readers: How Teachers and Parents Can Lead the Way.*

Thanks Tom Koerner (vice president of Rowman & Littlefield Education) for accepting the manuscript and expanding it into the book it is today. Thanks Kristina Mann (acquisitions editor) for your insightful comments, editing, and relaxed approach.

Thanks especially to James Jajac for his time and effort to create twelve incredible drawings and an outstanding book cover: they demonstrate how the power of illustration humanizes the book's concepts and strategies for motivating adolescent readers. This talented artist-cartoonist is now involved in teaching art education in the schools.

The source of my projects in reading, writing, thinking, creativity, and poetry involving intrinsic motivation comes from the works of Dr. Edward de Bono on "lateral thinking" (see the bibliography). Many years ago he referred to my method of inspiring thinking and poetry writing as "the trigger method of creativity." Dr. de Bono has written sixty-two books in the area of thinking and created courses that teach thinking as a skill, essential for all levels of educators, business leaders, and parents. (His website is http://edwdebono.com.)

A must-read for educators is Sylvia Ashton-Warner's classic book, *Teacher* (see the bibliography), which discusses an organic approach to learning and became the root for my views on self- or inner-motivation as a key to stimulating reading and writing.

I am truly grateful to Dr. Sally Humble (editor, writer, teacher of English/ American literature, and writing instructor) for her honest, exacting analysis and critique of the book's organization, structure, and content: it has made a huge, positive impact on the final version of the manuscript.

Thank you Arun Toke (editor/publisher of *Skipping Stones, A Multicultural Children's Magazine*) for your straightforward, in-depth comments and suggestions: they benefited and expanded the manuscript. The magazine, *Skipping Stones*, just celebrated its twenty-second year and is one of the top children's publications in the United States today (www.skippingstones.org).

Andy Rotherham (writer of the blog Eduwonk, cofounder and partner of Bellwether Education Partners, education journalist/writer) has taken the time to exchange ideas with me about the current state of teaching. I greatly appreciate his effort to read many of my projects developed over a long teaching career. His comments about my work and book illuminated the challenges teaching, teachers, and education face in the 2000s. (The websites for his blog and organization are www.eduwonk.com and www.bellwethereducation.org, respectively.)

Dr. Deborah Wooten (associate professor of theory and practice in teacher education, University of Tennessee, writer in collaboration with Bernice Cullinan of *Another Jar of Tiny Stars* and *Reading Children's Literature in the Elementary Classroom: An Invitation to Read*) is a teacher of teachers, a process which is an important issue in education today. Her comments about the book validated that my work as a classroom researcher, developer, and experimentalist has created inroads in the area of inspiring kids to read, as well as motivating educators, from neophytes to veterans, to become discussion leaders.

Esther Leiper (poet, writer, artist, "Poet-in-the-Schools") has a strong background in education, English, poetry, writing, and illustration, and with these credentials her positive analysis is valuable and meaningful toward the potential success of the book. Esther's column appears as a regular feature in *WRITERS' Journal Magazine* and she wrote *WIN! POETRY CONTESTS* among many other publications. She is poet laureate of the White Mountains in New Hampshire.

Many thanks to my daughter, Cynthia Pflaum, for your editing, formatting, and technical suggestions that helped make this project easier to complete. Thanks to Mat Pelrine for your assistance with technical and computer program issues that came up in writing the manuscript.

And a million thanks to another Pflaum, my wife, Alberta, an elementary school teacher, tutor, mentor, and reading specialist, for applying her knowledge to keep the book real, practical, timely, and educationally sound. Your incisive suggestions about motivating young readers and teaching the reading process helped me define and redefine the work: my sincere gratitude to a terrific veteran educator who should be recognized for her boundless skills and patience.

Hank Dodel (special education administrator, conflict mediator, and teacher) assisted in expanding the "implementing" sections in the original manuscript. The scheduling and procedures for the different grade levels play a key role in making the project teacher-friendly. As a teacher with much special education experience, his views about the book's potential value for mentally and emotionally challenged kids were well taken and very much appreciated.

Michelle Friedman (parent of middle/high school children) addressed the issue of parents mentoring children who are struggling readers. She felt that if the book's theories about the inner processes of reading were taught, it would help develop comprehension skills and an appreciation for literature. Parents would have enough information to work with reluctant readers who would benefit from these concepts and the many kid-and-parent-friendly questions on reading and writing. Her recommendation about question placement really improved the manuscript's organization.

Thank you Justina Conte (high school English language arts teacher, writer) for your perceptive comments about: the questions' challenging nature pushing kids to become creative and contemplative; power of words and how language stirs up emotions; student-centered approach; parents connecting with teachers when applying the materials to motivate kids at home; project being one of self-discovery and teaching a love of reading; and kids becoming stronger, more confident readers as a result of working on the questions.

Thanks to administrator and teacher, Rosalie Masarof, for an insightful overview of the one year project. Her description of the teacher-friendly approach notes its ease of implementation with minimal prep time needed for engaging students. The project also includes strong culminating activities and questions, where kids have a chance to express their thoughts and feelings about reading experiences via important teacher and student evaluations.

I am grateful to Andrea Volding (administrator, elementary/high school teacher) for her commentary about: the book providing the skill for implementing questioning techniques as a key in her district's current incentives; teachers on any level learning the strategies presented and helping kids see the choice to become life-long readers; and the book as a classroom resource for showing students how to become responsible readers.

Many, many thanks to writing/library teacher Haren Zwiebel for her knowledgeable observations about the materials: designed to get children thinking, a skill often overlooked by the glut of phonic programs currently marketed; based on the assumption that reading is about comprehension, that the interaction between student and text is needed for true reading to take place; start students thinking about reading as well as writing about reading; and spark ways to discuss reading. Also, I want to thank Mike Zwiebel for his technical assistance with processing my six "scary" drawings demonstrating concepts developed in the classroom.

My appreciation to Dara Kaplan (reading coach and classroom teacher) for her comments on how the materials will assist teachers in her schools to motivate students' reading lives: it is a "how-to book" for inspiring kids via questions, a goal of *Motivating Teen and Preteen Readers*.

Thanks to Robert Nussbaum (classroom teacher) for his positive observations about the book: Questions teach students how to use their imaginations and to be transported by the written word. The introduction is a free-standing guide for reigniting teachers' enthusiasm, a basic aim of the book. Questions will stimulate discussion and provide a "template" that functions as an annual lesson plan: it is akin to a "one-stop teaching tool."

Thank you Maureen Comiskey (teacher and parent of middle and high school children) for your comment that filling a house with "beautiful children's books" and reading to them does not always "make" kids like reading. For Maureen, the book is a parents' guide empowering parents to participate in their children's reading development via self-discovery and pre-Socratic methodology to facilitate the process: all purposes of my book.

Finally, my deep appreciation to the great kids of "Sweet 16," who, through their individual and collective worlds, helped make me a better teacher and person. Those experiences will always live in my mind and heart, and for this I am "internally" grateful.

Introduction

Education is the kindling of a flame, not the filling of a vessel.

— Socrates

ONE KEY TO IMPROVING READING: INTRINSIC MOTIVATION

Motivation meant something when I started teaching in an inner-city school in the late 1960s. Thirty minutes to inspire the class, add vocabulary words from basal readers, and the race began. To find the motivation, that channel into a story, became a challenge. After the preliminaries, the room turned quiet, relaxed, yet full of enthusiasm. Look at their eyes, their noses in the books: the kids were off to reading wonderland.

Motivating children to read came mostly from the outside. How can teachers hold students' attention, make them readers and lifelong readers, with less intrusion from the outside? Reading is an internal process, a world of solitude, peace, delight, and grace, after all the oral readings, book clubs, small-group reading, class discussions, and testing. How kids deal with themselves inside their reading worlds and imaginations becomes significant in reading today.

You may want to stop and ask: Who has the time for elaborate internal motivations when I have to raise reading scores? How much thought can I give to my class's reading sanctuaries, let alone their minds and imaginations? Reading in the 2000s is functional: to get grades on standardized tests.

You will get no arguments from me: reading now means drills, skills, and less thrills. And don't forget the electro-techno world. How can reading compete with iPods, video and computer games, DVDs, CDs, and the Internet? Statistics show us losing readers after the fourth grade; in fact, interest in reading decreases through high school. Leisure-time reading goes down for most adolescents to less than ten minutes a day.

To change this situation, return to motivation, not so much from the outside, but from the inside, or to inner or self-motivation. Happy readers entertain themselves in reading's "lonely pleasures" and will continue throughout life. When students search for and learn more about reading experiences, processes, and the imagination where all this stuff resides, they will rejuvenate their reading and reading lives.

MICHAEL, A RELUCTANT READER: HIS TALE BEGINS . . .

Consider the example of Michael, which comes directly out of the author's teaching experience: Michael's father felt frustrated because he bought all sorts of books for his son, who rarely picked up one and read it. "I don't understand it," his father lamented. "I buy him books and books but he never reads them. What am I doing wrong?" The father had hit on one of the primary challenges in reading today: he cannot *make* Michael read, and neither can Michael's teacher. Michael needs to find that motivation comes from inside himself. And that's essentially one big problem in education today: how do teachers and parents *make* them read?

An abundance of research studies proves that intrinsic motivation is more effective than extrinsic motivation. The organic, student-centered, holistic, humanistic approach to reading and reading life works from the inside out. The questioning-and-inquiry technique of *Motivating Teen and Preteen Readers* invites Michael to think about what happens inside himself while he reads—his thoughts and feelings, the images he sees or does not see—and the many reading experiences from the past, his beginnings as a reader. The questions ask about that time when he first learned how to read right up to the present, when he's either enjoying a good reading life or is conflicted about it. Does he enjoy reading or does he prefer being a couch potato who watches TV, plays video/computer games, surfs the Internet, or listens to music CDs? Diverse questions trigger a student's thoughtful responses about his reading life, what it's all about, and how vast a life it can be.

So many books written about reading describe its wonders according to that particular writer. However, the books of questions enable adolescents to search for and discover, independently and collaboratively, the amazing experience of creating their own reading lives. The strategy is age appropriate for preteens and teens because it satisfies their need to question things, to question everything, and their need for autonomy, with less control and extrinsic motivation by teachers, parents, and other adults.

Michael, by writing answers to original, challenging questions, and discussing responses with classmates (and teachers and parents), will discover the extraordinary power of reading. His reflections on reading, the thoughts and feelings he

Illustration 1. Michael, a reluctant reader, surrounded by books.
Illustration by James Jajac.

experiences as he responds to the questions, will help Michael develop greater awareness about his reading life. He will grow as a reader as he defines his own purposes for reading and awakens his own desire to read.

The mental and emotional power of the right question at the right time can change a teen's or preteen's attitude toward reading. All of a sudden the questions cast him off into thought and reflection, making them harbingers of new possibilities.

Visualize this young reader floating in a hot-air balloon through his own mind and imagination. He wanders in an infinite universe of ideas, beliefs, attitudes, opinions, meanings, feelings, images, memories, dreams, and reveries, all triggered by the books of questions on reading and reading life. He stops the balloon to look at the immense landscape and pauses for a moment, an instant in time, to re-view the multitude of reading experiences that happened in a short lifetime. He contemplates the endless roads to take and the possibilities presented to him by the stimulating questions.

Visualizing reading as an imaginary balloon voyage in a world of creative possibilities invites every school-age child (reluctant readers like Michel included) to revive the motivation to read through fresh, organic, realistic choices. If adolescents realize the opportunities brought about by reflecting, thinking, and writing responses to questions, they can rebuild their reading lives and passion for reading through their own creativity with a renewed sense of purpose, focus, and determination. Creativity, once triggered in kids, becomes contagious, and as discussion leaders, teachers and parents should try to connect to the youngster's enthusiasm and keep an open, imaginative attitude toward what the student writes and expresses about the reading life experiences during the discussions.

Michael's simulated journey, from his past to present reading experiences, will begin in a later chapter. At that time, you will find out how the books of questions, potentially, can impact Michael's reading in a positive way. *To be continued. . . .*

ORIGINAL CURRICULA TO DEVELOP INTRINSIC MOTIVATION WITH SUPPORTING RESEARCH

A realistic approach to motivate adolescent readers operates from *within*—call it intrinsic motivation—which helps young people to realize meaning in reading and its improvement through their own design. After thirty-four years of teaching experience, as well as developing innovative and progressive projects in reading, writing, thinking, creativity, poetry, vocabulary, communication, and emotional intelligence, I have discovered empirically that a student's desire, the hunger to read, is fundamental to becoming an effective, independent, confident reader. What is the saying? *"You can lead a horse to water, but . . ."*

The various projects I produced in my classrooms, all using the concept of intrinsic motivation, led to *Motivating Teen and Preteen Readers*. A poetry-writing curriculum started with brainstorming ideas in the form of titles (for poems) using photographs, giant posters, and slides of great artwork. This trigger method showed kids their own creativity, what the mind and imagination were capable of, stimulated thinking and feeling processes, and cranked up their inner or self-motivation to write poetry. Another original project, called "Contemplation Writing," led elementary school children on peaceful journeys of self-discovery via music, writing, and discussion. They learned to enjoy themselves in thought and that they had something important to say, and they motivated themselves to write (prose called "contemplations") about their lives from within: more intrinsic motivation that engaged students to express and discuss personal things with classmates.

Working with intrinsic motivational curricula changes the classroom environment. Adolescents become more self-aware and connected to their inner lives. They see the world with their eyes, mind, imagination, and experience. This is not Buddhism or Eastern philosophy. It's a commonsense approach to learning how to deal with the inside world, to understand and appreciate the outside world, and to make connections between school and daily life.

An article by Nancy Frey and Douglas Fisher titled "You Got More of These?" supports the major goals and rationale behind *Motivating Teen and Preteen Readers* (Frey and Fisher 2006, 7–12). Two significant findings show that intrinsic motivation to read is fundamental and essential to improving literacy in the United States. Cameron and Pierce, in their 1994 study, conclude: "The choice to read independently must ultimately be intrinsically motivated. . . . Several decades' worth of research on intrinsic motivation shows that outside rewards do not increase intrinsic motivation. While extrinsically motivating programs can increase reading for the duration of the program, they have less impact on developing lifelong reading habits" (Cameron and Pierce 1994, 10). Deci and Ryan (1985) found that "closely related to the concept of intrinsic motivation is the development of autonomy, defined as a sense of independence and self-rule. Notably, adolescence is characterized by the drive for autonomy. The need for autonomy is essential to learning as well. A sense of autonomy has been found to be an important influence on academic outcomes" (Deci and Ryan 1985, 11). Furthermore, autonomy and intrinsic motivation work in tandem, according to Boggiano et al. (1992). *Motivating Teen and Preteen Readers* initiates, develops, and expands intrinsic motivation in adolescents as a strategy to create independent, lifelong readers and learners. The four books of questions are a practical application of the above studies. They show connections between triggering intrinsic motivation and the resultant feeling of autonomy. Kids become actively involved, or proactive, from the inside out in their reading and reading lives, satisfying the need for self-determination and independence.

OVERVIEW OF *MOTIVATING TEEN AND PRETEEN READERS*

The four books of questions comprise over a thousand questions on reading and reading life. Students answer questions about their reading experiences—on a schedule determined by teachers and parents—and discuss the written responses afterward. Brief teacher/parent raps (given before and after the mini-lesson question) and mini-discussions (following written responses) examine their experiences. Class or one-to-one (parent-child) conversations bring out reading-world encounters and ideas. Student/child and teacher/parent evaluations—question-naires and optional chats—follow up each completion of thirty to seventy-five questions in the four books. Three final discussion lessons and an epilogue of prompts for brainstorming provide extra teacher/parent assessments on reading, reading life, creativity, imagination, and writing, concluding an entire year's questions, answers, raps, and dialogues. (See the chart/notes for a One-Year Journey through the Books of Questions in "Implementing Workable Schedules/ Strategies for Presenting Questions in Book 1" for further information about how the project works.)

The questions make reading brain-frying fun for adolescents through visual-ization, concentration, thinking, reflection, recalling, drawing, and writing: to look inside and realize reading's magic and mysteries and motivate themselves intrinsically. *Motivating Teen and Preteen Readers* combines innovative with conventional questions, showing kids the possibilities of what reading can do for them and what they can do for reading. Students find the reasons why they read, and think more about their reading lives and how they can change themselves as readers by experimenting. The books of questions supplement classroom and home reading instruction by helping young people connect passion to reading, ruminate on what they read, and gain insight and perspective about themselves as readers and their reading abilities.

PURPOSES AND GOALS OF THE PROJECT

The purposes of the diverse, entertaining, absurd, challenging questions are to:

- Show, describe, and increase awareness of what makes up reading life.
- Search, discover, review, and refresh reading and reading life.
- Motivate reading by heightening understanding of its processes.
- Demonstrate reading as a creative act impacting the imagination.
- Reveal the power of the written, spoken, and imagined word.
- Develop, improve, and expand the response to literature.
- Build self-expression via writing, listening, speaking, and drawing.
- Define reading as a process of self-communication.
- Make the reading-writing and writing-reading connections.

The greater and long-range goals are to:

- Develop critical-thinking skills for comprehension and responding to the questions.
- Deepen students' understanding of reading's affective side.
- Show the power of the mind's magic reading and writing theaters.
- Portray reading as a wonder-world through journeys of self-discovery.

Illustration 2. Reading is an "invitation."

Illustration by James Jajac.

- Reduce test anxiety and reader burnout and dropout.
- Have students take responsibility for their reading and reading lives.
- Enhance the reading environment with collaborating, focused readers.
- Create confident, intrinsically motivated, effective, independent, lifelong readers.
- Stimulate appreciation for reading's importance and meaning in everyday life.

GROWING READERS VIA QUESTIONING
AND FUNDAMENTAL SKILLS FOR LEARNING

After reading a capsule view of the overall project along with its short- and long-range objectives, the question becomes: How can we grow happy, responsive, insightful readers through an inquiry- and passion-based strategy? Some solutions this project offers are:

- Introduce inner or self-motivation to kids with the question-and-answer technique.
- Emphasize a self-directed and self-discovery approach.
- Teach fundamental prerequisite skills or tools needed to enjoy reading and learning.
- Make reading real, practical, vital, and fun by expanding its influence in daily life.

The questioning technique will create positive results because it boosts adolescents' motivation to read, improves their reading, and answers the crucial question: why read? The provocative questions will absorb kids and inspire them to write thoughtful responses. The strategy of asking questions and discussing answers with additional, probing questions from the discussion leader is the key to success in *Motivating Teen and Preteen Readers*.

From my past classroom experimentation, I have found that students don't get bored answering and discussing questions/responses concerning their lives, and that includes reading, reading life, and real life. They enjoy writing responses when taught fundamental prerequisite skills of visualizing, reflecting, creativity, concentration, and contemplation needed to dig up experiences and find answers to questions in reading or any other subject. These basic tools, often taken for granted or not given enough instruction time in school, help kids appreciate the "lonely pleasures" of reading.

The four books of questions will return meaning to reading. They motivate students to make sense out of reading and realize that testing is only a small part of it. By reflecting on and visualizing their lives as readers, they will answer the project's primary question: what's motivation got to do with it? Through the different questions and *self-questioning*, they become aware of their attitude toward reading, for better or worse; learn about their likes/dislikes in reading and books;

open up and expand their reading tastes; become more thoughtful; and make reading a habit and become lifelong readers.

An outgrowth of the inquiry- and passion-based questioning is the link to emotional intelligence. Responding to and discussing a variety of open-ended, imaginative, contemplative questions initiates thinking that increases self-efficacy, self-reliance, self-discipline, self-communication, self-awareness, self-understanding, self-knowledge, self-responsibility, and self-education. Raising students' emotional intelligence quotient (EIQ) is a big step to improving reading comprehension and enjoyment. The questions help them see new opportunities and openings, including connections between reading and living. Adolescents will see reading as one way to realize, advance, reinvent, and change their real lives.

AUDIENCE AND SETTINGS FOR THE BOOKS OF QUESTIONS

The audience for the versatile books of questions on reading and reading life is upper elementary, middle school, high school, and college educators throughout the United States and abroad—in urban, inner-city, suburban, and rural areas—with different levels of teaching experience. Classroom, resource room, remedial reading, gifted/talented, language arts, reading, English, library, special education, and college teachers, as well as literacy coaches, mentors, staff developers, curriculum coordinators, sports and arts teachers, librarians, before/after-school program teachers/tutors, and correctional facility teachers can use the diverse questions to fire up motivation for their particular populations. The project can be presented in professional development sessions and used for preservice and in-service courses for apprentice, neophyte, and veteran teachers alike. *Motivating Teen and Preteen Readers* works in public, charter, private, parochial, and alternative school systems.

The book is also for parents—from the inner-city to suburbia and beyond—who tutor their kids for enrichment purposes, as well as homeschooling parent-teachers. Parents and educators will appreciate that the innovative questions target *all readers*, from below average to gifted students of all ethnic groups and genders; at-risk and disadvantaged children; emotionally handicapped and learning-disabled kids; and they can accommodate any number of students, from one-to-one situations to small/large groups (class size up to forty).

REASONS EDUCATORS WILL APPRECIATE
AND IMPLEMENT THE BOOKS OF QUESTIONS

There are many reasons educators with all levels of teaching experience will value and use *Motivating Teen and Preteen Readers* in their classrooms:

- User-friendly, supplementary reading/reading life questions
- Clear strategy explanations for viewing and improving reading/reading life

- Over a thousand questions to choose from for grades 4 to 9
- Questions are valuable, downtime, transition lessons
- Questions get adolescents thinking about reading as an integral part of daily life
- Questions work with all levels and abilities: from struggling to reluctant readers
- Questions promote cognitive development and make kids independent thinkers
- Unconventional questions naturally generate dynamic, energized discussions
- Comprehension shown in depth: reflectively, emotionally, cerebrally, and visually
- Evaluation questions included for culminating assessments of reading progress
- Flexibility allows it to fit into most instructional schedules and settings
- Adaptable for homeschooling parent-teachers, literacy coaches, mentors, and tutors
- Neophyte teachers' tool for how to motivate a passion to read in students
- Develops thinking, visualization, reflection, and communication skills
- Grows a response to literature by expanding the affective side to reading
- Intrinsic motivation approach creates self-motivated, independent readers
- Trigger method of creativity develops imaginative/inventive young people
- Inner-eye visualization method allows kids to see beyond the mundane in reading
- Frameworks to reading process (inner eye, voice, and ear) create reading pleasure
- 3-D, virtual, holographic approach to reading competes with the electro-techno world
- Stimulates the reading-writing and writing-reading connections
- Improved student awareness of and insight into the reading process and reading life
- Enhances and revitalizes the classroom reading environment
- Literacy seen in humanistic light via inquiry- and passion-based strategies
- Complies with national reading and writing standards
- Timeliness and age-appropriateness help return comfort, passion, and fun to reading

The Mini-Lesson with All Its Parts

Questions focus our thinking. Ask empowering questions like: What's good about this? What's not perfect about it yet? What am I going to do next time? How can I do this and have fun doing it?

—Charles Connolly

WHAT MAKES UP THE MINI-LESSON?

The mini-lesson and all its parts, the rap, question, discussion, and optional homework question, will work for teachers and parents alike. Consistent, efficient presentations will create an environment of intrinsically motivated readers and learners, the main goal of *Motivating Teen and Preteen Readers*. The combination of the mini-lesson's parts will produce successful results in a one-year voyage through the books of questions:

- The rap, before and/or after giving the question, enlightens and inspires.
- The selected questions should be suitable to class/child's needs and desires.
- Discussions revolve around leader's ability to question kids to build, improve, and expand their written and oral responses.
- The homework question (optional) follows up and connects with the in-class question. They are discussed the next day and are as important as the questions asked in school. (More about assigning homework questions will be found in the "Implementation" sections of the books of questions.)

SAMPLE MINI-LESSON: RAP, QUESTION, DISCUSSION, AND HOMEWORK QUESTION

Rap: When you answer any question in *Motivating Teen and Preteen Readers*, take your time to review different reading experiences before writing a response. Many questions will push you to think things-through, to look at more than one experience to get the best possible or a thoughtful answer. Be open to all the pluses and minuses of your experiences to write a truthful response. How you evaluate or judge what has happened to you in your reading life can help you grow it. Relax and have fun in your search for answers, because these questions are not test questions. So enjoy the voyage, your "see cruise" through your mind, memory, and imagination when trying to figure out answers to the questions.

Question: How cool and calm are you when reading? Explain your answer.

Discussion (Discussion leader = DL; Student 1, 2, 3, 4 = S1, S2, S3, S4):

DL: Who would like to read their response to us? Okay, S1, go ahead. . . .

S1: I'm pretty cool when I read. I feel okay, not bothered by anything, kind of re-laxed, you know, just reading the book and getting into things. I can read even if there's a lot of noise and things going on around me. I don't mind—I just get into the book more.

DL (to S1): Why are you so relaxed and cool when you read?

S1: I don't know really. I just don't get uptight because it's only reading. And I like it. . . .

DL (to S1): How do you read with all that noise you describe?

S1: I read and read and keep my mind on the words; the noise fades away once I start.

DL (to S1): Describe "cool" in "I'm pretty cool when I read." What does "cool" mean to you?

S1: Chilled out; don't let things bother me.

DL (to class): Does someone have a question or comments about this written re-sponse?

S2: How do you concentrate with noise around you? I can't do that; it gets annoy-ing, like in my house with my little brother and sister running around screaming. Sometimes I can't take it and just throw the book on the floor and watch TV or play a video game. Then they don't bother me and I'm cooled out.

DL (to S2): So you just give up, quit, and forget about reading?

DL (to class): How do you get back into the book and read when there are dis-tractions?

S3: Say to yourself: "Concentrate harder."

S4: Yeah, more focus, less noise . . . you relax; it's better for reading.

DL (to class): When you say "concentrate harder," you're asking or telling yourself to pay attention and get back in there. Reading is about concentration. Let the noise be a challenge for it. Focus on concentrating, keeping it together so you can read.

Illustration 3.   Discussion leader asks kids to stop, reflect, think, and respond.
Illustration by James Jajac.

S5: If I concentrate harder on reading, will I be cooler and calmer?

S6: Yes, you will be doing what you're supposed to be doing.

DL (to S5, S6, and class): And your concentration will chill and relax you, because that's what it is, like this nice, cool breeze going through your mind when you read and helping you think. If you're not feeling "cool and calm" when reading, do something to change the feelings. For example, sometimes I ask myself questions like: "What am I doing? Why can't I read? Why can't I think? What's going on here?"

DL (to class): How will self-questioning help you relax and read?

S5: If you ask yourself a question, maybe you'll find out why you're not feeling that great.

S6: You will think about how you're feeling. . . .

DL: And?

S5: Maybe change it so you can read feeling less hyper and bothered by everything.

DL (to class): If you're cool and calm when reading, wonderful, but when you don't feel this way, if you feel pressured and tense, for whatever reason, then you should do something about it to change those feelings and get your head back in the book. Focus on being cool, calm, and relaxed when you read. Check yourself out before you start. Know where your head is so you'll understand what you're reading.

Homework question (taken from the books of questions): When is reading sweet peace for you? Explain your answer.

This is it: a mini-lesson with all its parts, including the rap, question, discussion, and (optional) homework question that follows up the class question. Parent discussion leaders should *reimagine* this class dialogue as a one-to-one situation. Similar to classroom teachers, a parent's role in the discussion is to make up impromptu questions in response to the written and oral responses to the mini-lesson question. Discussion questions will spark and advance the conversation. Think about what questions will expand kids' responses and get them deeper into their reading, reading life, and self-motivation. (More information about the questioning technique and discussions is found in this chapter and the "Not-for-Parents-Only Guide to *Motivating Teen and Preteen Readers*" chapter.) Use raps to pump up readers and review key points about the project (call them reminders or reinforcement) before the question is given. Teacher discussion leaders should try to connect homework to class questions. The follow-up question solidifies insights gained from the prior written responses and class discussions. Parents can also assign homework questions to expand knowledge from their one-to-one discussions.

Notes: Homework questions come only after kids are familiar with the question-and-answer process and their written responses show progress and growth. Teachers can assign homework questions on a class website to save time and further develop student understanding of the project. (More information about setting up a class website for giving homework questions is found in "Implementing Workable Schedules/Strategies for Presenting Questions" in Book 2.)

THE RAP IN *MOTIVATING TEEN AND PRETEEN READERS*

Raps before/after asking the mini-lesson question include anything about reading, reading life, question categories, and discussion leaders' personal reading-life experiences (always fun for kids). Talk about: understanding the questions, thinking before writing, responding to questions, supporting answers with reading experiences, stronger versus weaker responses (thoughtful/detailed versus automatic/cursory), improving written responses, obstacles to responding, nongrading of written responses, and concentrating during discussions.

Use raps to introduce the various question categories on reading and reading life prior to giving the day's question. Discussion leaders can also ask students to read *side trips* or *detours* written while responding to questions in *Motivating Teen and Preteen Readers*. The comments can be connected or unconnected to the given question. (More information will come on these rapping points.)

Be their coach and pump kids up during the quickie talks: "Anything you want to do will come from inside you. That's called inner or self-motivation. It's easy to do things you like, but what happens if you're faced with things you're not especially thrilled with such as reading and thinking? How do you motivate yourself?"

Question: How important are raps to trigger adolescent self-motivation?

Answer: Communicating positive thoughts and information to kids about reading life experiences and responding to the books of questions have a cumulative effect as the quickie talks continue throughout the (school) year.

Start an early, introductory rap with a question (not from the books of questions): "What makes up reading life?" Have each student make up a list of ten items connected to reading life. They write whatever comes to mind. Or, instead of individual lists, let the class/child brainstorm responses (fill the board or paper with answers). Everyone will be surprised at the many different responses articulated.

Try "Reading Tales 1 and 2" in your introductory raps: Print out copies or read orally to class/child and discuss them. See what kids think about the descriptions of the reading process. *Ask before reading the tales*: "Describe what each tale says about reading in your own words."

READING TALE 1

Reading is a journey, ride, trek, stroll, sprint, really a cruise, an excursion somewhere in your mind and imagination, a trip to yourself, to your home, to your best friend, a lifelong, never-ending odyssey, a great adventure of fun and seriousness, one that soars with wings and ascends through sky and clouds into the wild blue yonder, one that descends deep, deep into the depths of an ocean whose currents and tides pull you along in a comforting, peaceful light, leaving you with eyes wide open and ears popping with songs and music, alive with the sounds of different storytellers speaking the words you are waiting to hear about phenomenal worlds coming from writers' infinite galaxies, which lead directly to your heart, spirit, and life.

READING TALE 2

Reading helps you travel through your mind word by word, sentence by sentence, paragraph by paragraph, page by page, until you snap the language together and wrap up all those thoughts, images, feelings, meanings, and reflections into one clear, understandable chunk of knowledge and insight. By focusing your mental and emotional energy on words, you find yourself right there, inside a story or piece you're reading. When you feel the vibe from the book or your heartbeat, you're deep inside your reading world called the mind's magic reading theater, living and loving every moment of it, and just like your video games, songs, DVDs, CDs, you let your imagination rock on and on and on. . . .

Note: Read the tales twice (orally) if kids can't follow the different meanings, definitions, and descriptions of reading and the reading process.

TWO APPROACHES FOR MINI-DISCUSSIONS

Mini-discussions of five to ten minutes follow the written responses. Students exchange ideas and experiences on reading. Class dialogues and one-to-one parent-child exchanges describing phenomenal reading worlds become as important as the writing. Let conversations create a flow of thoughts that will affect young people's reading and real lives forever.

Introduce an early mini-discussion with: "Your reading life is a private life that happens inside your mind and imagination. When you read, you communicate with yourself (self-communication) by thinking, feeling, imagining, and experiencing. Our discussions will reveal these private reading worlds, from your awareness of an incredible reading life to an amazing reading process, and inspire a passion for reading and a desire to express your experiences. Exchanging these experiences opens up your reading worlds and helps you appreciate other reading worlds. What you say and how you listen in the discussions will make a difference in your written responses and in reading ability."

Two suggested approaches for mini-discussions are: student-centered approach and teacher/parent-directed approach. In the student-centered approach students read aloud written responses. Get in as many as possible in the short time frame. The strategy helps break the ice for discussions; it ends students' hesitancy to talk about their experiences. As kids listen to classmates' responses, it gets easier to say things. The dialogues become a way to describe, compare, and incorporate different reading ideas, attitudes, and experiences into their own.

Recap student-centered discussions with your questions: "What did you learn about your friends' reading lives? Did their experiences tell you something about your reading? Did you find out anything new or unusual about reading?"

Note for parents: To use a student-centered approach, ask your child to reread responses silently and orally after writing about five answers, and then adapt and apply the above discussion questions. However, one-to-one mini-discussions work mostly with the upcoming teacher- or parent-directed approach.

Teacher/parent-directed approach: This teacher/parent-as-discussion-leader strategy probes written responses with questions to increase understanding of reading/reading life. Also, when responses fall short, question the writer and class about them. Encourage others to ask the writer questions. Let the class collaborate to fill in the missing pieces. The approach clarifies and improves responding. Use discussions to motivate imaginative written responses and illuminate reading. *Think*: How can discussion leaders guide kids to meaningful, exciting, and entertaining reading worlds?

Sample general discussion questions for teacher/parent-directed approach:

- Did you understand your classmate's response?
- Did the response answer the question?
- Is it detailed enough?
- Did the writer stop too soon?
- Could she add anything to make the answer more complete?
- What feelings, thoughts, and pictures came to your mind after listening to the answer?
- Did her responses make you think about your response?
- Did her answers make you think about your reading and reading life?

Note for parents: Adapt and ask the above questions, for example: "Did your response answer the question? Could you add anything? What feelings, thoughts, and pictures came to mind after reading your response?" (Parents and teachers can find more information about discussion and the questioning technique used in the "Not-for-Parents-Only Guide to *Motivating Teen and Preteen Readers*.")

Vary the approach from discussion to discussion (for teachers): Make one day student-centered (more oral readings, less questioning) and switch to a teacher-directed approach (more questioning) the next day. Or switch the approach within any discussion, where students read several entries orally (with no questions), and then, intermittently, choose responses that need work or are exceptional and question the writer and class about them.

The sample mini-lesson used a teacher-directed approach (which is the most frequently used strategy for whole class mini-lessons): a response was read orally followed by teacher discussion questions delving further into it. If this fictitious lesson were extended, other responses would have been read aloud and expanded through the questioning technique.

Notes for teachers and parents: Teachers should pick their spots, that is, a meaningful response connecting with most students' experiences and expand on it via the questioning technique. After listening to many different answers, teacher discussion leaders will know which approach to use or a combination of the approaches. Parents, on the other hand, would stick to a parent-directed approach to keep the dialogue going in a one-to-one situation.

IDEAS AND CONCEPTS FEATURED IN MINI-DISCUSSIONS

The organic approach of *Motivating Teen and Preteen Readers* reveals what kids experience inside when they read. In discussions and raps, model and illustrate visualization, a key skill needed in the reading process and for answering the questions. Demonstrate how the inner eye sees word-images on an imaginary TV screen in the mind (see figure 1).

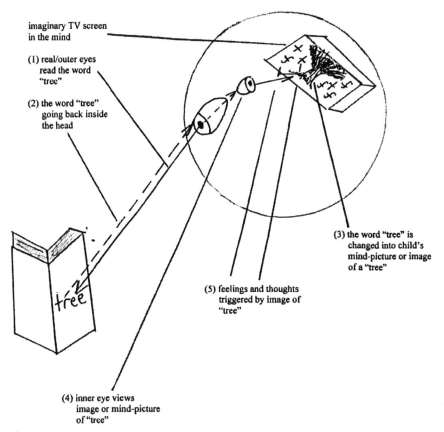

imaginary TV screen
in the mind

(1) real/outer eyes
read the word
"tree"

(2) the word "tree"
going back inside
the head

(3) the word "tree" is
changed into child's
mind-picture or image
of a "tree"

(5) feelings and thoughts
triggered by image of
"tree"

(4) inner eye views
image or mind-picture
of "tree"

Figure 1.

Make it simple: Draw a diagram (on the board for teachers or paper for parent-teachers) of reading the word "tree" from a page with their real eyes and how it is changed into a mind-picture viewed by the inner eye. Sketch a profile of a face (circle) with one arrow going from the real eye(s) to the word "tree." Draw a second arrow (broken line) from "tree" through the real eye(s) and going inside the head to an imaginary TV screen (rectangle), where a picture of a "tree" is drawn, and an inner eye views that image (indicating the reading process of changing a word into a mind-picture).

Discuss the imaginary inner reading voice that reads words subvocally from a page (as detailed in the upcoming Thomas Lux poem). The inner eye and voice—mind-pictures and silent sounds—combined with feelings conjured up by both, make reading into a magical event. *Ask*: "What does your inner reading voice sound like when you read?" These silent sounds are narrators of all the things they read. Without this voice, reading's silent sounds would seem more like white noise to kids.

Include in your discussion the imaginary inner ear (as depicted in the Lux poem). *Ask*: "What listens to and hears all those sounds?" The imaginary inner eye, voice, and ear are a big part of reading. Keep your definitions, descriptions, illustrations, and explanations simple. Students will appreciate the concepts because they provide a framework to view and define the reading process. Have your class/child read the outstanding Thomas Lux poem that describes the imaginary inner reading voice silently reading the words and the ear listening to them:

THE VOICE YOU HEAR WHEN YOU READ SILENTLY

> is not silent, it is a speaking—
> out-loud voice in your head; it is *spoken,*
> a voice is *saying* it
> as you read. It's the writer's words,
> of course, in a literary sense
> his or her "voice" but the sound
> of that voice is the sound of *your* voice.
> Not the sound your friends know
> or the sound of a tape played back
> but your voice
> caught in the dark cathedral
> of your skull, your voice heard
> by an internal ear informed by internal abstracts
> and what you know by feeling,
> having felt. It is your voice
> saying, for example, the word "barn"
> that the writer wrote
> but the "barn" you say
> is a barn you know or knew. The voice

in your head, speaking as you read,
never says anything neutrally—some people
hated the barn they knew,
some people love the barn they know
so you hear the word loaded
and a sensory constellation
is lit: horse-gnawed stalls,
hayloft, black heat tape wrapping
a water pipe, a slippery
spilled *chirr* of oats from a split sack,
the bony, filthy haunches of cows . . .
And "barn" is only a noun—no verb
or subject has entered into the sentence yet!
The voice you hear when you read to yourself
is the clearest voice: you speak it
speaking to you.

—Thomas Lux

Motivating Teen and Preteen Readers looks at different levels of thinking: Readers sort out many things by slowing down, looking, listening, and concentrating on hundreds of words and sentences coming at them. They view their reading worlds through images produced in the mind's magic reading theater and will, at times, sketch/draw them. The resulting drawings and even cartoons mirror back their reading lives in entertaining and absurd ways. The unexplored reading territories motivate adolescents to keep an open mind when responding to experiential questions on reading and reading problems: to get things out and change them through writing and discussion.

The books of questions explore the peace reading and books bring in contrast to the anxiety created in today's testing climate. Reading means a home away from home, a buddy to confide in and rely on when everyday life gets rough. This private world turns into a luxurious suite, where reading becomes comfort food for the mind. Thought-provoking questions take adolescents inside different areas of reading life and produce positive advertisements for reading: from the search for knowledge to inspiring self-examination and using reading as a temporary escape from the world. Dialogues following the writing create an open forum for ideas about habits in and attitudes toward reading. Teachers and parents can finish discussions with a basic wrap-up question: "Did you realize something new or different about reading in this lesson?"

Note: Use the motivational preface for students/child titled "Dazzling Your Mind with Reading" in an early rap. Make copies or read orally and discuss its ideas and implications. At the same time, don't forget to read the motivational preface for educators and parents titled "Hello Reading Life, Wherever You Are" to get yourself psyched up as a discussion leader for *Motivating Teen and Preteen Readers*. Your engagement is wanted and needed.

ADDITIONAL STRATEGIES FOR
IMPLEMENTING THE BOOKS OF QUESTIONS

In addition to the mini-lesson approach, teachers and parents have other options for presenting questions on reading/reading life. Discussion leaders can try:

- *Duets*, where kids pick partners for writing and discussing answers to a question.
- *Three-student brainstorming*, featuring groups of three, who brainstorm responses orally to a question followed by a discussion of what was expressed and learned.
- *Early question/late response*, which starts with a mini-lesson question given in the morning work and answered later in the day (parents can vary this at home by presenting a question in the afternoon that is answered later in the evening).
- *Relax-and-respond*, where kids pause for a one-minute relaxation break before responding to a question.
- *Music hour*, where teacher/parent discussion leaders play light background music (not heavy metal, rap—more like Top 10 sounds or instrumental) so

Illustration 4.   Duets: An additional strategy for presenting questions.
Illustration by James Jajac.

students/child can search for and discover the best possible answers to a question while feeling more peaceful.

- *Double answers*, which shows adolescents that there can be more than one answer to open-ended questions. They first write answers to a mini-lesson question and then stop for a few moments to conjure up a different, potentially stronger response. To see if the questions have initiated a passion for reading in their kids, discussion leaders can give them the opportunity to make up their own original questions in reading. (See *Create your own questions*.)

- *Question triggers question*, where students work from a mini-lesson question to create a second, new question that may be similar to or different from it. The best questions go in a "bonus box" (kids get extra credit for answering them in their free time during the day), and/or are used in class/small-group mini-lessons. (Parents can still use this activity with their child. Go to "Implementing a Workable Schedule for Book 2" for more information about the "bonus box" and its applications.)

- *Create your own questions*, where kids conjure up questions based on their reading experiences and responding to the mini-lesson questions. A panel of student judges and/or the teacher selects the ones deemed suitable for use in lessons or the bonus box. Top questions are rewritten on three-inch by five-inch index cards and become part of the pool of questions from *Motivating Teen and Preteen Readers*. In the evaluation questions and the books of questions, students are also asked to create their own questions about reading/reading life.

One of several strategies for concluding each of the four books of questions is:

- *Read-aloud-marathon* in which students answer either their original questions or questions given by the teacher in a typical mini-lesson. After writing responses, kids take turns reading them aloud to classmates for approximately fifteen minutes. They discuss their answers for ten minutes following the read-aloud. By the end of the school year, if the questions from the lessons inspired a passion for reading, the class should be riveted on the readers and their writings: It won't be boring. . . .

Notes: Teacher and parent discussion leaders can refer to "Implementing Workable Schedules/Strategies for Presenting Questions" in Books 2, 3, and 4 for more information and procedures about the different strategies for presenting, answering, and discussing questions, as well as creating original questions by students. The grade levels for each activity are indicated at the end of the descriptions. Teachers, from elementary through high school, can to choose approaches they feel would work with their classes (those that are age appropriate and timely). Parents pick strategies relevant to one-to-one instruction such as: early question/late response, relax and respond, music hour, question triggers question, and create your own questions.

Illustration 5.   The music hour strategy for presenting questions.

Illustration by James Jajac.

How to Answer the Questions on Reading and Reading Life

It is the supreme art of the teacher to awaken joy in creative expression and knowledge.

— Albert Einstein

HE WHO HESITATES IN *MOTIVATING TEEN AND PRETEEN READERS* IS NOT LOST

The questions propel preteens/teens to recreate their reading lives by searching, probing, ruminating, and contemplating. Certain questions need more critical and creative thinking. To stop and ponder means a student/child wants to dig for an answer, and that's a good thing in this year-long project. He or she who hesitates will not be lost in the books of questions. As discussion leader, *model how to answer questions* in complete, clear, candid sentences. Students write mini-lesson questions, the book number where they came from, and record their responses in a separate notebook.

Problem responders, those who "see only black" when searching for answers, must be patient and use their creativity until something moves across the imaginary TV screen in the mind; or they can jumpstart their own creativity by brainstorming ideas, word-storming (free-associating) words, and/or picture-storming images. In a classroom situation, students can wait for the discussion to see if it sparks a response. (To learn more about problem responders and storming techniques, see the upcoming sections. Also, a class website would have additional information to help kids who are coming up short in their written responses. See "Using Technology to Implement the Books of Questions" in Book 2 for how to set up a class website.)

Illustration 6.   The reader as a thinker enjoying himself in thought.
Illustration by James Jajac.

When questions ask to "explain your answer" or "why," they give reasons for the written responses. *Stress* using critical-thinking skills such as finding the main ideas, drawing conclusions, and making judgments to come up with answers.

If questions ask to "describe" or "describe your experience," kids provide details of the reading experience. For example, they can use creative-thinking skills such as visualization, reflection, and storming techniques. Repetition of word-prompts reminds students to think twice before writing, as annoying as they may seem at times. (See figures 1 and 3 for illustrations of the visualization in the reading process and an "inner-eye scan for book memories" for more information about these important skills.)

When questions ask to "describe your experience," *emphasize* using inner eye scans to search for images and memories (see figure 2). This imaginary eye becomes a spotlight to find and illuminate the mind's many pictures. Students connect inner-eye observations to their descriptions, a key to responding to the questions, and also relevant to the reading process. *Ask*: "What are you looking at and focusing on with your inner eye?"

FUNDAMENTAL PREREQUISITE SKILLS
NEEDED TO ANSWER THE QUESTIONS

Model thinking skills in your talks needed for responding to questions by defining each:

- Visualize: to form an idea or picture in the mind.
- Reflect: to give serious thought to or check over carefully and deliberately.
- Recall: to bring back a past image, event, or idea to the mind.
- Concentrate: to focus attention steadily and evenly on one thing.
- Analyze: to take things apart and examine them for better understanding.
- Synthesize: to put ideas, experiences, and things together to make sense out of them.

Another helpful thinking skill for answering questions is contemplation. It means staying with something for a longer time to experience and examine it carefully and continuously. This sustained concentration improves all thinking abilities and will renew interest in reading.

Follow up the definitions with a practical application by asking kids which thinking skills they would use to respond to:

- How do you find the main idea of a paragraph? (*Possible answers*: visualize, recall, reflect, concentrate, analyze, synthesize)

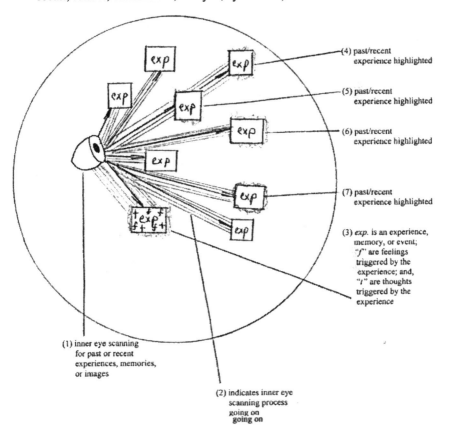

Figure 2.

- How would you describe your reading life: fun, work, boring, or painful? (*Possible answers*: visualize, recall, reflect, analyze)
- Find a word that makes you angry. (*Possible answers*: recall, reflect, analyze, visualize, contemplate)
- Describe a real or an imaginary place that brings you peace. (*Possible answers*: visualize, reflect, recall, contemplate)
- Recall a poem that made you feel good. (*Possible answers*: recall, reflect, visualize, contemplate, analyze)

Emphasize: "You can use different processes to answer the same question, and you can use more than one process to answer a question." *Ask*: "Describe the thinking skills you applied to the questions. Support your responses by giving reasons for how you solved each question." Again, this is an example of thinking about thinking. It might be a little tedious discussing the processes, but worthwhile and fun for kids in the long run.

Note: To be successful, the fundamental prerequisite skills for learning how to learn, combined with storming techniques and inner visualization strategies, have to be integrated into the process of answering reading life questions and reading. Take a few moments (time permitting) in raps and discussions to have a student/child demonstrate how they applied these fundamental skills and techniques to respond to a particular question. The class website would be another place to post examples of how to search for and find answers to the questions.

STORMING TECHNIQUES TO ANSWER QUESTIONS: THE TRIGGER METHOD OF CREATIVITY

Demonstrate the trigger method of creativity to jumpstart a fast-paced stream of ideas, thoughts, words, pictures, or sentences needed for responding to the questions. *Define and model* the following techniques:

- Word-storming: to trigger one word after another in the mind starting with a spark word.
- Picture-storming: to create one picture after another in the mind connected to a word, place, scene, thing, or idea.
- Brainstorming: to produce one idea after another in the mind to answer a question or resolve a situation, predicament, conflict, or problem.
- Sentence-storming: to conjure up one sentence after another in the mind for a writing activity.

For example, picture-storming initiates a chain of images. Kids create many pictures (as many as they can) viewed by the inner eye to find an answer to: "Draw a picture of the most ridiculous place to read." *Explain*: "Picture-storm

Illustration 7. Word-storming: The trigger method of creativity.
Illustration by James Jajac.

silly places to read before answering. Make it fun by putting yourself in the different places. Hang out in your imagination for a minute and enjoy the trip making up goofy places to read, ones you would never read in, and draw one."

Model a picture-storming response to the question. *Sample author response*: "I see myself reading in a cloud; on top of a cloud; in outer space; under water; on top of a tree; inside a giant bubble; floating on a balloon; on the moon; on a shooting star; in a cave with a family of bears sleeping; inside a frozen lake; in a dresser drawer; and, inside an empty bottle drifting on the ocean."

Try oral picture-storming with kids: Let them storm absurd places, scenes, settings orally; write responses on the board/paper; and, to make things interesting, ask to expand on the ridiculousness of the stormed environments.

Word-storming, or triggering a stream of words, starts with a spark word that initiates more words. Apply the strategy to solve this simulated word question: "List ten or more words that come to mind when you think about the word 'snake.'" *Author's sample response*: scary, slimy, sneaky, fever, tongue, slithering, grass, forest, woods, bite, fangs, attack, poisonous, faint, collapse, sweating, fear, fever, die, dying, death, horror, hate. *Explain*: "Let your imagination explode with words. Light it up with more and more words, until your mind overflows with them. See where the word-storming takes you. Experience the freedom and fun the process allows you. You'll be surprised at how many words are in your head and can be stormed. . . ."

Model storming techniques to answer this writing question: "Write a sentence that gets your heart beating or pounding." *Author's sample, stormed responses*:

- Brainstorm ideas: getting lost in a storm; driving in a NASCAR race at 2,000 mph; or looking down at New York City atop the Empire State Building. Take one idea, visualize it, and write a sentence.
- Picture-storm images rapidly in the mind by visualizing: sunsets, sunrises, fireworks, snowflakes, gardens, forests, parrots, kittens, burritos, or blizzard floats. Take one image and visualize it by zooming in for greater details and write.
- Word-storm words with the spark word "run": speed, fast, fly, zip, trip, fall, injury, fight, violent, punch, beat, blow, explode, ignite, explosion, fire, scream, cry. Pick one word, visualize a mind-picture for it, and write a sentence.
- Sentence-storm sentences by jumping right into creativity: Make up one sentence after another. Create a burst of sentences flying out of the mind and imagination. Have the class sentence-storm collaboratively or individually at their seats. *Model sample sentences*: (a) The mad dog ran after the boy down the dark alley. (b) The winter sun blazed through the icy windows and made rainbows on the white walls. (c) The children did not stop crying until the floor turned into a river and they floated out of the classroom. *Explain* sentence-storming: "Push your mind and imagination to come up with sentences.

Just keep writing sentences until you find one you really like and that answers the question. Test the sentence by visualizing or imagining it in your mind. What do you see? Does it work?" Each storming technique triggers the start of creativity. Which technique gets kids to a sentence that stirs the heart?

DEALING WITH PROBLEM RESPONSES AND RESPONDERS

If a student's/child's answers show a lack of effort, use a discussion/rap to model a fictitious student response that needs work or possibly an example from a specific book.

Sample question: Why do you keep reading a book?

Sample fictitious student response: "I keep reading a book because it's interesting. I'm really into the book. I like it."

The response does answer the question, but in a cursory manner. Responses should be supported by reading experiences or possibly a specific book recalled. Meanings of words like "interesting," "like," or phrases such as "into a book"

Illustration 8.   Roadblocks to responding and reading.
Illustration by James Jajac.

need to be expanded by the discussion leader to answer the question "why": "Why is it 'interesting'? What makes books 'interesting'? Why do you 'like' it? What does 'like' mean in your reading world?"

Notes: Reread the sample mini-lesson dialogue to see how the discussion leader draws out a more detailed response from the kids through the questioning technique. Also, check out the "Not-for-Parents-Only Guide to *Motivating Teen and Preteen Readers*" for more information about the questioning technique.

To create a more in-depth response, *ask* students/child to:

- Slow down, think, and reflect before writing.
- Use greater concentration during the inner eye scan to find a book.
- Focus on the memory of the book's story/plot and let it write the answer.

Go to figures 2 and 3 for illustrations of "Describe your experience" and an "Inner eye scan for book memories." Draw these simplistic sketches in raps/discussions to remind kids of the processes involved when searching for answers to questions.

After explaining how to improve their responses, collaborate with the class/child about completing an answer. Discuss specific reasons why they keep reading books via your questions. Get at their thoughts and feelings with these basic questions: "What did the book make you think about? What mind-pictures do you recall from the book? Why did the images stay in your mind? What feelings did the book trigger inside you? Why did the book stir up or awaken your imagination?"

Let students model their thinking processes for responding to help others who have difficulty. *Ask*: "How did you come up with that answer? Describe the thinking that got you your response." This is more student-modeling of meta-cognition: thinking about thinking. Teachers and parents can also model how they would find answers to the questions.

Teacher discussion leaders should spot check written responses in reading notebooks from time to time to see which students understand *Motivating Teen and Preteen Readers* and those who just don't get it. Use their written and oral responses from discussions to determine the stronger versus weaker responders. Talk informally about how to improve answers, writing skills, and reading life.

Challenge kids in a rap with: "Push yourselves to visualize, reflect, and think when responding. Pay attention during our talks. Let classmates' answers serve as models for your responses to the questions. You can always bring your thinking up a notch with the effort, so demand a lot from yourself and concentrate hard."

Remind students: "Check out the class website for examples of ways to improve weak written responses. Examples of strong responses will also be posted to help you with your answers." (See the "Implementation " and "Using Technology" sections in Book 2 for more information about using a class website.)

Written responses will increase in quality and length as kids answer and discuss more questions. *Cross-fertilization of ideas* from class and one-to-one parent-child talks improve writing as well as understanding, enjoyment, and awareness of a reading life. As discussion leaders, inspire your kids by pointing out the creative connections to printed, spoken, and imagined words, which come organically through the plethora of word and word activity questions (see the "Not-for-Parents-Only Guide to *Motivating Teen and Preteen Readers*"). In your raps, plant positive, expansive seeds of thought about reading to reduce test anxiety.

Not-for-Parents-Only Guide to
Motivating Teen and Preteen Readers

Reading has always been life unwrapped to me, a way of understanding the world and understanding myself through the unknown and the everyday. If being a parent consists often of passing along chunks of ourselves to unwitting—often unwilling—recipients, then books are, for me, one of the simplest and most sure-fire ways of doing that.

—Anna Quindlen

Note: The "Not-for-Parents-Only Guide" is for both parents and teachers. All educators can substitute students/class for "child" and apply the information to their particular situations.

WHAT IS *MOTIVATING TEEN AND PRETEEN READERS*?

Motivating Teen and Preteen Readers includes over a thousand questions about reading and reading life. By the time you finish asking and answering questions from Books 1 to 4, your child will have a greater understanding and appreciation of reading and how much he or she really wants to read.

Each book grows an awareness of reading life, where it fits in and how it affects real life. The books bring up everyday reading experiences that go beyond tests and test scores. A variety of fun, creative, challenging questions shows the awesomeness of reading life experiences that are often taken for granted. *Motivating Teen and Preteen Readers* starts a genuine journey to energize and inspire a passion for this extraordinary world. As a discussion leader, *stop*, *think*, and *reflect* on the following questions to see if they will *open up* your child's reading world: What happens in your mind when reading? How far and deep can reading take kids? Is reading imagining and dreaming? Is reading still fun? Are words important? What is the solitude of reading? How can reading create a peaceful mind? How much energy is expended reading? When does reading become boring? Can kids who don't like to read, or read because they have to, create a love for reading and motivate it by themselves? Whose responsibility is it to read? What can readers do for their reading and reading lives to improve them?

Have the questions gotten your attention? Can they jumpstart your child's mind to see reading in a fresh, positive light? Even at this early stage in life, many reading experiences live inside your child's mind or remain hidden in memory. This book of questions will trigger and bring them to the surface. Let it be your literacy coach to help unravel the story of your child's reading life, from the earliest days to the most recent times.

REASONS THE DIVERSE QUESTIONS WILL ENGAGE PARENT DISCUSSION LEADERS

Motivating Teen and Preteen Readers will be valued by parents in urban, inner-city, suburban, and rural areas. Parents who tutor for enrichment, home-schooling parent-teachers, as well as parents of ADD/ADHD children will use the book for similar reasons as educators. The diverse questions will engage *you* because they:

- Open up communication with your child about reading.
- Inform you first-hand about your child's reading/reading life.
- Are clear, easy-to-use, valuable home resources.
- Naturally generate dynamic, energized one-to-one discussions.
- Illuminate your child's reading life history and trace problem areas.
- Supplement, compliment, and advance the school reading curricula.
- Inspire creative thinking, critical thinking, and comprehension.
- Build and increase the motivation to read and write.
- Prevent judgmental thinking when dealing with your child's reading.
- Trigger experimentation as a strategy to find out about your child's reading life.
- Provide new ways to enjoy different reading experiences.
- Initiate reflection on and renewal of your reading/reading life.
- Connect parents and teachers through the project's accessibility.
- Unite parents and teachers in the struggle to motivate adolescent readers.
- Help parents of middle and high school students gain insight into motivating kids in reading.
- Work on all levels/abilities in reading, from struggling to top readers.
- Build fresh awareness in reading for all levels of reluctant readers.

SAMPLE QUESTIONS WITH ANSWERING TIPS

The questions examine reading life by dropping teens and preteens right in the heart of it.

Examples: Describe the silent world of reading as you read to yourself. Do you get uptight when you don't understand what you read? Do you remember your earliest feelings about reading? Do you feel you get smarter the more you read? How do you get yourself to read if you're not in the mood? Does reading wake you up? Can reading and books be hazardous to your health? How would your kid respond?

Give tips for responding in raps: Read all questions carefully to make sure you understand what they ask. Translate or change any unusual words, phrases, or expressions into your own words before answering. For example: Does reading wake you up? What does "wake you up" mean? Do you follow what this question asks? *Clarify* any question you ask if it creates a thud, like: "Huh, what are you talking about?"

Emphasize to think, recall, reflect, visualize, and concentrate before "describing the silent world of reading." Ask your child to use the inner or imaginary eye in the mind to search for and scan this "silent world of reading to yourself." Let it spotlight the experience and memories. As discussion leader, make the question clearer, if necessary, by asking: "What goes on inside when you read to yourself? What's happening?"

Explain: "In the beginning, describing your reading world may seem a little difficult. But that's okay, because the skill improves with practice in searching for answers to questions: You begin to see more and more. Another example would be 'describing your earliest feelings about reading.' Take your time and be patient when scanning your memory; let the inner eye have a chance to look for answers." Give advice, suggestions, hints, and reminders in your raps prior to asking the mini-lesson question.

Emphasize to state reasons clearly when a question, for example, asks to "explain whether reading makes you smarter the more you read." Remind your child to review reading life memories with the inner or mind's eye to dig up any experiences, knowledge, and insights to create a response.

Some questions are easy to answer such as: "Why do you keep reading a book?" *Suggest* taking a second look, to think harder, deeper, and appreciate why he or she keeps reading a book even if the question and answer are simple. Ask your child to find specific reasons by scanning reading-life experiences with the inner eye, from recent to not-so-recent books read.

Certain questions sound similar, for example: "What book has opened your heart?" and "What is the connection between reading and feeling?" Distinguish between the two: The first asks to discuss a book that made you really feel and care about things. The second asks: Where do feelings enter reading? In fact, they are the glue that keeps kids interested and engaged in a book. As a discussion leader, pay attention to similar sounding questions in your selections. Stop to see their differences by answering the questions yourself. Even if questions ask the same thing in different ways, your child's answer on Monday may not be the same as Wednesday. *Suggest* to search the mind for potential answers and to support them with reading experiences. Let kids experiment and discover new possibilities that could impact their reading lives. The question-and-answer process is all about breakthroughs.

Point out that students can go to the dictionary and/or thesaurus to define words and find synonyms, especially when a question gives a "hint" at the end to use them. A child may know a word, but still needs definitions and/or synonyms to clarify its meaning. For example, the word "solitude" in the "solitude of reading" question needs more understanding to realize how it affects reading. Think about it: Some kids may not like the "lonely pleasures" of reading. *Suggest*: "Build a habit of looking up words for definitions, synonyms, and antonyms: a gift you give to yourself, one that does not stop giving back in your reading life and *Motivating Teen and Preteen Readers*." *Repeat* this statement in raps and discussions until your child goes to the reference books without thinking about it.

How much do I have to write? This question usually comes up. *Discussion leader response*: "Write a thorough, thoughtful answer, from three to six sentences (short paragraph) to half a page (even a full page if totally into it). There is no set or assigned length to your response. Answer in complete sentences: clearly, simply, and handwriting counts. Reread your written responses to see if they make sense, and, answer the question. Use fiction or nonfiction reading and books to answer questions, unless they specifically ask for a novel, short story, fairy tale, fable, myth, poem, memoir, or biography." Compared to classroom teachers, parent discussion leaders in one-to-ones have less limitations and restrictions on time and scheduling. This is an advantage where a child has extra time to finish an expanded response to a question.

Imagine that: Your child has trouble answering a question. He goes blank trying to recall an early reading experience or book: What to do? *Suggest*: "Relax for ten seconds, go slow, and continue your inner-eye scan for memories. Visualize yourself reading. Search for an image or mind-picture of the event. Discover a book you really loved. Find a page in it, an illustration that pops out at you. What thoughts and feelings are triggered by the mind-picture(s)?" If a book recall question totally stumps the reader, let him or her find an answer by searching the Internet or at a home library. This is not a test. A disadvantage of one-to-one versus classroom discussions is: Kids can listen to their friends' responses—an exchange of ideas—to stimulate experiences when they're at a loss to answer certain questions. Parents, on the other hand, can trigger responses via their suggestions and discussion questions without the help of other kids.

Detour! Detour! Side trips through reading worlds: Slowing down to ponder reading life brings back memories, at times, unrelated to the questions, which is great. This shows how the questions from *Motivating Teen and Preteen Readers* inspire thinking and reflecting on reading experiences. *Explain*: "If your mind wanders to an experience not connected to the question, you can write about it in a separate response in the reading notebook. Any ideas, feelings, thoughts, mind-pictures, and insights can be entered in the back of the book: Call it a 'side trip' or 'detour' and date it. For example, 'describing a favorite fairy tale' may take you on a ride through your imagination and other enjoyable tales. The unexpected side trip becomes an adventure in your reading world, so why not write about it?" These detours show an increased passion for reading slowly building up.

Discussion leader quickie rap: "Your effort to answer questions makes or breaks the value of the four books of questions. After writing and rereading a response, ask yourself: 'Have I given enough thought to the question? Have I rushed my answer just to get it done?' Be honest and sincere when responding, because one goal is to open up and reveal your reading life: past, present, and future. The questions and answers will return the effort by raising awareness of your attitude toward reading and create a love of reading."

QUESTION CATEGORIES, RESPONDING TIPS, AND DISCUSSION QUESTIONS

As discussion leader, it's important to look over the question categories in Books 1 to 4 and additional answering tips to make your travels through the question categories more enjoyable and understandable:

- *Common, everyday reading experience questions* focus on familiar events that happen during routine reading activities. *Example*: Do you have to fight yourself to read at times? How does the battle end? Are you the winner or loser? Why? *Stress* the search through those difficult times using an inner-eye scan to see herself on an imaginary TV screen in the mind and to review the events. As discussion leader, ask your child to "look in the mirror of reading life" to see what happens, for better or worse. Kids learn to face their reading conflicts and solve them. Use this as an eye-opener. Reinforce applying inner-eye scans until it becomes a habit.
- *Reading process questions* take kids on a trek to see what occurs inside the mind and imagination while they read. *Example*: What is the magic of reading that gets a reader so absorbed in a book? How does this happen? *Rap*: "First, figure out what the 'magic of reading' means. Second, describe how this 'book magic' absorbs readers. The question is all about the magic of reading. What is it? Think, reflect, and visualize before writing your response." As discussion leader, show your child that he is the magician creating shows in the mind's magic reading theater.

- *Opinion questions* let young people express their beliefs, feelings, and ideas about reading/reading life. *Emphasize*: "Get it out, whatever you have to express, and back it up with your reading experiences. Avoid snap or automatic judgments, even though you might have strong feelings about your response. Try to be objective, fair, and honest. *Think about this*: Can books boost your confidence? Why or why not?" What the question really asks is: How powerful are books? Can books change kids? *Rap*: "Step back before answering and return to past books to see if the question holds true for you. Is there a connection between reading books and real life?" This question will create a lively one-to-one dialogue, where you probe the child's reading life with more questions about books that might have increased confidence. Keep going after feelings, thoughts, ideas, mind-pictures, memories, and meanings that triggered a change with your questioning. *Sample discussion questions*: What idea from a book affected your life? How did it change you? What mind-picture from the book remains in your memory? What feelings and thoughts does the image trigger? How can readers use mind-pictures from books to impact or change real life?

- *One-line statement questions* (author's original quotations) about reading/reading life ask to explain what they mean or suggest. *Example*: Read and move to the beat of the world. Explain. *Discussion leader*: "Before responding to the statement, try to make sense of the phrase 'move to the beat of the world.' *Think*: How does reading help readers 'move to the beat of the world'? Add your own ideas and experiences to complete the answer—that's a good thing to do." This is not an easy question because kids have to be connected to and have a passion for reading to write a strong response. One-liners, like opinion questions, give your child a chance to air views about reading and are considered important in *Motivating Teen and Preteen Readers*.

- *Book recall questions* are searches for books that have been read. Like many questions in the books of questions, readers are asked to revisit old, but not completely forgotten, reading experiences (and also recent ones). *Rap*: "Use an inner-eye scan to find books. Once a book or book memory comes to mind, visualize and concentrate on it, and write a response." *Example*: Recall a book that showed how people could be mean or cruel to each other. Describe one scene. What were you thinking, feeling, and imagining? What were your reflections at the end of the book? There's lots of visualization here (describe a scene) with emotions/thoughts attached to the images/imaginings, followed by a reflection, "thinking back about the story": Call it a response to literature. As discussion leader, get your child to fill in the details of the recalled mind-pictures, as well as the surrounding thoughts, ideas, and feelings connected to them. *Sample discussion questions*: Can you visualize the characters' faces? Describe them. How did the characters act? What do you see them doing? What did you think and feel? What really stands out in your mind? Define the story's cruelty in your own words. Were you able to put yourself in any scene from the story? Did your mind and imagination make the story come-to-life? Do you like to get so close to a story you're reading? Does the story ever seem like 3-D? Keep asking questions to help kids make their reading worlds into virtual, holographic realities, alternate universes: Show them how to enjoy themselves in the mind's magic reading theater.

Illustration 9.   3-D, holographic, virtual reading realities.
Illustration by James Jajac.

- *Nonfiction reading questions* help readers discover their likes/dislikes in this relevant reading genre. *Rap*: "Why is reading nonfiction so important? Subjects like history and science will follow you all the way through college. *Think about it*: Big fat textbooks will haunt your life until school and standardized tests are over. Nonfiction questions will open up your mind to different worlds you didn't think interesting. Is it possible to discover new, fascinating subjects? I'll let you decide." As discussion leader, start the rap by posing the original question about the importance of reading nonfiction: Find out your child's knowledge of this vast reading area. *Examples*: Describe a book, reading, or an article you read about nature. Was it a good read? Explain. Or: Recall a magazine article where you found something new on almost every page. Give an example. *Ask*: "Where can nonfiction reading take you?" *Sample answer*: Just about everywhere. . . . Let your child fill in "everywhere" by brainstorming ideas.

- *Hypothetical reading situation questions* set up fictional or imaginary reading events to analyze and resolve. *Rap*: "Put yourself in the various situations described in these questions. Make believe you're the person and answer this *sample question*: If you were teaching a child to read, what would be the most important idea you would communicate about reading? Why? And imagine, yeah, imagine: create a way out of it by reflecting on your reading life. What would *you* say to this child?" Hypothetical questions are fun problem-solving situations that challenge kids to search their reading lives for answers. The written responses really answer questions and provide insights about their attitudes to and understanding of reading. *Discussion leader*: After you hear one idea, ask if there is a second, third, or fourth idea she would try to communicate: "What is another important idea you would present to the child?" Keep pushing and probing with your impromptu questions following the original response. You're always trying to show kids the different possible answers with open-ended questions.

- *Quotation questions* combine and connect key reading life experiences into one statement. *Example*: Explain the meaning of: "Take up and read, take up and read" (St. Augustine). *Rap*: "Rewrite the quotation in your own words to make sense out of it, but don't change the intended meaning. Next, try an inner-eye scan to recall and connect your reading life experiences to the quotation. Pause to search your reading life to come up with a response for quotations." *Discussion leader*: Quotes are useful as "closers" when completing any of the four books of questions. They put things about reading/reading life into perspective. *Sample discussion questions*: What picture comes into mind after reading the quote? What feelings does the quote trigger? What does it make you think about reading? Expanding the quotation's ideas will develop greater insight and take kids on extended journeys (sidetrips) through reading life. You allow them to take control of their reading destinies through an inquiry-based approach.

- *Past, early reading experience questions* need more effort. *Rap*: "Ask your child to use recall, reflection, and concentration skills to handle these *examples*: What changed inside yourself once you learned to read on your own? Can you improve reading by yourself? Before answering, review your reading life to see what has changed. Hold off a second to examine experiences thoroughly to reveal your reading life to *you*." *Discussion leader*: The first question's response will need probing with: "What did you think once you could read on your own? How did you feel about yourself?" And for the second question, ask: "How can you improve your reading by yourself? Have you ever tried? What were the results? Do you depend on school and your teachers to improve your reading? Do you have responsibility in improving your reading ability?"

- *Poetry reading life questions* look into the genre of poetry. *Examples*: Why read poetry? Do you read poetry? Is there a poem you return to again and again? The questions make kids aware of their connection, or lack of one, to poetry. *Rap*: Start off with questions to trigger his/her mind on the subject: "How much do you like or dislike poetry? Do you think it's dumb, silly, or a waste? Who needs it? How can it help you in reading or on reading tests?" Is rap poetry? Prepare kids with these questions and present one of the examples in a mini-lesson. By surveying demanding and potentially "uninteresting" areas in reading, you help your child rethink his attitude to and passion for them. The books of questions are about expanding adolescents' views (positive or negative) about reading-life experiences. *Note*: But what if *you're* not a big fan of poetry? How would you talk about it? *Possible answer*: Why not read some poems together? Why not struggle a bit with your child to see the effort that it takes to handle tougher reading genres?

- There are, throughout the books of questions, "*deeper thought questions*" (not a question category), which need greater consideration. A question like "How is reading an invitation?" triggers another question: invitation to what? The question also includes a "hint" at the end to look up "invitation." Make sure the hint is taken. *Rap*: "Before responding to the question, check out definitions and synonyms for 'invitation.' Use the dictionary and/or thesaurus whenever you need more information about a word that will help you answer the question. The meanings and synonyms will give clues to answering the question. Once you understand 'invitation,' think about its connection to reading and reading life." *Discussion leader*: Ask your child, "What does reading invite you to do?" *Sample answers* (Let her brainstorm a list of "invites."): Reading is an invitation to think, feel, and imagine, and to enjoy yourself in your own world. It's an invitation to forget about your self and escape from the real world. Reading is an invitation to find out about yourself, who you are, your identity. Reading invites you to find out about worlds beyond your own neighborhood. The list can go on and on. However, if the question confuses your child, start her off with an answer to spark a list of brainstormed responses. Child and parent can also feed off each other with an exchange of responses. Why not? This is an advantage of one-to-one discussions.

Some questions may seem unusual at first glance, for instance: "Reading takes courage. What do you think?" *Rap*: "Now you might be thinking to yourself: What courage do I need for reading? Does it take courage to read? Why/when would I need courage to read? In what situations is it needed? Are there connections between reading and courage? The question forces you to think back in your memory, yes, try another inner-eye scan and search for a time you needed courage to read. What do you come up with? Take your time and imagine the connections." *Sample answers*: You need courage to take reading tests to fight the pressures of getting a good grade. Courage is needed to keep reading when you're wiped out and you have to finish the assignment. Courage is needed to read and understand difficult books. Courage is not something ordinarily thought about in connection to reading/reading life. And sometimes, kids are scared when it comes to reading; they're uptight and won't admit it to anyone, including parents, teachers, and friends.

Discussion leader rap (about questions, answers, and how to answer): "Many questions from different category areas are *open-ended*, which means there is more than one 'correct' answer for any given question. One-line, hypothetical, and quotation questions are examples of mostly judgment calls on your part. Prove your answers by supporting them with reasons from reading experiences. Be ready to hunt for responses about what happens inside your reading world. Although instant, fast answers may seem convincing at first, certain questions need to be explored further. Take a minute of 'think time' to slow down and bring back important events in your reading life."

Rap: "Be careful about making quick responses to opinion questions such as: Should books with a lot of violence be read? or What is your definition of a good book? *Think about it*: How many possible answers are there for each question? If you hesitate, pause, or stop, you're not lost because you're reflecting and concentrating—and that's what you want to do."

Rap: "When questions ask, 'What do you think?' or 'What comes to mind?' respond with your understanding and knowledge of a particular reading subject. Again, there isn't a right answer here. Your best responses are backed up with reading life events." *Example*: A good book is not hard to find. What do you think? Is it easy or hard to find a good book? What has been your experience? *Discussion leader*: Ask your child to relate different experiences in searching for and finding a "good book" to read. With millions of books on library shelves, any reader can have trouble getting their hands on the "right one." *Discussion question*: "Why is it hard to find a good read with so many books out there? How did you find your last good book to read? Was it still a 'good book' after you finished it?" Parent and child can certainly exchange experiences and ideas about answers to this question.

The four books of questions look at the pluses and minuses of reading and reading life. *Rap*: "Be open and honest about experiences, even negative ones. It will help you realize and fix a problem that may be affecting you right now. Have the courage to face your reading hassles, so they won't hurt you in the future. Get rid of your demons now and feel the freedom reading offers you." *Example*: Can you recall a difficult experience you had when first learning how to read? *Discussion leader*: Keep promoting candidness in written/oral responses so kids can make headway in the books of questions and reading life. Let them get up close and personal about reading life and see it through fresh eyes. Model what you mean by "openness" and "honesty." Give your answers to the question. They like to hear about your experiences expressed in an open, truthful way. Young readers can take the cue from you.

WORD, SENTENCE, AND WRITING QUESTIONS WITH ANSWERING TIPS AND DISCUSSION IDEAS

Rap: "What would reading life be without words? Reading is about knowledge of and the appreciation for words. Are words important to you?" *Sample introductory word question*: Are words just black-on-white, or are they something more to you? *Ask*: "Do you ever think about this? Where do words fit in to your daily life?"

Word and word-activity questions empower readers to see words creatively and how they affect them emotionally, cerebrally, and psychologically. Consider imaginative searches for answers to these questions: (a) snow: What do you see, think, feel, and wonder? (b) What happens when watermelons and tomatoes collide? (c) Think of a word that makes you feel good; say it over and over to yourself, and describe the experience.

Think about it: The word "snow" brings up a lot of associations, images, words, feelings, thoughts, experiences, and memories, which create a fun one-to-one conversation. As discussion leader, motivate preteens/teens by talking about your response to the word question (think about answers mentally to anticipate the written response). The silly question about "watermelons colliding with to-matoes" gives kids a chance to visualize an outrageous mind-picture and show them the power of image-making (the imagination). Word questions stimulate a passion for reading and writing. The word activity question, "saying a word over and over again that makes you feel good," shows the power of words, the feel-ings, thoughts, and images they're capable of cranking up in the mind. Remind them of the repetition in song/rap lyrics.

Another example of how far a word can take kids or how far kids can take a word is: "Find a word that makes you hungry and contemplate it for a minute.

Where does it take you? Describe the journey." *Discussion leader*: Contemplation means giving much more attention and energy to discover a word's life, its various meanings, connections, mind-pictures, emotions, and ideas. What can these word workouts, fueled by contemplation, do for your child's reading and reading life? *Sample discussion questions*: How did contemplating the word affect your experience? Did you feel hungry or hungrier? Were you able to taste the word? Did you smell it? Describe the mind-picture of the word. Did you see it really close-up? What did you learn about words you didn't know before the activity? What does contemplation do? What is it?

Word journey questions continue with *sentence journey questions*, where a group of words forming a complete thought becomes a quick flick or movie flashing on an imaginary TV screen in the mind's magic reading theater. *Example*: The two dogs, one big and one small, ran in circles chasing after each other's tails. *Discussion leader (to child)*: "Visualize this sentence in your mind. What do you see? Does the sentence turn into a little comedy picture show in the mind's magic reading theater inside your head?"

This sentence activity becomes self-amusement because kids can "toy" with the various images created inside. *Sample discussion questions*: What kind of dogs do you imagine? What do they look like? How big is the big dog and how small is the small one? How fast are they running? What does that look like? Do they create a blur? Are they angry with each other or just playing? Do you feel you're a spectator viewing what happens in the sentence? The mind-pictures visualized, described, and drawn can be real, surreal (fantasy-like), goofy, however it is imagined.

Can your reader become a writer and produce "a scary sentence originating completely from the imagination"? Can you, as discussion leader, take your child from the mind's magic reading theater to the mind's magic writing theater, where images are changed into words? How can he make up or create a sentence purely from his head? *Model making up sentences* by: brainstorming scary ideas (the last day on planet Earth); picture-storming frightening images (the sun exploding); word-storming words triggering fear (tornadoes, lightning/thunder, tsunami, earthquakes); and/or sentence-storming horror-filled sentences by pumping up one scary sentence after another ("The devil looked at me with his eyes on fire"; or "The ghost was breathing down my neck as I walked down the dark hallway"). As you lead your child through these processes, he might want to join in and you can "storm" together until some creepy-sounding sentences are created. *Experiment* with different storming techniques to find one or more that sparks an answer.

Discussion leader: Try this goofy writing activity question together with your child: Visualize, write, and then draw a silly, ridiculous sentence. What comes to mind afterward? Inventing absurd sentences ignites the imagination: to put funny pictures on an imaginary TV screen in the mind viewed by the inner eye, which are then changed into words. Build sentences by focusing the inner eye on one image before starting to write, draw, and reflect. This exchange of silly sentences, drawings, and reflections should make both of you laugh out loud together. Conjuring up different images in the mind means the writer is picture-storming.

Discussion leader: You can jumpstart responses to past, early reading experiences by picture-storming. The author recalled a memory by first visualizing a "maroon-covered book" he liked to read and look at the pictures as a young boy. To spark a more detailed experience, images were picture-stormed from memories of the book:

- Image 1: A thick, warped book with pages stuck together and pried apart to read.
- Image 2: Watching a young boy with a happy face running through open green fields.
- Image 3: Smiling at the contented child on the page.
- Image 4: Reading the book in the bathtub.
- Image 5: Seeing the book of stories about the little boy fall into the bathwater.
- Image 6: The water-logged book saved by his mother drying it out on the radiator.

Once again, you both trade memories: His picture-stormed memories would likely involve you and mirror back how you communicated a passion for reading at an early age. Children enjoy listening to parent/teacher stories of their early reading lives. This conversation invites a warm, loving communication, a connection, which leads the way for motivating preteen/teen readers.

MORE CREATIVE-THINKING QUESTIONS WITH ANSWERING TIPS

Creative-thinking questions present fun, absurd—yet serious—reading situations to solve. Keep in mind that wacky-sounding questions may have a real purpose. *Mini-lesson question*: If bees could read, what books would they take out of the "buzzing library"? Create some titles. *Rap (to child)*: "How would you respond to the question? Which storming technique(s) would help make up titles for the bees' books?" *Answer*: Brainstorm ideas, word-storm words, picture-storm images, and/or sentence-storm sentences. Amuse yourself by searching for creative responses and ideas for titles.

Discussion leader: How would you create book titles for bees? What books would they like and take out of the "buzzing library"? *Here are methods with sample answers*:

- Brainstorm ideas: They buzz a lot; make honey; live in a bee hive; sting and cause pain; and annoy people. What titles would come from the ideas and interest bees? *Sample answers*: "Make Money with Honey"; "Bee Hive Living Magazine"; "How to Annoy Humans"; "Sting Time for Bees."

- Word-storm words: Start with the spark word "bee": buzz, buzzing, honey, hive, sting, pain, annoying, scared, run, scream. Use the words to create book titles. *Sample answers*: "The Buzz Around Town"; "Buzzing Away Your Life"; "How to Sting and Live to Tell the Tale."
- Picture-storm images: Bees buzzing and flying around your head; a bee stinging you (ouch!); running away from a bee that's coming after you; bees flying into their hive; jars of honey on the grocery store shelf; and a picture of a bee in a science book. How can the images become book titles? How can these images be changed into book titles bees would enjoy? *Sample answers*: "The Bees Are Coming, The Bees Are Coming"; "Hive Five"; "Honey, Honey: Saga of a Bee's Life"; "Honey, Honey, I Got Stung by a Bee"; "I Fought the Bee, and the Bee Won."

Discussion leader: What does the question hint at about choosing books to read? *Think*: How would you connect the question to kids choosing books to read? What are their reasons for picking books? Can they find new reasons for choosing books to read? Discussion leaders broaden adolescent reading worlds by taking them to genres rarely considered. *Rap*: "Expand your interests by experimenting. Try something different for a change and see if you like it. You'll never know until you try. . . ."

DRAWING QUESTIONS WITH ANSWERING TIPS

Drawing and art have been part of reading and reading life starting from kids' earliest days in school and at home. Drawing pictures of words learned or sketching mind-pictures from a story read in class are examples. Drawing questions help preteens/teens see and grow passionate about their reading lives in a fun way. They inspire readers to enjoy the delights of reading in color (markers, crayons, and colored pencils) and black-and-white (pencil and pen).

Example: Zoom in on the eyes of a reader. Draw those reading eyes. What does your finished picture make you think about or ponder? *Rap*: "Scan your mind for images of young people reading. When you find one, focus closely on the details of the eyes, whatever you can see and remember, and then draw your visualization. This is a workout for the mind's eye. You want to move in for a close-up of reading eyes. What do you see? What if you can't recall or find reading eyes? What can you do? *Imagine* what these or your eyes look like when reading. Visualize an original image in your mind, put it on the imaginary TV screen for viewing, and draw what you see. *Think about it*: What would these eyes show?" *Sample answer*: The pencil-sketch might show intensity, concentration, excitement, engagement, peace, relaxation, and calm in a reader's eyes.
Discussion leader (optional): Start reading a book and let your child draw what he sees (focus on face and eyes). *Ask*: "Describe the look in my eyes when I read.

What words would describe my reading eyes? Are my reading eyes the same as yours or different?"

Example: Can you find and draw a mind-picture of a beloved book that is falling apart? *Rap*: "Let the image from memory and imagination draw the book. What? You're a lousy artist? *Imagine* the picture before drawing to make the question easier to answer and more fun."

Visualize what this question asks: Draw a self-portrait of you reading in your favorite place. What do you see in your mind? The example gives kids a chance to see what they look like when reading (self-portrait). *Discussion leader follow-up questions*: Extend the self-portrait drawing with: Why makes this your favorite place? What feelings does it create? How does it affect your reading? What would be your ideal dream place to read? What is your worst place to read? Can you read in the library?

Sample comical drawing question: Draw a cartoon of you wrapped up in a book. *Rap*: "Enjoy yourself in the mind's self-amusement park called the imagination. Let your inner eye become a camera snapping the pictures. Develop or pencil-sketch an image on paper. Your picture can be serious, funny, silly, or dreamlike. It's the idea communicated through your drawing that counts. Masterpieces are not necessary." *Discussion leader follow-up questions*: "What does 'wrapped up in a book' mean according to your picture? Describe this experience. What feelings are you experiencing in the picture? What are you thinking? What was the last book you were wrapped up in? Why?" Are you getting the picture now?

QUESTIONS ON RATING READING AND READING LIFE WITH ANSWERING TIPS

Kids have opportunities to rate different areas in their reading lives throughout the project. There are no right or wrong answers here, only honest, genuine evaluations. *For instance*: How much energy do you put into your reading? Rate it on a scale from 0 to 10, where 0 = no energy, and 10 = a great amount or total energy. Give reasons for your rating. *Rap*: "Rating questions need reflecting and thinking. Scan your reading experiences and 'add them up' to measure the energy level. How much energy—effort, concentration, and feeling—do you normally put into reading? *Caution*: Watch out for snap judgments to rating questions. There are many experiences you have to search quickly to get an idea of how much you really 'give.' Back up your 'mark' with reasons. A snap response might not add up to what you do daily." *Discussion leader*: This self-rating, if truthful, will tell you about a child's motivation level. (Energy rating scale: 8–10 = good to excellent; 5–7 = fair; 1–4 = needs pumping up.)

Ask follow-up discussion questions: "Is your energy level the same all the time? Do you have to give a lot to get something out of your reading? Can you read with feeling and understanding without great effort? When do you need to raise your reading energy level? How high is your energy level for big reading tests? When are you reading at your highest energy level? Can you crank up your reading energy level whenever you need it? What tells you that your reading energy level is low? Which subject do you give the most energy in reading?"

Discussion leader: To create follow-up questions in *any* question category, answer the questions in your head before asking them. Once experiences have been scanned and reflected on, you can use these journeys to anticipate and make up challenging, but do-able, follow-up questions. Tap into your reading life to tap into her reading life.

Some rating questions don't ask for a number rating/mark. *Example*: Do you feel confident about your reading ability? Explain your answer. This self-evaluation depends on an objective, truthful response. *Rap*: "Can you be honest about what you really feel? Look at the pluses and minuses of your confidence level. Use the inner eye to find different experiences in reading to write a realistic answer. Look at the pictures/memories and describe your confidence (without numbers) in reading ability. If it helps, use a number rating and then describe how confident you are in reading." *Follow-up discussion questions*: "When is your confidence in reading ability low? When is it high? Has your confidence improved or gotten worse as you grew up? Can practicing reading help your confidence in reading? Has a teacher, parent, brother, sister, relative, or friend helped you increase your confidence in reading? Do you believe you are a good reader? What feelings can hurt your confidence? Does a low reading-test score hurt your confidence in reading?" Throw out a few of these questions and say to your child: "Ponder that for a moment. . . ."

SELF-EVALUATIONS IN READING/READING LIFE:
THE STUDENT QUESTIONNAIRE

You can jumpstart the evaluation part of the project or any mini-lesson with questions. *Rap*: "How much effort went into your journey through *Motivating Teen and Preteen Readers*? How much was found out about reading? What did you realize? How pumped up did you get about reading life? Did you improve your reading life? Were there any changes in your desire to read? These are some questions you will respond to in the student questionnaire. It's a survey to find out about your experience."

Kids self-evaluate their work by answering a series of twenty questions about reading, reading life, and the books of questions after thirty to seventy-five questions have been completed. A discussion about the responses to the questionnaire follows the written part.

Rap: "Before responding to the questionnaire, reread all your written answers to the questions from your reading notebook. After receiving the questionnaire, we'll read over the questions together to make sure you understand what each is asking. Respond to the questions by thinking things through. Honest, thoughtful answers make your self-evaluations worthwhile. The four student questionnaires have different evaluation questions. Stop to recall many experiences you described in your reading notebook. The final questionnaire has one essay question out of five to answer instead of a series of questions."

TEACHER AND PARENT ASSESSMENTS: STUDENT-TEACHER/PARENT CHATS 1 TO 4

Each book of questions ends with a student-teacher/parent chat. A brief interview follows your child's rereading of the written responses and completing the student questionnaire. *Rap*: "In a five- to ten-minute meeting, I will talk to you about answering and discussing questions on reading like we've been doing all along. Our chats are simple question-and-answer conversations. Each of the four chats will be different. The last interview, chat 4, changes: there will be one question to answer orally. Chats and questionnaires are not tests to grade your work. Both evaluations will expand your understanding and enjoyment of reading/reading life and the questions."

THE EPILOGUE: ONE LAST ASSESSMENT

To conclude an entire year's work in *Motivating Teen and Preteen Readers*, hold three or more fifteen-minute brainstorming sessions in the final week. All sorts of prompts on reading, reading life, creativity, imagination, and writing are in the epilogue for brainstorming ideas. The prompts or sparks wrap up insights and wisdom gained after your child has written answers to over a hundred questions and discussed them with you throughout the year. As an option, join in with your child and brainstorm responses together, which should be fun after all the questions, writing, and talks.

For example: "Reading is not just reading. . . ." Present this prompt for brainstorming. *Think about it*: If reading is not just reading, what else is it? *Sample answers*: Reading is thinking, feeling, imagining, dreaming, remembering, concentrating, reflecting, analyzing, synthesizing, contemplating, wonder, curiosity, experiencing, motivation, passion, attitude, open-mindedness, visualization. . . . As discussion leader in a one-to-one situation, add fuel to the fire by throwing in a brainstormed idea or two to keep the dialogue going. Let your child feed off you if necessary. Make it an exchange of ideas between parent and child.

IMPORTANT NOTES FOR ALL DISCUSSION LEADERS

Encourage your child to ask himself questions about reading life and the minilesson questions. *Self-questioning examples*: "How can I improve my answers?

What else can I say and reveal about my reading life? How serious am I about reading?"

There are many questions in Books 1 to 4 to keep kids involved and smiling. Determine which ones work best to increase motivation and responding by perusing the chapter titled "Skimming the Four Books of Questions" for a sampling of questions the author found by skimming the books. Also, check all the suggested survey samplings of questions in the "How to Use" sections in Books 1, 2, 3, and 4 before using them.

Can the questions be leveled according to grade? Which questions are appropriate for elementary, middle, and high school? Teacher discussion leaders must skim, review, and reread their selections to see if their kids can answer them. Parent discussion leaders should experiment with their question choices to find out which are doable in a one-to-one session. An "easy" question for the elementary grades might also work for middle and high school students. You never know exactly which questions are going to be a hit with adolescents, so you just have to play with it to discover the right stuff.

Discussion leaders can make up their own questions, especially after reading and asking so many of them. This initiative shows engagement as a questioner of kids' reading lives. Examine questions to see if you can find new questions starting from an original one. Check out how to extract and create other questions from an original question. *Sample book question:* In what ways is reading about silence? *New sample questions created by discussion leader:* Do you play music when reading? Why? In what ways is reading about "noise"? What "noise" is there while you read? What do you hear? Describe it. Is the "noise" distracting? Why or why not?

Keep an open mind when listening to responses, because discussion in *Motivating Teen and Preteen Readers* is an open book. If adolescents learn to keep an open mind toward reading, do the same to create a luminous atmosphere conducive to all learning.

The key word for all discussion leaders is *listening*: Listen to answers closely, ruminate on what is expressed, and then listen to yourself: What are you hearing? What is your child saying? How can it be interpreted? What questions will expand the response? How can answers be expanded to get kids on the right motivational track? How can I, as discussion leader, remove boredom, disinterest, distraction, and apathy from my kid's reading life? How can preteen/teen emotions change through questions and answers?

Motivating Teen and Preteen Readers, in a nutshell, is a question-and-answer project: You ask the questions and your child answers them. Discuss and expand upon the responses through your impromptu questions. Make things up, take your child on a ride, and keep the dialogue moving toward inner or self-motivation. A key long-range goal of the mini-lessons is that parent and child can accompany each other into reading's compelling magical world and share its "lonely pleasures" together.

MORE IDEAS, PROCEDURES, AND
REMINDERS FOR DISCUSSION LEADERS

Motivating Teen and Preteen Readers works with one child at home or forty students in a classroom. It remains the same for parents, with some adaptations, to the number of questions presented (parents can ask more), one-to-one discussions, and the evaluations. As a parent discussion leader, when reading the instructions for teachers, *reimagine* the situation for one person and substitute "child" for "class" or "students" (as has already been done). Here are ideas, points, and reminders when presenting the project: *Explore* your reading and reading life first. Review experiences by self-questioning: What is my reading life like? How did it start? How much do I read each day? Do I make time for reading? How much do I really enjoy reading? (See the motivational preface for parents and teachers titled "Hello Reading Life, Wherever You Are" for more self-examination questions.) After reviewing your reading life (to get a "read" on you), think about how much passion your child shows for reading. *Ask yourself:* How much motivation does my child need? How much do I want and expect from her? Which questions will inspire and grow reading life?

You might want to add friends and classmates, both motivated and unmotivated readers, to form a small group with your child. Have group meetings in your home when convenient for all. After introducing the project, let the kids answer two or more questions and discuss their responses; or, to save time in the mini-lesson, e-mail the questions in advance before the next live group meeting. *Stress* the importance of combining talks with writing to trigger a love of reading. When working with a small group, follow the same procedures used by teachers in whole class mini-lessons.

One-to-one and small-group lessons have the advantage of closeness, privacy, and manageable size. Parents may have extra time to extend discussions and enrich learning. Student-parent chats are easier because dealing with one child/small group as opposed to thirty kids means less pressure and more time to know the children.

One-to-one/small-group instruction, like class mini-lessons, focuses on written and oral responses. For example: Does the response answer the question? Are responses showing greater thought and reflection as more questions are asked and answered? Is my child or group listening carefully during discussions? Do the written responses reflect past discussions and raps? The mini-lesson's main goal is to excite kids about reading. Motivated readers are happy readers, and happy readers, regardless of age or ability level, want to read and improve their reading.

Demonstrate and model techniques and strategies for answering questions: Illustrate changing words into images and scanning reading experiences/memories using the inner eye and imaginary TV screen (see figures 1, 2, and 3, the same procedures used by classroom teachers). Let your child describe the mind-pictures viewed by the inner eye and how he or she finds them. *Rap*: "Reading is a trip to another world that goes on inside the mind's magic reading theater (an alternate universe, perhaps?), while everyday life fades away quickly on the outside.

How to handle the situation if kids don't understand a question has been previously discussed (see "Dealing with Problem Responses and Responders"): Explain the question again if there's confusion, or drop the question if it's too difficult or is for older kids. Use common sense and preview anticipated responses to questions: If you're coming up blank, chances are they will, too. As teacher/parent discussion leaders, have several questions on hand to ask the kids.

However, don't back off a challenging question too quickly. Let them think and reflect to see if they can find and/or create an answer to the question. Use that fuzzy moment to inspire teens and preteens to think, concentrate, and give more effort in the search for a strong response. Remind them to use storming techniques and the fundamental prerequisites for learning how to learn when responding (see "Storming Techniques to Answer Questions" and "Fundamental Prerequisite Skills Needed to Answer the Questions").

PROCEDURES FOR PARENT-TEACHERS OF HOMESCHOOLED KIDS

For one-to-one/small groups of preteens/teens in homeschooling situations, parent-teacher discussion leaders should follow procedures for parents and classroom teachers. Add and combine whatever works best in your circumstances. The homeschooling parent-teacher, tutor, mentor, and coach as discussion leader, has more leeway in scheduling compared to classroom teachers. Supplement reading skills lessons, test practice, and independent reading with motivational questions to complete your instructional curriculum. Work sequentially from Book 1 to 4 or use randomly selected questions from the books. Finish about two hundred questions per year via a survey approach for questioning. *Motivating Teen and Preteen Readers* can run in consecutive years from grade 4 to 5, 5 to 6, 6 to 7, and 7 to 8. The four books of questions will compliment all types of reading lessons and will certainly enrich, stimulate, and expand kids' enjoyment of the "lonely pleasures" of reading. This is an ideal project for homeschooled children.

PROCEDURES AND NOTES FOR PARENT
DISCUSSION LEADERS OF ADD/ADHD KIDS

Discussion leaders should follow procedures and notes for parents applying to one-to-one child-parent mini-lessons. There are only small changes for ADD/ADHD kids that will be explained in the upcoming instructions.

Ask two questions per session, twice a week, prefaced by parent raps, and follow up with short discussions. To expand attention span, slowly increase the number of questions per lesson after a month of responding (only if your child can handle it). Add one extra question each day for two days and see how he responds. Have mini-lessons every other day if that works best. If he can handle three questions a day, add a fourth question two weeks later. *Experiment*: Feel out the enthusiasm, patience, and control and work from those vantage points. The purpose of this approach is to gradually build up the ability to stay on a task longer, as well as pumping up a desire to read. Play with your schedule and the number of questions asked.

This inquiry- and passion-based strategy would work effectively with ADD/ADHD kids, in this writer's opinion, because:

- One-to-one nature: A quieter, peaceful environment affords less distraction, pressure, and more time to ask questions than a classroom teacher.
- Appeals to the creative imagination: Explaining the imaginary structures of the inner eye, TV screen in the mind, and the mind's magic reading theater motivates children to discover more about the processes, experiences, and their impact on reading and reading life. Through the magic theater, they realize that reading is a fun, quirky trip to a virtual world, where imagery, action, and lives of words come together and are enjoyed. The same points can be made about writing, writing life, and the mind's magic writing theater.
- Storming and creative strategies used to answer questions: The trigger method of creativity connects kids' spontaneity by creating freedom to express themselves via the different storming techniques. Visualization connects with the creative imagination, especially the theoretical, ideal concept of reading as a holographic reality (think of computer game imagery). They learn to appreciate the incredible picture shows, which stimulate and increase attention spans for longer periods of time, reducing hyperactivity and boredom. Again, these same ideas can be applied to the writing process and the mind's magic writing theater.
- Innovative questioning links openness to new ways of seeing and doing things: Kids are challenged by creative, funny, absurd, advanced placement, and good-for-dudes questions (more about the latter two questions in "How to Use Book 4"). ADD kids' openness is a potential step to change and a goal of *Motivating Teen and Preteen Readers*. *Rap*: "Keep an open mind to reading experiences as a way of changing your reading and real life."
- Intrinsic motivational approach needs good concentration to keep up interest: It embraces spirit, sensitivity, and flexibility. The children like expending energy to search the mind for experiences. Dynamic questions focus them on the task at hand. Attention, control, and drive build as more answers are written and discussed. The cumulative effects of the questions compel all students to slow down by recalling and reflecting before responding.
- Problem-solving needed for discovering self-motivation to read: Throughout the books of questions, kids try to solve the puzzle of motivation in reading

and how to increase attention span via their written and oral responses. They will not pass up the opportunity because it appeals to a desire to seek solutions and changes to reading and real-life hassles.

Most ideas presented here will work with *all kids*. *Reread* the above notes to see there aren't any boundary lines.

FINAL THOUGHTS ABOUT
MOTIVATING TEEN AND PRETEEN READERS

The four books of questions take your child's reading life, from the start to the present, and into the future. They answer important questions: How well do you know yourself as a reader? Does reading equal power? How good has your reading life been so far? What would your real life be without a reading life? Where do you see your reading life heading in the future? Do you see yourself as a lifelong reader?

The weekly raps, questions, writing, and discussions about reading motivate expression and communication of reading life experiences as well as family closeness. Reading, writing, thinking, creating, and feeling become releases, beginnings, and possibilities for all kids. Many questions turn into mindful, emotional, visual, and pleasure cruises through adolescent reading worlds.

Rap: "The questions show connections between reading and thinking. As a reader, you learn to think, think for yourself, and, to separate yourself from authors' thoughts. Reading and books are *mirrors* to see your thinking, how you think, your thoughts, as well as your self and the world reflected back to you. When answering questions, look into your mirror of reading life to uncover what has happened. By combining reading life with your written responses and writing, learn how to improve and appreciate critical and creative thinking, reflection, recall, concentration, and visualization skills, and most important, how to respond to literature. The reader and writer inside you will happily meet through the books of questions. Imagine the amazing power of your reading and writing lives. . . . Any questions?"

Skimming the Four Books of Questions

Opening Up Reading and
Reading Life for Teens and Preteens

If a seed of lettuce will not grow, we do not blame the lettuce. Instead, the fault lies with us for not having nourished the seed properly.

—Buddhist Proverb

SKIMMING THE FOUR BOOKS OF QUESTIONS FOR ANSWERS

Motivating Teen and Preteen Readers creates dynamic, open-minded, open-ended class raps and discussions where kids connect with their reading lives as well as their classmates' experiences. After responding to diverse questions in Books 1, 2, 3, and 4, they start to see and set goals for reading via self-discovery, self-motivation, and self-determination. At the end of a year, and after responding, hypothetically, to a hundred or more questions, they have a much better idea of their real interests in reading and books.

The books of questions are not only about student engagement, they are about teacher and parent engagement, because you can't have one without the other. The selected upcoming questions came from skimming the four books. It is recommended that all discussion leaders do this before introducing them to adolescents. The chosen questions are not directed at a specific child, group, or selected with any class in mind. Those that popped out at the author and would pump up kids—questions working from inside out and pushing them to tap inner resources and experiences in reading and reading life—are listed. Wait before skimming the books and presenting questions, at least until students' abilities in and attitudes (likes/dislikes) toward reading and reading life have been discovered. Then experiment with a plethora of questions.

Skim the books and go for questions that inspire thought and reflection. As a discussion leader, see if your choices would motivate or pump up *your* reading life. A fast skim will not necessarily come up with all the questions that would be used. After the initial skimming, apply a second review for the final selection of questions before starting each book. If trying a random approach to question choices — going through all four books to find questions — you can use the following strategy: For example, you've already picked questions by skimming and want to review your selection. Reread the questions in groups of three to five at a time and contemplate answers to them. Take a few moments to think about answers. In this way you can foresee or have some understanding of what your kids might express in their written responses. The technique helps to generate discussion questions. whether they're for a class, small group, or one-to-one parent-child situations.

In between the upcoming skimmed questions, there will be prompts in italics such as:

- Discussion leader: Stop, recall, and contemplate.
- Discussion leader: Pause, reflect, and think.

Teachers and parents should use this method with the following questions to see if they would fire up a class/child to probe inside their reading worlds. Anticipate what their overall effects/affects would be on teen and preteen reading lives.

SAMPLE SKIMMING OF BOOKS 1, 2, 3, AND 4

Book 1

Read for fun? Do you? Explain.

Visualize and draw a happy reader in his or her reading world.

What was the first book you remember reading by yourself? What thoughts are triggered by the book? What feelings come back to you?

Discussion leader: Stop, reflect, and contemplate.

Think of a word that makes you feel good. Silently say the word over and over again to yourself. Describe what you experienced.

How cool and calm are you when reading? Explain your answer.

Describe a lousy day in reading.

Discussion leader: Stop, reflect, and contemplate.

Other worlds are possible — read. Explain.

What book would you give someone to turn that person on to reading? Why?

Would you rather look at the imaginary TV screen in your mind or the big screen TV in your living room? Why?

When you read silently, there is an inner imaginary reading voice that mouths, speaks, says, and reads the words. Describe your inner reading voice.

Discussion leader: Stop, reflect, and think.

Book 2

How is a book an invitation?

Always read as if it is your first time. Explain.

How does the outside world fade away so quickly once you begin to read? How does this happen? Is it an easy or hard switch for you to make? Why?

What is the connection between reading and feeling? Give an example.

Discussion leader: Stop, reflect, and ponder.

Recall a time you chose to be alone with a book and away from your friends. Why did you choose reading over your friends? Was it a good choice? Why?

Were you rewarded for reading when you were much younger? Explain. Give an example. Did the reward motivate you to read more or to like reading more? Explain.

What is the longest you have read at one time? What kept you going? Why?

Can music get you into reading if you feel tired? Explain your answer.

Does history *come to life* when you read a history textbook? Why or why not?

Discussion leader: Stop, recall, and reflect.

How is reading on a reading test different from other reading experiences?

Do you daydream, at times, while you read? Why? Give an example.

Is reading searching? Explain your answer.

Discussion leader: Stop, recall, and reflect.

Do reading and books teach you to think for yourself? Explain your answer.

(a) Make up an absurd, ridiculous, silly sentence and write it. (b) Visualize the sentence and then draw or sketch the picture created in your mind. (c) What thoughts come up after you finish the activity?

Athletes say they're "in the zone" when playing at their best. Describe your reading when you're reading "in the zone."

Discussion leader: Stop, reflect, and contemplate.

Book 3

Reading every day quietly changes your world. Explain.

"Take up and read, take up and read" (St. Augustine). What does the quote mean? What does it suggest? Why does he repeat the line? Is the quote important to you? Explain your answers.

How can you improve your ability to read?

Did a teacher ever challenge you to become a better reader? How? Why? Did the challenge work? Explain.

Discussion leader: Pause, reflect, and think.

How are you living a story when you read it? How is this possible?

The English poet, William Wordsworth, called reading a book a "lonely pleasure." What did he mean? Do you think it's something negative? What is he getting at?

How good are you at changing words into mind-pictures (images)? Rate yourself on a scale from 0 to 10, where 0 = poor ability, and 10 = excellent ability. Give reasons for your rating.

When does reading become boring? Explain.

Discussion leader: Pause, reflect, and ruminate.

Do you ask questions about what you read? Explain.

How can you instantly increase your concentration when reading?

Does reading make you more aware or unaware of your real life? Explain.

Discussion leader: Pause, reflect, and deliberate.

Read for power. Explain. (*Hint*: Look up "power" in a dictionary or thesaurus for definitions and synonyms before answering.)

You are what you eat, but, are you what you read? Explain.

Read to dream. . . . Explain.

Poets are teachers. Explain. Give an example of what a poet has taught you.

Discussion leader: Pause, recall, reflect, and contemplate.

Book 4

Mind-pictures: reading's little miracles. Explain.

Reading seizes the moment. Explain by giving an example.

I read to escape from the real world. Imagine a dreamlike, surreal, absurd, or fantasy image for the statement. Picture-storm images and sketch one you really liked.

Let your feelings breathe—read. Explain the statement's meaning. Does it have meaning for you? Why?

Discussion leader: Pause, reflect, and contemplate.

Think about this: Reading is about attitude. What do you think? Explain. (*Hint*: Look up "attitude" in a dictionary and thesaurus for definitions and synonyms before answering.)

Tiny words = jumbo jets. Explain.

How are readers like thrill-seekers? Give an example.

Discussion leader: Stop, recall, and ponder.

Imagine that: Reading televises your mind back to you. Explain.

What is your biggest problem in reading right now? Why? Give a solution.

How is your mind like a vacuum cleaner in the reading process?

Discussion leader: Stop, recall, and contemplate.

Think about this: Mary was confused about reading: some days she liked it, and on other days she disliked it. How would you, as the reading guidance counselor, help Mary to end her confusion and make a decision about reading? What would be your rap to her? Why?

Visualize the word "butterfly." Picture one in your mind. Now picture another one and more and more until they completely fill your mind. Stop: look at the mind-picture you created. Describe what you see and then draw the image.

Do you feel, at times, like you're in a "bubble" when you read? Explain.

Discussion leader: Stop, ponder, and visualize.

How is reading like playing sports?

Words heal; words hurt. Explain.

Read to live, but don't live to read. What does the statement suggest about reading and its possible consequences? What do you think: agree or disagree? Why?

When is a reader born?

Discussion leader: Stop, think, and contemplate.

SKIMMING NOTES

Skimming Books 1, 2, 3, and 4 produced an eclectic list of questions. It should inspire teacher and parent discussion leaders because they trigger many extraordinary experiences in reading and reading life. My mind and imagination flooded with thoughts about what would come next to evoke phenomenal, magical reading worlds. Numerous experiences lay dormant and scattered inside, but were now revealed through the inquiries. Are the choices viable for reenergizing adolescent reading lives? Imagine that . . .

The skimmed choices came mostly from reading process, common, everyday reading experiences, and one-line statement questions, with several handfuls from past reading experiences, opinion, drawing, hypothetical reading situations, word/word activities, book recalls, nonfiction, poetry reading life, rating, quotation, and writing questions.

A rationale for the question selections' relevance is: As a discussion leader, you want students to fully understand the reading process, because with greater insight into imagery, emotion, and thinking, they increase their passion for, and learn to see, reading more as a virtual reality. Examining what happens in the mind when reading gives kids feedback about its nature and power, which makes or breaks motivation and a response to literature. Questions on everyday reading experiences are not always discussed in class or at home and can initiate the stimulus for a renewed desire to read. A student/child has an opportunity to write about and discuss the human side of reading. One-line statements give preteens/teens time to reflect on their ideas and beliefs about reading/reading life. They get a platform to express themselves, and what they have to say should be respected by discussion leaders. Past reading experience questions help students reconnect with early reading life roots and give them insight about their beginnings, whether positive or negative. If questions bring up bad attitudes toward reading, that's okay. As discussion leader, it's your responsibility to deal with their thinking. Let kids realize and encounter their reading gremlins: It might save their reading lives.

Another practical way teachers and parents can use the skimming chapter is: Starting with Book 1, skim the questions to see which would appeal to preteens/

teens and suit their needs. Also, think about the questions that appeal to you as discussion leader. After skimming questions in Book 1, reread and respond to them carefully to be more selective in your choices. Pick thirty or more questions from Book 1 and ask them over a two-and-a-half-month period.

Notes for elementary through high school teachers: To make classroom life easier and to expedite the project, type your questions and photocopy them for the class. Students get copies of Book 1's questions and tape each question in their reading notebooks as they come up in the mini-lessons. Elementary school teachers can use this *suggestion* to reduce the extra time copying questions from the board, especially the longer ones. In fact, to make it simple, just photocopy the longer questions intended for use and hand out. This is directed at middle and high school teachers to save time and effort. Teachers, if they prefer, can write the shorter, chosen questions on the board in the morning for students to copy prior to the day's mini-lesson.

All questions should either be handwritten or taped in the reading notebooks. Students, when rereading their responses for the self- and teacher/parent evaluations, will need the questions in front of them in order to appreciate their answers.

A note and anecdote about skimming: Teachers and parents can use the information, ideas, and knowledge found in the numerous questions to create original questions of their own. Use the skimming technique, along with reflection and thought, to trigger more questions that might be a better fit for your class's or child's needs.

Think about this: A TV chef, while talking about her recipe for meatballs, said it started with a cookbook recipe. She added her own creative choices (other ingredients) to it and, in her opinion, improved the original recipe for meatballs.

Discussion leaders can do the same thing in *Motivating Teen and Preteen Readers*. Take questions from the four books and let them jumpstart original questions. As teachers and parent-teachers with lots of background, experience, and wisdom in reading and reading life, empower yourself by opening up to your creativity by brainstorming ideas, word-storming words, and/or picture-storming images to discover new questions not found in the book. By creating fresh, novel questions, teachers and parents demonstrate a strong commitment to, and engagement in, pumping up preteen and teen readers.

SKIMMING AND THE CONTINUING TALE
OF MICHAEL, THE RELUCTANT READER

Consider how the skimming technique can assist Michael (remember him, our reluctant reader?) on a real voyage (not an imaginary hot-air balloon ride) through his mind and imagination. My aim as discussion leader is to take Michael on a trip through his experiences by asking questions that mirror or reflect back what's happened to him, and how he can make changes and take control of his reading life. With this objective in mind, I skimmed the books of questions for an eclectic sample of questions (called a survey approach) to break down his reluctance to read. Remember that there are many ways a series and sequence of questions can be presented to adolescents to weaken their resistance to and build a passion for reading.

Skimming allows me to find the questions specific enough to complete a one-year journey through his reading worlds so he can connect with these experiences to realize and appreciate their relevance in his reading life. As discussion leaders, feel your way through the dissidence of preteen and teen reading lives by making things up: Experiment with your question selections. My choices in the upcoming chapter titled "Why Won't Michael Read? One Solution . . ." will hopefully inspire him to pick up a book because he wants to read: Call it intrinsic or self-motivation, the last stop in the project for all readers.

Why Won't Michael Read?
One Solution . . .

No matter how he may think himself accomplished, when he sets out to learn a new language, science, or the bicycle, he has entered a new realm as truly as if he were a child newly born into the world.

—Frances Willard, *How I Learned to Ride the Bicycle*

THE QUESTION-AND-INQUIRY TECHNIQUE
AND INTRINSIC MOTIVATION

The introduction started the tale of Michael, a reluctant reader. He wasn't interested in reading no matter how many great books his father bought him. As discussion leader, I wanted this sixth-grade student to find the motivation to read from the inside by taking him on an imaginary hot-air balloon ride through his imagination via provocative questions about reading. Once inside his reading world he can attempt to find answers to his reading conflict. Can the books of questions help reinvent Michael as a self-motivated reader? Will he become the master of his fate and determine his reading future? Can Michael revitalize his lost interest in reading?

In my trek through the books of questions I searched for channels to Michael's reading world. An eclectic array of skimmed questions was chosen because I did not know exactly what was going on inside his head. (See the suggested sample approaches for presenting questions in Books 1 to 4 for more examples of survey strategies.) Keep in mind that the upcoming skimmed questions offer only a partial solution to Michael's tale and his reading problem. There would be many other questions asked to build passion and inner motivation during the year.

The big question for me and all discussion leaders is: Can choosing the most appropriate and timely questions in *Motivating Teen and Preteen Readers* rekindle Michael's, or an adolescent's, reading life? By skimming the questions and testing them through trial and error, I would see which ones get the strongest responses and make a difference in his reading life.

THE BEGINNING OF MICHAEL'S JOURNEY: PAST READING EXPERIENCE QUESTIONS

To start Michael's journey, I skimmed the questions to find one that would take him back to his forgotten early reading life. *Sample skimmed question* (from question category "Reading Experiences"): "What was the first or an early book you remember reading by yourself? What thoughts and feelings come back when you think about it?" Return this sixth-grade student to those memories and see what emerges. Invite Michael to reflect on his experiences, the good and bad times. Get him to ponder and feel the events to discover new insights into his reading and reading life, a view that increases his motivation to read.

BRINGING MICHAEL TO THE PRESENT: EVERYDAY READING, ONE-LINE, AND HYPOTHETICAL QUESTIONS

I decided to return Michael to his current reading life with questions skimmed from the "Reading Experiences/Everyday Reading" category: "Why do you read?" and "Read for fun? Do you? Why or why not?" By probing early on his reasons for reading or not reading, you find out right away how motivated he is: Does he enjoy the reading experience or is he conflicted about it? The questions allow Michael to review his present reading situation.

Move Michael further into his reading life with a skimmed one-line statement question: "Reading brings peace. What do you think? Explain." This is another question to find clues about his desire to read. Let him see reading as a peaceful journey (even if he might not agree at this point), something that is self-entertaining, a relaxing thing to do when alone, and not just a subject about drills and tests. Discussion leaders should stop to contemplate a response to the statement and add their own questions to expand and enrich the ideas brought out by it. *Sample questions* are: Do you remember a time when you experienced peace while reading? What were you reading? What were you thinking and feeling at the time? Does it happen often? Does school reading bring you peace? What kind of reading brings you peace?

In a classroom situation, collaborative reflection on this mini-lesson question triggers an exchange of ideas on how reading brings peace, enabling students such as Michael to see different roads to, or possibilities for, positive reading

Illustration 10.   Reading ain't heavy, it's your friend. . . .
Illustration by James Jajac.

experiences. His classmates' responses may rub off on Michael and make him re-evaluate his own reading experiences to see the times reading brought him peace. Maybe he can uncover a negative attitude toward reading in his review. (In one-to-one discussions, parents can add *their* experiences to their child's answers.)

But there were other one-line statement questions found on a skimming cruise to keep Michael reflecting on his reading life: "Reading takes courage. What do you think?" These short statement questions pose speculative ideas on reading which require a thoughtful response. He has to learn to pause before responding to avoid automatic answers.

Poor Michael must be feeling a little bit of heat now, but alas, he's not finished with his trip yet, he's only just begun. A hypothetical question (category: "Reading Experiences") was found describing a fictitious reading situation—corresponding to his own—that needs solutions. Skimmed question: "Mary was confused about reading: Some days she liked it, and other days she disliked it. How would you, as the reading guidance counselor, help Mary end her confusion and finally make a decision about reading? What would be your rap to her? Why?"

This question will affect Michael and probably a lot of other kids. Hypothetical reading situation questions will connect with unsuspecting reluctant readers. If the question stirs up Michael's mind and imagination about his ambivalence toward reading, that's fine. A discussion leader's role is to activate inside worlds by jumpstarting a kid's internal monologue as well as class or one-to-one dia-logues. *Extract more details with added questions*: Do you think your response as student-counselor to Mary's problem will work? Why or why not? Do you think it's realistic? How do you handle those days when you're not in the mood to read? How do you move past it? Or, do you? The handful of skimmed questions should gradually penetrate his attitude toward reading and make him think about it a little more.

LIGHTEN THINGS UP WITH
CREATIVE-THINKING AND DRAWING QUESTIONS

Hit reluctant readers like Michael with some toughies to confront his reading demons. However, as discussion leader you don't want to scare off kids too soon with heavy questions. Skim for creative-thinking and drawing questions to lighten up the mood for adolescent readers (question category: "Writing, Draw-ing, and Creative Thinking"). Present absurd, imaginary reading scenes requiring inventive responses. *Sample skimmed question*: "My teacher once told us that she always carried a pet book around with her. She never wanted to be away from it: that's how much she loved her pet. Imagine carrying a pet book with you all the time. Which book would you pick? Why?"

Michael has to go creative to come up with a pet book, something he would always have in his back pack to keep him company, a true blue friend. Using the inner eye to scan book memories (see figure 3), he can conjure up imaginative ideas about his book choice and reasons for it, and positive thoughts, feelings, and images about reading and reading life. Discussion will expand on the pluses of reading, books, and reading life.

And while working on Michael's imagination, drawing questions (same as the previous question's category) were skimmed to introduce real and fantastic reading experiences which are visualized, illustrated, and contemplated. *Sample skimmed question*: "Visualize the most ridiculous places to read. Picture-storm places by triggering one image after another in your mind. Pick the silliest image (one you like and can draw) and pencil-sketch it. Your drawing can be a cartoon with a short caption."

This skimmed question addresses a less serious side to reading life: It's about having fun and easing the stress coming from the current testing climate. *Expand the question with:* How would the place affect your reading: for better or worse? What are the craziest or most ridiculous places where you have read? Describe it and the effects on your reading. I went from surreal to real reading places to see Michael's ability to concentrate in exceptional situations, and also to find out how strong his motivation to read is. Teacher discussion leaders, working with an entire class, can put on an art show in the discussion by having students tape their finished sketches on the board—and remember: Masterpieces are not necessary.

WHAT MICHAEL SEES: QUESTIONS ON WORDS AND THE READING PROCESS

Now that Michael's smiling from his funny pencil-sketches, I skimmed questions from the "Word and Word Activity" category, which can increase his appreciation for the building blocks of reading: words. The unconventional questions in this category tap Michael's capacity to think creatively about words by changing them into mind-pictures, thoughts, ideas, and feelings: for example, "Tiny words = jumbo jets." (See figure 1, "The Reading Process," for an illustration of visualizing the word "tree.") Questions on words help preteens like Michael to enjoy the power, beauty, and fun they create in the mind/imagination.

Sample skimmed word and word activity questions:

- Are words just black on white, or are they something more? Explain.
- Think of a word that makes you feel good. Say it over and over again to yourself. Describe what you experienced.
- Snow: What do you see, feel, think, and wonder?
- What word stresses you out instantly? Why?
- Strawberry shortcake; vanilla and chocolate milkshakes; peppermint candies; hot cinnamon buns with vanilla icing; hot dogs with ketchup; cheeseburger

deluxe; peanut-butter-and-jelly sandwiches. Describe what you experienced after reading this list.
- How powerful are words? Explain your answer by giving examples.

From imaginative questions on words, I skimmed for questions that would feel out Michael's knowledge of the reading process: what he does when reading and how he does it.

Sample skimmed questions on the reading process:

- Read a page from a book (fiction) and describe any thoughts, feelings, and images triggered.
- Does your reading pace ever change? Why? Give an example.
- What is concentration? How important is it in reading? Why?
- When you read silently, there is an inner, imaginary reading voice that mouths, speaks, says, and reads the words. Describe your inner reading voice.
- Describe how you remember what you read while you read.
- Reading can get you lost in world of thought. Recall a time when reading got you lost in a world of thought. What were you reading? What were you thinking? Where did your thoughts take you? Was it worth the trip? Why?
- Did you ever get lost in a crowd of words while reading? Describe what happened. How, or did you, find your way out? Explain your answer.
- Do you pause for a moment to think about or reflect on what you read? Why?

QUESTIONS ON WRITING LIFE RETURN PASSION TO READING LIFE

But this book of questions is not only about reading: It also attempts to engage teens and preteens in writing. Word and word-activity questions prepare Michael for future questions on writing. If he increases his motivation to read and discovers a new appreciation for words by changing them into mind-pictures and has fun doing it, he's ready to write, to express himself in words. The questions help Michael to make the reading-writing connection organically. And once he is motivated to write, he'll return to his reading life with greater enthusiasm through a writing-reading connection.

Sample skimmed questions to stimulate Michael's writing life:

- Can reading motivate you to write? Why?
  (a) Make up three ridiculously silly sentences.
  (b) Use sentence-storming (trigger one sentence after another) to find answers.
  (c) Visualize each sentence and briefly describe what you see.
  (d) How can creating silly sentences help you become a better writer?

- Relaxation time: Put your head down and close your eyes for two minutes. When you finish, write about your experience. Describe what came to mind in fifty words or more. Do your words—or description—give an accurate account of what happened while your eyes were closed? Why or why not?
- Imagine that: What happened to the child who never stopped reading? Write an imaginary tale in one hundred words or more. Illustrate the story with one or more sketches. (*Hint*: Picture-storm images and brainstorm ideas before starting your story.)

Writing questions will inspire passion in Michael's reading life. If he grasps the value of words in his writing, to see them, ideally, as a three-dimensional, holographic, virtual reality (as he would in the reading process), then he would come back to reading with a rejuvenated attitude and understanding. Words become more meaningful for him via the creative and demanding writing questions. They initiate a fresh experience in the mind's magic writing theater where creative ideas and images hang out. Their importance is also connected to the mind's magic reading theater: Call it the writing-reading connection, the reverse process of the reading-writing connection.

MICHAEL ASSESSES HIS READING AND READING LIFE WITH RATING QUESTIONS

Michael's really being tested, that's for sure. After all his hard work, he will have a chance to grade himself on his reading prowess with rating questions skimmed from the four books of questions. These questions allow him to assess his reading skills and how much effort he gives during the reading process via honest, objective, thought-out answers. The question category develops an emotional awareness about reading and reading life through his marks, something a reluctant reader needs to do.

Sample skimmed questions:

- Rate your ability to think about and reflect on what you read on a scale from 0 to 10, where 0 = giving no thought, and 10 = giving a lot of thought. Give a reason(s) for your rating.
- How good are you at changing words into mind-pictures (images)? Rate yourself on a scale from 0 to 10, where 0 = poor ability, and 10 = excellent ability. Give reasons for your rating.
- How well do you communicate with yourself while reading? Rate your ability on a scale from 0 to 10, where 0 = poor, and 10 = powerful self-communication. Give reasons for your rating.

QUOTATIONS TO SUM UP READING-LIFE EXPERIENCES

Michael has answered diverse questions on reading and reading life. Now, as discussion leader, I wanted to finish his reading journey with quotation questions to sum up his experiences. Quotations compel him to pause, recall, scan, visualize, and refresh his memory. Besides the search for key experiences to answer the quotation, he first translates and understands it in his mind, without changing its meaning.

Look over the following skimmed quotations to see if and how they fit into Michael's current reading life and if they can help him find a way to a better attitude toward reading and realize new inspiration:

- "Take up and read, take up and read" (St. Augustine). What does the quote mean? Why does he repeat the lines? Is the quote important to you? Explain.
- Explain whether or not the quotation is good advice to improve your reading, reading test scores, and reading life: "Resolve to edge in a little reading every day, if it is but a single sentence. If you gain fifteen minutes a day, it will make itself felt at the end of the year" (Horace Mann).
- "I read my eyes out and can't read half enough. . . . The more one reads the more one sees we have to read" (John Adams). What does the quote mean? Has this been your experience? Explain by giving an example from your reading life.
- "A word after a word after a word is power" (Margaret Atwood). Explain the quote's meaning: How does "a word after a word after a word" become power? What creates this power?
- "I am not a speed reader. I am a speed understander" (Issac Asimov). Why does Asimov choose speed understanding over speed reading? Do you? Explain.
- "Books can be dangerous. The best ones should be labeled 'This Could Change Your Life'" (Helen Exley). What does the quotation mean? Do you think books have that much power? Explain.
- "Read in order to live" (Gustave Flaubert). Explain the quote's meaning. Write an essay about the quote in one hundred words or more. (*Optional*: Instead of an essay, write a fairy tale, fable, or myth about the quotation in one hundred words or more.)

How do the skimmed quotations encourage Michael to face his reading life experiences?

STUDENT AND TEACHER/PARENT EVALUATIONS OF READING PROGRESS

Michael's self-interrogation, this question-and-inquiry strategy, to reach the heart of his reading life isn't over yet. There are three more phases, evaluations of the books of questions called the student questionnaire, student-teacher/parent chat, and the epilogue.

After completing every thirty to seventy-five questions (in one or more books), Michael rereads and assesses his progress in reading, reading life, and the questions through a student questionnaire (of twenty questions) and then discusses his responses. Call this questionnaire a "self-evaluation," the kind preteens and teens like because they do the evaluating and it's all about them.

Here are *sample skimmed evaluation questions*—determined by the previous questions—for Michael's hypothetical student questionnaire (see "Evaluation Questions" for Books 1 to 3 for more assessment questions):

What thoughts and feelings come to mind after rereading your responses?
Did you learn anything new about (your) reading?
Can the questions improve reading? Explain.
Which question triggered many reading life experiences?
What have you learned about words?
What have you realized about negative reading experiences?
Do you believe you can motivate yourself to read? Why or why not?
Where does motivation come from: the outside and/or the inside? Why?
What, if anything, has changed in your reading life? Explain.

Check out *sample skimmed questions* for a hypothetical student-teacher/parent chat (See "Evaluation Questions" for Books 1 to 3 for more chat questions):

Are the books of questions fun for you?
Do the questions make you think and reflect?
What surprised you about the questions?
When you think of the word reading, what words come to mind?
Are you more aware of what goes on inside yourself while reading?
Do you read more after school these days?
Has a question helped you with your reading life?
Can the questions motivate a child to overcome a reading problem?
Has your imagination improved after answering the questions?
Is there a secret to becoming a successful or good reader?
What do you think is the magic of reading?
Do you see yourself becoming a lifelong reader?
Can the questions change an unhappy reader into a happier reader?

EPILOGUE PROMPTS ON READING/READING LIFE, CREATIVITY/IMAGINATION, AND WRITING

At the end of the year, complete the cycle of evaluations by skimming for prompts from the epilogue so Michael can integrate and really appreciate the accumulated insights. The prompt categories are reading/reading life, creativity/imagination, and writing. Prompts are presented to the class/child in each area for oral and/or written brainstorming (See the epilogue for additional prompts and brainstorming procedures.)

Sample skimmed epilogue prompts on reading/reading life:

Reading is all about the action in the mind's magic reading theater.
Books = teachers, counselors, poets, parents, brothers, sisters, friends, and pets
Reading is not just reading. . . .
Can a word beat you up?
Reading as a window to your heart . . .
Reading in the zone: hypnotic concentration

Sample skimmed prompts for creativity/imagination:

The power of creativity . . .
Experimenting = the creative life
"Everything you can imagine is real" (Picasso).
Read and imagine and imagine and imagine . . .
Creativity = mind magic

Sample skimmed writing prompts:

Write to connect.
Write to celebrate yourself.
Write to know yourself.
Writers and readers = communicators

ADDITIONAL STRATEGIES FOR PRESENTING MICHAEL QUESTIONS ON READING

How would the new strategies for asking questions affect his reading/reading life? How can teacher/parent discussion leaders apply these approaches to liven things up for Michael? For instance, a little mellow music might soothe him back to his early book memories when he first learned how to read by himself. A question such as "Why do you read?" can be enhanced with three students brainstorming responses to it; or, a duet with Michael and a motivated reader/buddy bouncing answers off each other. Wouldn't that be nice? (See the "additional strategies section" in the mini-lesson chapter for more information about all the techniques discussed here.)

What about one-line statement questions such as "Reading brings peace" and "Reading takes courage": How would he be influenced by working with a partner

Illustration 11. Reading is an adventure.
Illustration by James Jajac.

in a duet activity? The early question/late response technique could help Michael with the hypothetical reading situation where Mary was also a reluctant reader (à la Michael), sometimes liking it and other times not so thrilled about it. Letting the question incubate in his mind gives him a chance to envision potential answers, new possibilities — for *Michael*.

"What are some of the most ridiculous places to read?" was another question that could be jumpstarted with a three-student brainstorming session and would bring greater pleasure and humor into his dull reading life.

The writing question that asks "to make up three ridiculously silly sentences" would be more fun in a three-way brainstorming session with classmates: It might trigger a stronger response and positive attitude toward writing and thinking. Duets can work with this question as well. Michael could "rate his ability to change words into images" via: relax-and-respond, the music hour, and a duet with a knowledgeable partner to initiate new insights to his visualization skills, a key component to enjoying reading and understanding the reading process.

And finally, quotations about reading could be enriched through the music hour, relax-and-respond, and early question/late response strategies.

Try out these different approaches to presenting questions via trial and error and see what happens: How would Michael respond to the questions if you mixed things up?

IMAGINE A NEW READING LIFE FOR MICHAEL

The books of questions empower Michael to find a route to a better reading life. Teachers and parents have the option of skimming and choosing questions that

Illustration 12.   A new reading life for a reluctant reader.
Illustration by James Jajac.

work with individuals, small groups, and/or an entire class. As discussion leaders, pick questions that work best to help kids help themselves.

The skimmed questions allow Michael to slowly engage himself in reading. Will Michael ever read in peace because he likes to read? This short study shows how a small sampling of questions on reading, reading life, and writing gives a preteen the opportunity to take charge of his reading destiny. Imagine where he would be in his reading life after a year's worth of questions, for example, three each week for forty weeks, along with follow-up discussions? Imagine presenting five questions a week for an entire year: How would it affect adolescent readers? And what would happen after kids evaluate their growth in reading and reading life? What would they see? Where would they be in their reading and real lives? And that's a lot of questions that can be answered in the books of questions: So pump it up, Michael!

REASONS PRETEENS AND TEENS
WILL ENJOY THE BOOKS OF QUESTIONS

Young people will find reasons for answering many questions on reading/reading life:

- Entertaining, imaginative, challenging, diverse questions
- Discovering, independently, their purposes for reading
- Expressing personal opinions about reading and reading life
- Thinking skills developed to make reading more interesting and do-able
- Finding affective side to reading sparks stronger, inner response to literature
- Rediscovering the creative imagination needed for reading and real life
- Learning to understand their thinking/thoughts while reading
- Kids coming first in this organic, student-centered, holistic approach
- Responses focusing on reading life experiences, not "correct" answers
- Reading becoming a new, exciting, virtual 3-D reality
- Building self-confidence and self-belief in reading abilities
- Confronting reading demons in order to change them
- Reducing stress coming from test mania and test anxiety
- Self-evaluations of progress/growth in reading and reading life
- Seeing themselves as readers and uncovering reading's possibilities
- Taking responsibility for being in charge of their reading lives and fates
- Leisure-time reading becoming a viable choice to the electro-techno world

Book 1

Once children learn how to learn, nothing is going to narrow their mind. The essence of teaching is to make learning contagious, to have one idea spark another.

—Marva Collins

ABOUT BOOK 1

Skimming, Surveying, and Question Categories

Book 1 serves as the introduction for Books 2, 3, and 4. Most questions are basic starter prompts that motivate kids to think about reading and reading life. As discussion leaders, teachers and parents should constantly remind students not to answer questions automatically without stopping to think. Tougher questions require greater visualization, recollection, and reflection. Skim the questions first to get a feel for the different question categories and see which ones would fit in with the class's/child's needs. *Motivating Teen and Preteen Readers* complements a classroom reading program as valuable downtime instruction and a transition mini-lesson of ten to fifteen minutes.

A survey approach for Book 1, or thirty to seventy-five randomly selected questions from the four books (call it Round 1), is recommended to cover a wide range of topics. Book 1 has the following question categories, appearing in order of most to least frequently asked questions:

- Reading Experiences: Common (Everyday), Past (Early), and Hypothetical
- Reading Reflections: Book Recalls, Nonfiction, and Poetry
- Words and Word Activities
- One-Line Statements and Opinions

- Reading Process
- Writing, Drawing, and Creative Thinking
- Ratings and Quotations

The categories are not absolute. One question can jibe with several categories. *For example*: Get into what you read and enjoy yourself in thought. Do you? Why or why not? This question fits in the categories of: one-line statement; reading process; and common, everyday reading experiences, in the author's opinion.

BOOK 1 QUESTIONS

Note for all discussion leaders: When reading the questions for Book 1 follow the strategy used in the skimming chapter. Read three to five questions and pause for a moment or two to contemplate responses. The questions shouldn't be read like a textbook because it would be too much to comprehend and assimilate at one sitting. Instead, try to be more deliberate in your approach: It will give you an idea of what answers to anticipate in mini-lessons and potential follow-up discussion questions to the written responses. Take time to ponder, ruminate, reflect, and think about responses every few minutes as you read the questions in Books 1 to 4.

Reading Experiences: Common (Everyday), Past (Early), and Hypothetical

1. Why do you read?
2. Read for fun? Do you? Why or why not?
3. What makes you grab a book off the library or bookstore shelf instantly?
4. How did you learn to read?
5. Describe the kind of stories you like to read.
6. Do you read for fun at night? Why or why not?
7. Did anyone give you a book that turned you on to reading? Who? What book? Why did it get you to enjoy reading?
8. What is the right time for you to read? Why?
9. Does where you read affect your reading? Why?
10. What is a good place for you to read? What makes it so good?
11. Does reading wake you up? Explain.
12. What do you like the most about the book you are reading now?
13. Do you feel excited when you're about to start reading? What feelings do you normally experience before you begin? Explain your answers.
14. How cool and calm are you when reading? Explain your answer.

15. Can you read when you're stressed? Why or why not? How do you manage to read and comprehend the material? How do you motivate yourself to continue reading?
16. Do you have to be relaxed or at peace when reading? Why?
17. Did you ever feel that reading was a waste of time? Explain.
18. Think of a book you first read by yourself: What memories are triggered?
19. How did your reading life begin?
20. Think about this: You had help in learning how to read: parents, teachers, siblings, and friends. What have you done to teach yourself how to read? How did you educate or help yourself in reading?
21. Do you enjoy the solitude and silence of reading and your reading world? Explain your answer.
22. Describe your earliest feelings about reading. Have they changed since then? Why?
23. Is the title important when you select a book to read? Why? How can a title motivate you to read a book? Give an example of one that got you going and explain why.
24. Do you like happy or sad books (fiction or nonfiction)? Why? Give an example.
25. Do you like to read easy or hard books? Why?
26. Do you like to reread easy books? Do you reread books? Explain your answers.
27. Why read novels totally different from your own life?
28. How do you choose a book to read?
29. Why did you pick the last book you read?
30. What do you bring to any book you read?
31. What book did you want to read aloud over and over again when you were very young? What can you recall: images, feelings, thoughts, and words?
32. Have you ever read a book over and over again? Why?
33. How do you find something to read when you don't know what to read?
34. Do you look forward to reading at the end of a school day? Explain.
35. Can you read after a bad day? Why or why not?
36. What do you read to chill out? Why?
37. When is reading sweet peace for you?
38. Do you feel a sense of accomplishment after you finish reading a book? Why? What is accomplished or realized?
39. What is the reading magic of someone reading aloud to you?
40. Which activity would you choose in your free time: reading, TV, music, video games, computer (Internet), hanging out, or sports? Why? When would you choose reading over the others? Why?
41. When is reading entertaining? Explain.
42. When is reading work? Explain.

43. Describe a lousy day in reading.
44. Do you like books that challenge your mind to think hard? Explain.
45. Describe what happens if you try to read a book you are not ready to read.
46. Do you have memories of someone reading to you at bedtime when you were little? What comes to mind?
47. Imagine that: Can a book or reading stop your world? Explain. Give an example.
48. Recall your earliest reading memory: Find the picture(s) and describe what you see.
49. Recall a positive classroom reading experience or memory. What comes to mind: pictures, feelings, and thoughts?
50. What is difficult about learning how to read in school? Visualize a school memory and the thoughts and feelings it triggers.
51. How often do you read on your own? What is this reading world like?
52. Do you discuss books with your friends when you are not in school? Why?
53. Think about this: You want to do two things: read a book and listen to music, but not at the same time. Which activity would you do first: read or listen to music? Why? Does it matter which one you do first? Should you read and listen to music at the same time? Explain your answers.
54. Are there days when you hate to read? Why?
55. When you learned how to read, you also learned about patience: Why?
56. What did you think the first time you stepped into a library? What did the library look like to you? What were you feeling?
57. Did your reading life change once you got a library card? Why or why not?
58. Where can't you read? Why?
59. Recall a time your hard work in reading paid off. What were you reading? What hard work did you put into your reading? Why so much energy? What did you accomplish?
60. Would you call reading hard work or hard fun? Explain.
61. Do you feel frustrated or disappointed at times after you finish reading a book (fiction or nonfiction)? Why?
62. Describe your way of relaxing with a book.
63. How is summertime reading different from reading during the school year?
64. Do you read when taking a long trip by car, bus, train, or plane? Why or why not?
65. Can a reading journal help you with your reading and reading life? Explain.
66. Do you like to read the newest, hottest books out? Explain.
67. Think about this: Is a book dead or alive when you read it? Why?
68. Do you read comic books and/or newspaper comics? Why or why not?
69. Have you read an entire book series or many books by one author? Why or why not? Give an example, if you have one, from your reading life.

70. Recall a time when thoughts about hanging out with friends interfered with your reading homework. How did you handle the situation? What did you resolve?

71. How much time do you spend reading on your own and for fun each day: zero, five, ten, fifteen, twenty, twenty-five, or thirty minutes? Why?

72. Do you have memories about reading in the first or second grade? What mind-picture(s) can you see? Describe any connected feelings and thoughts.

73. Recall an early reading experience at home. What mind-picture(s) pop up? Why?

74. Was learning how to read fun? Why or why not?

75. Recall a time when learning how to read made you feel bad (angry, sad, upset, anxious). What happened? Did the event make you dislike reading? Did you resolve the feelings? Explain your answers.

76. What is a reader? Are you? Explain.

77. What is the magic of reading that gets you involved in a book? How does this happen?

78. Can reading motivate you to draw, paint, or create something? Explain by giving an example from your reading and real life.

79. Is reading good for your health? Why?

80. What happened to the boy who had trouble reading and said to himself: "I think I can't, I think I can't, I think I can't read." Explain your answer.

81. What would be a good first book for a child to read? Why?

82. Would you read poetry to a baby? Why?

83. Would you rather watch the imaginary TV screen in your mind or the big screen TV in the living room? Why?

Reading Reflections: Book Recalls, Nonfiction, and Poetry

84. Describe the last book you read.

85. Recall a story you enjoyed listening to when it was read out loud.

86. What book would you call a buddy or companion? Can you count the ways? Give examples.

87. Visualize the first book you wanted to own or possess and explain why you felt this way.

88. Recall a book that made you laugh and then describe a funny scene from it. Pencil-sketch the mind-picture you visualize and see.

89. What poet do you like? Why?

90. What fairy tale do you enjoy? How does it hook you into its world?

91. Do you like reading fantasies? Why? Share an example from your reading life.

92. What did you read last summer? Why?
93. Do you read poetry on your own? Why or why not?
94. Recall a book you read with ease. What made it so easy? Explain.
95. Recall a book you started reading, but gave up on. Why did you give up? Did you start reading the book again? Explain your answers.
96. How can a book or reading increase your understanding of friendship?
97. Why read magazines? Do you? Give an example.
98. What magazine(s) would you like to read? Why?
99. Is reading the newspaper any fun? Why or why not?
100. Do you believe everything you read in the newspaper? Why or why not?
101. Is newspaper reading like book reading? Explain your answer.
102. Do you read nonfiction for fun? Why or why not? What fun is there in nonfiction books or readings? Give an example.
103. What poem makes or made you feel good? Why?
104. What book would you give someone to turn that person onto reading? Why?
105. What great action scenes from books (novels, stories, nonfiction) still remain in your mind? Visualize, describe, and draw one image you can recall.
106. Recall an incredible landscape or setting from a book (fiction or nonfiction) that remains in your memory till this day. Describe what you see. What thoughts and feelings come up? Draw the mind-picture you visualize.
107. Recall any book you read and describe your feelings at the beginning, middle, and end. Did your feelings change from the start to the finish of the book? Why?
108. Describe a book (fiction or nonfiction) that shocked you.
109. What book made you angry? Why?
110. Recall a book that made you feel both love and sadness. Describe this experience.
111. Recall a book that made the world seem strange. What strangeness? What thoughts and feelings come to mind?
112. Recall a book that made the world seem extraordinary and miraculous. How did it do this? What ways? What thoughts and feelings were triggered?
113. Did you ever reread a baby book? What's that like?
114. Recall a ghost story you read or that was read aloud to you. What mind-picture(s) do you remember? Why? Draw one image.
115. Do you remember reading a poem that rocked your world? What was it about? Describe a mind-picture and how it affected you.
116. Does reading poetry make you feel like writing poetry? Why or why not?
117. What have you read that you will never forget? Why?
118. Recall a book you could not wait to finish. Why couldn't you wait?

Words and Word Activities

119. Write whatever words come to mind when you think of reading. Word-storm a list of ten words by triggering one word after another.
120. Are words just black on white, or are they something more? Explain your answer.
121. Think of a word that makes you feel good. Say it silently over and over again to yourself. Describe what happened. (*Optional*: Say the word out loud over and over again and write about what happened.)
122. Think of a word that makes you feel bad. Say it silently over and over again to yourself. Describe what you experienced. (*Optional*: Say the word out loud over and over again and write about what happened.)
123. Think of a word that brings up deep feelings and thoughts. Describe what happens inside.
124. Think of a word that warms your heart. Describe how it affects you: pictures, feelings, thoughts.
125. What word stresses you out instantly? Why? Describe what happens.
126. What words do you use to pump yourself up in sports? How can words get you into the game and thinking positive?
127. What were the first words you remember your mother or father saying to you? When you think about the words now, what comes to mind: pictures, feelings, thoughts—anything?
128. Snow: What do you see, feel, think, and wonder?
129. Certain phrases or expressions really pop out in the mind. Use your imaginary inner eye to view the following and then write a short description of each image you see. Include your thoughts and feelings for each phrase.

   • broken glass
   • puffy clouds
   • angry eyes

130. Check it out: Read 'em, visualize 'em, and write descriptions to make the mind-pictures pop out:

   • sunflower forest
   • lonely girl
   • peace train

131. Zoom in on these phrases and describe the images, feelings, and thoughts they trigger:

   happy clowns
   • images
   • feelings
   • thoughts

abandoned shack

- images
- feelings
- thoughts

French fries

- images
- feelings
- thoughts

rainy morning

- images
- feelings
- thoughts

132. Contemplate the phrase "reading life" for thirty seconds. What comes to mind? (*Hint*: Contemplate means to view or consider with careful and continued attention.)

133. How carefully do you choose words to express yourself and your experiences in a reading journal? Do you use the first words that come to mind, or do you search for the best words before writing? Explain the answers.

134. Strawberry shortcake, vanilla and chocolate milkshakes, peppermint candies, hot cinnamon buns with icing, hot dogs with ketchup, cheeseburger deluxe, peanut-butter-and-jelly sandwiches. Describe what you just experienced.

135. What does the word "baby" create in your mind? What do you see, feel, and think?

136. Say the word "fun" silently over and over to yourself. Describe what happens. Why is it happening?

137. What words can you taste in your mind? Make a list of five words (or more). Pick one word and describe how delicious it tastes. (*Hints*: Wordstorm words by triggering one word after another, and picture-storm images by triggering one image after another before answering.)

138. What ideas do the following words trigger? Write one idea for each word:

- tunnel
- drums
- hide
- smoke
- perfect
- gold

139. What word messes up your mind as soon as you hear it? Why?

140. Your name is very important to you. To prove it, say your full name silently over and over to yourself for sixty seconds and see what comes to mind. Write whatever you remember. (*Optional*: Say your name out loud for sixty seconds and see what happens. Another example would be to say a friend's name out loud and/or silently to yourself. Use an enemy's name and say it over and over again. Write whatever you recall for all the options.)

One-Line Statements and Opinions

141. I read, therefore I think. Explain.
142. Demand a lot from yourself when reading. Do you? Why or why not?
143. Reading takes courage. What do you think? Why?
144. A good book is not hard to find. What do you think? Why?
145. Reading brings peace. What do you think? Explain.
146. I read, therefore I imagine. Explain.
147. Reading is an instant cure for being alone or lonesomeness. Why or why not?
148. Warning: I brake for hard words. Explain. Do you? Why?
149. The more you read the better your concentration becomes. Agree? Disagree? Explain.
150. Get into what you read and enjoy yourself in thought. Do you? Why or why not?
151. Other worlds are possible—read. Explain.
152. Readers get more words. Explain. (*Hint*: "Get" means to understand.)
153. Warning: If you see me reading, see me later. Explain.
154. Do you believe that you should read every day? Do you? Explain your answers.
155. Read: Give your mind a charge. Explain.
156. Be daring and adventurous when choosing books to read. Why? How would this attitude affect your reading life?
157. Every reader is a magician performing magic acts in the mind's magic reading theater. Are readers magicians? What is the mind's magic reading theater? Explain your answers.

Reading Process

158. What's all the action about in reading?
159. What happens to the words read from a page?
160. Read a page from a book (fiction) and describe thoughts, feelings, and images triggered.
161. If someone were to take an x-ray of your mind while you read, what would they see? Describe this map of your reading mind.

162. What is concentration? How important is it in reading? Why?
163. Reading books and watching TV both need concentration. Compare your concentration when reading books to your concentration when watching TV.
164. Does your reading speed or pace ever change? Why? Give an example.
165. What is the hardest thing about the reading process? Why?
166. Describe how you remember what you read while you read.
167. When you read, do you put all your energy into it? Explain.
168. When you read silently, there is an inner imaginary reading voice that mouths, speaks, says, and reads the words. Describe your inner reading voice.
169. How can reading trigger real-life dreams?
170. Describe a real-life dream sparked by a book you read.
171. Imagine that: Why can a minute of reading last forever? How could that happen? Did you experience this in your reading life? Describe the event.

Writing, Drawing, and Creative Thinking

172. Visualize and draw a portrait or cartoon of a happy reader in his or her reading world.
173. Visualize someone in your family reading in his or her favorite place and then draw the image. Look carefully at the finished drawing and describe your thoughts and feelings.
174. What is a bookworm? Draw a portrait, cartoon illustration, or fantasy sketch of this person. After completing your picture, take a few seconds to look at and reflect on it. Write what comes to mind.
175. Visualize and draw a cartoon of Speedo Reader.
176. Picture in your mind an imaginary chair made especially for reading. How will it make reading more fun? Draw a cartoon of the chair with you sitting in it and reading. (*Optional:* How would the chair help you read something very difficult? How would it work? What would it do differently?) Draw a second cartoon showing the chair working. (*Hints:* Before answering both parts of the question, picture-storm images by triggering one image after another and brainstorm ideas by creating one idea after another.)
177. If bees could read, what books would they take out of the "buzzing library"? Create some titles.
178. Create a sentence that makes you feel peaceful. Draw or sketch the mind-picture triggered by the sentence. Look at your drawing: Does it relax you? Explain.

Ratings and Quotations

179. "Few things leave a deeper mark on a reader than the first book that finds a way into his heart" (Carlos Ruiz Zafon). What does it mean when a book "finds a way into your heart"? How does that happen? Did your first or an early book find a way into your heart? Explain your answers.

180. "Books became my world because the world I was in was very hard" (Alice Walker). What is the quotation suggesting to you about the importance of books? How would a "very hard world" make books so valuable to the writer? Explain your answers.

181. How much imagination goes into what you read? Rate your imagination's role in reading on a scale from 0 to 10, where 0 = little use and 10 = strong use of it. Give the reason(s) for your rating.

182. How alert are you when reading? Rate your alertness while reading on a scale from 0 to 10, where 0 = a low level and = a high level. Give reasons for your rating. (*Hint*: Look up "alert" in a dictionary and thesaurus for definitions and synonyms before answering.)

183. "Reading removes sorrow from the heart" (Moroccan proverb). What does the proverb mean? Has it happened to you? If it did, describe your experience. (*Hint*: If it did not, imagine how it would work. Make up an example.)

184. "You cannot open a book without learning something" (William Scarborough). What do you think? Explain.

185. Books can be dangerous. The best ones should be labeled 'This could change your life'" (Helen Exley). What does the quotation mean? Do you think books have that much power? Explain.

HOW TO USE BOOK 1

One Suggested Sample Survey Approach for Presenting Questions with Notes

Begin with ten openers students can easily relate to on common, everyday reading experiences. Get them psyched up with this *example*: What is a good place for you to read? What makes it so good? Where do you hate to read? Why?

Ask questions on past reading experiences such as: How did you learn to read? These will get students emotionally involved in their reading lives because the visualizations and reflections will, hopefully, rekindle positive memories. Pick five blasts from the past and scatter them throughout your questioning. Kids will love responding.

Check out their reading lives with recall questions about books read in the past and present. The questions trigger more positive visualizations and inspiration. *Example*: Recall a book that made you laugh and describe a funny scene from it. Pencil-sketch the mind-picture(s) you see. Pick five book recalls and spread them out amongst the other questions.

If they can't come up with a book for a particular question, add extra choices. Oral class readings (fiction or nonfiction) are acceptable for book recalls; however, they should limit taking responses from them and opt for books they have read. Students should avoid using the same book too many times to answer recalls, although that might not be a problem because they would get deeper into a book, making it a quality read.

Lighten things up by asking: (a) drawing questions so kids can illustrate (pencil-sketch) their reading experiences; (b) absurd creative-thinking questions for brain-frying fun; and (c) hypothetical reading situation questions to motivate curious minds. *Examples are*: (a) Imagine, visualize, and draw a cartoon of Speedo Reader. (b) If bees could read, what books would they take out of the "buzzing library"? Create some titles. (c) What happened to the boy who had trouble reading and said to himself: "I think I can't, I think I can't, I think I can't read"? Explain your answer. (See the second half of Michael's tale in the previous chapter for more similar examples.) Mix five lighter questions with book recalls, and past, as well as everyday reading experiences. Use a variety of question categories to keep things interesting.

Insert opinion questions to empower kids to be captains of their reading lives. *Example*: Do you believe that you should read every day? Do you? Explain your answer. Try five opinion questions and use them intermittently throughout Book 1.

Push the buttons in their heads and hearts more often with one-line statement questions to challenge assumptions, ideas, attitudes, and knowledge about reading and reading life. *Example*: Other worlds are possible—read. Explain. Pick five one-liners; they'll eat them up.

Keep mixing up questions, going from heavies to lighter ones, and back to heavies such as reading process questions, involving the students' search into what happens in the mind's magic reading theater, where all the action of reading takes place. *Example*: If someone were to take an x-ray of your mind while you read, what would they see? Describe this map of your reading mind. Introduce at least five reading process questions from Book 1, because Book 2 continues to expand student inquiry into this relevant area.

Enrich the reading process with word and word-activity questions, where a class/child, for example, changes words into images (mind-pictures), thoughts, and feelings and sees them three-dimensionally as a virtual, holographic reality. Let words take on new meanings through reading-and-visualizing-words questions such as: What does the word "baby" create in your mind? What do you see, think, and feel? (See figure 1, "The Reading Process," for more information about visualization.) Create greater self-entertainment with word-activity questions like: Say the word "fun" silently over and over again to yourself and describe what happens. Pick five word/word-activity questions to initiate a fresh, heightened sense of language.

Poetry reading life is an important category area both teachers and parents can add to a survey approach: (a) Do you read poetry on your own? Why or why not? (b) What poem makes or made you feel good? Why? Select three and begin a dialogue about poetry and its connection to real life. As discussion leaders, use the questions to initiate open-mindedness about poetry. It's cool—just look at all the poetry slams and rap songs.

Add nonfiction questions to your repertoire about reading habits in the genre, specifically kids' likes and dislikes for reading newspapers and magazines. *Example*: Is reading a newspaper any fun? Why or why not? There are many nonfiction questions in Book 2, so start off a class/child with them in Book 1.

Conclude Book 1 by summing up their experiences with quotation and rating questions:

- "Books can be dangerous. The best ones should be labeled 'This could change your life'" (Helen Exley). What does the quotation mean? Do you think books have that much power? Explain.
- How much imagination goes into what you read? Rate your imagination's role in reading on a scale from 0 to 10, where 0 = little, and 10 = lots of use. Give reason(s) for your rating.

The questions require synthesizing chunks of reading experiences before responding to find out, respectively: How powerful are books? How deep inside the imagination or the mind's magic reading theater do they travel when reading? To be answered successfully, the questions in the different books, from whatever category chosen, need some rumination.

Teachers and parents will appreciate how the questions address motivation in adolescent reading lives and prepare them for Book 2. Make sure your kids begin the next round of questioning feeling good about themselves as readers, reading, reading life, and *Motivating Teen and Preteen Readers*.

KEY INFORMATION AND PROCEDURES FOR
ASKING AND ANSWERING QUESTION CATEGORIES

Teachers don't have to target the whole class with their question choices: Individualize them as mini-side lessons for one child or a small group(s), who would benefit from a particular series of questions. The books of questions can be adapted to most classroom—and at-home—situations and for most teachers/parents. Create an original approach by shaping questions according to your students/child. Use the numerous choices to your advantage.

To increase involvement in reading life, ask rating questions about key reading experiences/processes and let them evaluate what they do. Probe their critical-thinking skills with one-line statement and quotation questions that integrate many reading-life experiences in a sentence or two. Let the questions push them further into their reading lives. Stress to examine carefully what happened in the past and what is happening in the present in order to realize how much they've accomplished in a relatively short time, and where they might be headed in their future reading lives. They will start appreciating their reading experiences through self-discovery, self-motivation, self-efficacy, and will determine their reading fates.

The quotation category is somewhat tougher to answer. Consider the quote about the best books being dangerous because they could change your life: Kids use several thinking skills to grasp its meaning, and then search many reading experiences to see if and how books caused a real change in real life. Have books or reading changed *your* life? Was it for better or worse? The question begs for serious thought and reflection by all discussion leaders.

Book 1's introductory poetry reading life questions survey students' preferences in the subject and are easy enough to answer. However, do not underestimate poetry's capacity to motivate reading. It teaches teens/preteens about the reading process by taking them deeper into the power of words, imagery, feeling, and thought. When they return to prose, whether fiction or nonfiction, kids will have greater insight into language, including a more effective and affective response to literature. Let the few poetry questions gradually open their eyes—and *yours* as discussion leaders—to the genre and ignite fresh thinking about poetry and prose.

Many recall questions ask students to discuss books that, for instance, "made them feel sadness and love." They become tricky because the responses depend on a child's ability to remember a book he or she may have read a while ago. Finding details via visualization becomes difficult if the memory of the book is fuzzy.

To offset the problem, demonstrate how the inner eye finds mind-pictures of, let's say, action scenes and settings from different books. Sketch a quick, informal diagram with the inner eye inside a big head (see figure 3). Draw arrows coming out of this imaginary eye to indicate it is searching for past or recent book memories. The eye illuminates whatever images it sees on an imaginary TV screen in the mind (or the big head/circle). The inner eye looks at and examines the lit-up memory to discover enough details for a written response, or at least one detail to start. Along with the image or book memory, there are also connected feelings and thoughts (symbolized by *f* and *t* surrounding it in the illustration.) Repeat the simple diagram in your raps/talks whenever they have trouble coming up with answers to book recalls. It is a framework for the visualization process and helps responding to this question category, as well as their response to literature.

Word questions should not be asked randomly, that is, skipping around haphazardly to whichever one seems appropriate at the time. They begin with simple

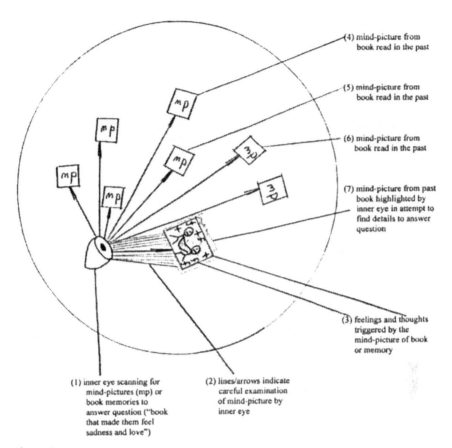

Figure 3.

introductory questions and get progressively tougher. To start off, students change words and phrases into images, thoughts, and feelings, and then play and have fun with words in word activity questions.

Take the earlier example of "what the word 'baby' creates in the mind": To respond, they visualize, find or create, images of "babies"; view them with the inner eye; and connect feelings and thoughts to the mind- or word-pictures they see.

The tougher word questions require increased visualization-concentration skills to create the different mind-pictures and find details. When kids zoom in for a closer look at images of an "abandoned shack" or "French fries," more *inner sight* is needed. Or, when they're asked about ideas triggered by "tunnel," "drums," "hide," "perfect," "smoke," and "gold," they must pause and reflect on the meanings, thoughts, and concepts the words trigger in the mind and imagination. Call it a word-workout.

Word questions continue and get more advanced in Books 2, 3, and 4. In Book 1 they visualize single words and phrases, and move on to two-word sentences, both real and absurd, and longer sentences in Book 2. The questions motivate reading and writing. They stimulate the reading-writing connection in an organic, practical way: great for students, teachers, and parents. The word-and-sentence questions are purposely made simple so adolescents see the visualization process in its most basic, broken-down form: Don't assume anything, even if kids say, "This is easy."

Make sure to include word and word activity questions in Book 1; they help develop strong responses to future creative writing questions (see Book 4), which depend on the foundation set up here. For instance, a writing activity in Book 1 relies on this: It asks students "to create a sentence that makes them feel peaceful and draw the mind-picture it triggers." They first visualize or find a mind-picture to make them feel peaceful (using the inner eye to highlight that image on the imaginary TV screen), and second, change the mind-picture to words in a sentence. In the writing process, images are turned into sentences to produce a complete thought. The reading process is the reverse: Words are changed into images.

Nonfiction questions on magazine and newspaper reading round out a survey approach by exploring how connected kids are to the real world and how much nonbook stuff they read on the outside. Are they interested in sports, fads, entertainment, movies, food, money, politics, celebrities, video games, and what's happening in the world? Nonfiction reading describes real people, places, events, and things. It takes young people out of their hoods to the worlds beyond them. Tap into as many genres with your questions as possible. Interest teens/preteens in new subjects they didn't think would excite them: the advantages of a broad-ranging approach to questioning by discussion leaders.

After finishing the questioning in Book 1 or Round 1, go to "Evaluation Questions for Book 1." Review specific information and procedures about the student questionnaires and student-teacher/parent chats. See this section for suggested evaluation questions on the kids' growth and progress in reading, reading life, and Book 1's questions in the questionnaire and chat.

IMPLEMENTING WORKABLE SCHEDULES/STRATEGIES FOR PRESENTING QUESTIONS IN BOOK 1

How many questions should be selected for each lesson? How many mini-lessons are given each week? How much time should be allotted for each mini-lesson? When can the mini-lessons consisting of a rap, question, writing, and follow-up discussion be given? Suggestions for teacher and parent discussion leaders are:

- One mini-lesson every other day (ten to fifteen minutes per, max)
- One daily mini-lesson (ten to fifteen minutes per, max)
- One in-class mini-lesson and one homework question every other day (fifteen minutes for in-class rap, writing, and discussion, plus a brief five-minute discussion of homework question responses the next day)

- One mini-lesson for three consecutive days (ten to fifteen minutes per, max)
- Two mini-lessons each week whenever class schedule/time permits (ten to fifteen minutes per, max)

Notes: Middle and high school teachers (English and remedial reading) must be selective and practical with the above suggestions. Based on five forty-five-minute periods per class/section, getting in two mini-lessons a week makes sense. However, being very realistic, one mini-lesson each week would be okay and better than nothing. Hopefully, by May or June, teacher discussion leaders at these levels will have more time to present two or even three mini-lessons per week. The end of the school year is a fertile time to motivate reading over the summer months.

Suggestions for scheduling mini-lessons in the elementary school classroom are:

- Start off the day as part of early-morning work
- Before class instruction lesson in reading
- After reading test practice lessons
- Before lunch as beneficial downtime assignment
- After lunch to energize afternoon work
- Before dismissal as a closer to the day
- Use *whenever* motivational "filler" needed as a transition lesson

Notes: Middle and high school teachers can begin or end their classes with a quickie question-and-discussion session, whatever works best for that scheduled period. Teachers must figure out through trial and error the best time(s) to get in a mini-lesson. For example, a quickie lesson might come after test practice or grammar lessons. If a motivational project is needed for certain classes, teachers in middle and high school can devote one or two forty-five-minute periods a month to asking three to five questions on reading and reading life followed up by mini-discussions. Once *Motivating Teen and Preteen Readers* has started, and the kids are acquainted with the inquiry- and passion-based strategy, homework questions can be assigned and briefly discussed the next day in class. Questions can also be posted on class/section website. (See "Using Technology to Implement the Books of Questions" in Book 2 for more information about class/section websites.) This is one way to add another mini-lesson without taking up too much class time.

When implementing the books of questions, elementary school teachers in grades 4 to 6, and also parents working one-to-one with children of the same age, should keep the following points in mind:

- Use the format that works best for all concerned, as long as two or three mini-lessons are taught each week.
- Don't overdo it by inundating the class/child with too many questions, especially in the beginning (Book 1). Start out with one question per mini-lesson.

Well-chosen questions and quality responses are keys to *Motivating Teen and Preteen Readers.*

- Be consistent in presenting mini-lessons, when possible. *For example*: Have three lessons a week with one rap/question/discussion per lesson, and stick to this routine throughout the year. Add an extra question when the situation calls for it: for instance, if one question is fairly easy to answer, or, when the kids' enthusiasm has increased, go for it; that is, throw in another question and see what they can do.

Final notes for teachers from elementary through high school and parents:

- *Emphasize* when assigning homework questions: "Give the same effort to your responses as those written in class." However, if answers are weak (as shown in the follow-up discussion the next day) or their efforts are lackadaisical, stick with in-class questions only for the time being. Later in the year, after they answered fifty to sixty questions (by Book 3), and the responses have generally improved, return to using questions for homework again and see how students respond. Also, teachers can post examples of stronger written responses on the class or section website.
- Use teacher/parent raps strategically when needed to pump up inspiration and passion in reading and reading life, as well as to briefly discuss class's/child's written responses and the various techniques applied to answering the questions.

ONE-YEAR JOURNEY THROUGH THE BOOKS OF QUESTIONS

Here are some important points connected to the above table discussion leaders should remember when implementing *Motivating Teen and Preteen Readers*:

- If three lessons each week prove too much under the time constraints, work with two.
- If four evaluations (questionnaires plus chats) are not feasible, use two: at mid-year and the end of the year, if that works within your schedule. Chats are optional for classroom teachers; however, they should still interview struggling students and spot-check students' notebooks (with written response) from time to time to see if an "intervention" is needed. Chats are not optional for parent discussion leaders and homeschooling parent-teachers because there are less time and scheduling restrictions. (See "Not-for-Parents-Only Guide to *Motivating Teen and Preteen Readers*" and the upcoming "Evaluation Questions for Book 1" for more information and procedures on student questionnaires and student-teacher/parent chats.)

	Book 1	Book 2	Book 3	Book 4
Time Period	September to Mid-November	Mid-November through Mid-February	Mid-February through April	May to June
Mini-lessons	Three per week including a rap, question, and discussion	Three per week including a rap, question, and discussion	Three per week including a rap, question, and discussion	Three per week including a rap, question, and discussion
Evaluations[1]	• Student Questionnaire 1 • Student-Teacher /Parent Chat 1	• Student Questionnaire 2 • Student-Teacher /Parent Chat 2	• Student Questionnaire 3 • Student-Teacher /Parent Chat 3	• Student Questionnaire 4 • Student-Teacher /Parent Chat 4
Final Wrap-ups				Final three discussion lessons given after student and teacher/parent evaluations
				Epilogue prompts; last week of brainstorming sessions to conclude the four books of questions

This chart is based on a 40-week school year consisting of three lessons each week; 120 questions should be completed within a full school year.
[1]Evaluations should be scheduled at the end of each book's time period.

Table 1. One-year journey through the books of questions.

- Elementary school teachers (grades 4 to 6) can use the four books of questions as a supplementary reading and motivational project. Remedial reading, teachers, resource teachers, literacy coaches, mentors, tutors, and before/after-school program teachers can have three lessons per week in one-to-one and small-group situations. Cluster teachers in language arts should try to work in one to two mini-lessons each week.
- Middle school remedial and resource teachers can start or end their periods with a mini-lesson. School librarians can add a ten-minute mini-lesson to their classes if the circumstances and students' needs call for it. Twenty mini-lessons a year, beginning in the sixth grade and going through seventh and eighth grades, would provide the necessary continuity for the books of questions and add up to a positive step toward motivating teen and preteen readers before leaving middle school.
- High school English teachers for grades 9 and 10 can implement the project, and remedial reading resource teachers can squeak in questions throughout the school year in order to make an impact. Once again, as kids move from ninth to tenth grade and beyond, there would be continuity and progression

leading them to increased motivation. Teachers can highlight or ask specific question categories targeting areas their classes have trouble comprehending, ones that would trigger greater enjoyment in their reading lives. The beauty of *Motivating Teen and Preteen Readers* lies in its flexibility of the diverse, creative, and innovative questions which can be appropriated for various ability levels, backgrounds, and groups of students. The questions become catalysts for the lesson of the day, and, ideally, would wake kids up, get them thinking, feeling, and reflecting about reading and reading life, exactly what teachers would like and want them to do.

- Parent discussion leaders and homeschooling parent-teachers can implement the one-year schedule more easily than classroom teachers. (More information for parents about procedures, strategies, and techniques for working with kids one-to-one is found in "Not-for-Parents-Only Guide to *Motivating Teen and Preteen Readers*.")

EVALUATION QUESTIONS FOR BOOK 1

Evaluations: Student Questionnaires and Student-Teacher/Parent Chats

Motivating Teen and Preteen Readers breaks for students to reflect on their written responses. They evaluate their progress after finishing every thirty to seventy-five questions in each book, or the same number asked randomly from more than one book, two to four times a year via student questionnaires and student-teacher/parent chats.

Introducing Student Questionnaires 1, 2, 3, and 4

Start the assessment by saying to students/child: "The questionnaire shows what progress you've made so far in the books of questions. Your responses to the questions give you an idea of where you have been and what you have been doing in reading. By reviewing and evaluating your interest in *Motivating Teen and Preteen Readers*, you will see how it has affected your reading life, for better or worse. This is not a test. Your answers increase your understanding of and appreciation for reading, reading life, and the questions. Respond to the assessment questions with the same effort and concentration used to answer the weekly questions. Think before writing. Stay away from snap judgments. Write in complete sentences. Keep your responses between several sentences to a short paragraph. You will discuss the questionnaires once the answers are checked."

Procedure for Student Questionnaires 1, 2, and 3

Step 1: Students reread their written responses slowly and reflectively.
Step 2: Class reads questionnaires silently and orally.
Step 3: Students write responses to the questionnaire.

Step 4: Questionnaire results are read by the teacher (or parent, as the case may be) and commented on (with no grades); returned to students/child; and discussed in class/home for twenty minutes. *Ask*: "What have you learned or realized about reading, reading life, and the questions from Book 1/Round 1?"

Note about rereading responses prior to answering questionnaires 1 to 4:

Book 1: Students reread responses to Book 1 (or Round 1).
Book 2: Students reread responses to Books 2 and 1 (or Rounds 2 and 1).
Book 3: Students reread responses to Books 3, 2, and 1 (or Rounds 3, 2, and 1).
Book 4: Students reread responses to Books 4, 3, 2, and 1 (or Rounds 4, 3, 2, and 1).

See the end of each book for suggested questions to use in student questionnaires 1, 2, 3, and 4. Pick those that cover the questions asked in one book or randomly selected from several books.

Suggested Questions for Student Questionnaire 1

1. How did you feel after rereading your responses? Why?
2. What thoughts came to mind after rereading your responses? Why?
3. Did you learn anything new about reading and reading life? Explain.
4. What was your favorite question? Why?
5. What was your least favorite question? Why?
6. Which question was easy to answer? Why?
7. Which question proved difficult to answer? Why?
8. Which question made you think the most? Why?
9. Did you make many snap responses to questions instead of thinking it through before responding? Explain your answer.
10. Were your responses to the questions honest and sincere? Explain your answer.
11. Describe the effort and concentration you put into answering the questions.
12. Do you enjoy the mini-discussions? Why or why not?
13. Does discussion of your classmates' experiences help you to understand your own reading and reading life? Explain your answer.
14. Can the questions improve reading? Why or why not?
15. Do you like answering the questions? Why or why not?
16. What do you dislike about answering the questions? Why?
17. How would you describe your experience of answering the questions up to now?
18. How important is passion in reading and reading life? Explain.
19. Have the questions affected your reading life at all? Explain.
20. Make up an imaginative or creative question about reading or reading life.

Notes: Teachers/parents can use all of the above twenty questions for student questionnaire 1; or select ten to fifteen questions from the suggested examples and add your own created questions. Original questions can be made up by discussion leaders to conform to their kids' reading life experiences and their written and oral responses in class and one-to-one dialogues.

Teacher/Parent Preparation for Student-Teacher/Parent Chats

After kids complete a book and a questionnaire, discussion leaders should have an idea of their attitudes toward reading/reading life and progress in *Motivating Teen and Preteen Readers*. Conclude evaluation of questions' impact with:

Step 1: Collect notebook(s) after questionnaire has been completed.
Step 2: Skim responses to see development, change, and growth.
Step 3: Check responses for detail, thoughtfulness, and enthusiasm.
Step 4: Comment on individual's work in notebook.
Step 5: Conduct five-minute chats with students/child.

Notes: Book 4's student-teacher/parent chat has one assessment question: *Why do you read?* Kids have five to ten minutes to take notes and brainstorm ideas before the interview. Student-teacher chats are optional, depending on teachers' time and energy to talk about things. Teacher discussion leaders can hold timely chats when there's uncertainty about an individual's progress or may want to meet with struggling students. Student-parent chats are not optional.

Procedures, Suggested Questions, and Notes for Student-Teacher/Parent Chats 1 to 4

- All interview responses by students require explanations and support.
- Tailor questions according to an individual's needs. Focus on questions that are keys to that child's progress and success.
- Chat questions are only suggestions. Make up your own questions based on your class's or a child's written and oral responses. The suggested questions get the interview started by breaking the ice of a one-to-one encounter.
- If answers bring out important facts about a student's/child's reading life, get more details by digging deeper and expanding the responses through further questioning. Concentrate on one part of an individual's reading notebook and stay with it for the whole meeting.
- By the time the first chats start, teacher/parent discussion leaders have already reviewed questionnaire responses and skimmed the notebooks, providing insight to their work and knowledge about which questions would be appropriate for different students.

• Keep enthusiasm high throughout the meetings. Create a lively interview atmosphere to counteract the seriousness created by the testing climate in reading. Integrate the harmonizing nature of reading life and the questions with current reading realities. Make the questions work for the kids—and yourself.
• Chat and questionnaire questions overlap at times because both measure students' awareness of their involvement in and commitment to reading, reading life, and the books of questions. Discussion leaders can *interchange* questions between the two types of evaluations.

Suggested Questions for Student-Teacher/Parent Chat 1

1. Are the questions fun for you to answer?
2. Do the questions make you think and reflect?
3. What does it mean to be a reader?
4. Do you consider yourself a reader?
5. What makes up your reading life?
6. Are you enjoying reading more since starting the book of questions?
7. Describe what happens inside yourself when you read.
8. Have your written responses improved as you answered more questions?
9. Describe a response to a question you remember really well.
10. Describe an unforgettable image from your reading life used in a response.
11. Are there too many questions to answer?
12. Where do you enjoy writing your answers more: in class or at home?
13. Do my comments about your written responses help you to understand the book of questions?
14. Did student questionnaire 1 help you to evaluate your progress in the book of questions?
15. Which storming techniques did you use to answer the questions?
16. What did you think of your responses to the questions?
17. What stands out in your mind about your answers to the questions?
18. What surprised you about the questions?
19. Are you thinking more about your reading life since starting the book of questions?
20. Are you looking forward to answering more questions?

Book 2

Good teaching is more a giving of right questions than a giving of right answers.

—Joseph Albers

ABOUT BOOK 2

Continuity, Surveying, Skimming, and Question Categories

The same question categories in Book 1 on reading and reading life are found in Book 2. The questions expand on and advance the questions answered in Book 1, so there is continuity and progression between books. After completing questions in Book 1 (or Round 1 of randomly selected questions), discussion leaders should have a better understanding and appreciation of which questions will or will not work in class or at home.

Book 2's questions are a little more challenging. *Explain* any that seem more involved or wide ranging or if students struggle to respond. With over three hundred questions, it increases your options for examining teen/preteen reading lives. Continue a survey approach with a wide range of questions on reading habits, preferences, and experiences.

Skim questions in Book 2 or the other books to see which would connect with your class/child and continue where things left off after the first thirty to seventy-five questions. *Again, get a feel for the questions by stopping, contemplating, and responding mentally after reading every three to five questions to anticipate potential student written and oral responses in your dialogues.*

Book 2 has the following question categories, appearing in order of most to least frequently asked questions:

• Reading Reflections: Book Recalls, Nonfiction, and Poetry
• Reading Experiences: Common (Everyday), Past (Early), and Hypothetical
• Reading Process
• Words and Word Activities
• Writing, Drawing, and Creative Thinking
• One-Line Statements and Opinions
• Ratings and Quotations

BOOK 2 QUESTIONS

Note for all discussion leaders: If you decide to skim the questions first, check off the questions that stand out because they fit the class's/child's needs at the moment. Second, reread the selected questions deliberately by following the aforementioned procedure. Do not attempt to read all of Book 2's questions in one sitting.

Reading Reflections: Book Recalls, Nonfiction, and Poetry

1. Do you like to read short stories? Describe a story you read and why you enjoyed it. What was the story's theme? What did you learn about its main character? What conflict did he or she have to resolve? Was it resolved: for better or worse? Explain.
2. Recall a book or reading (fiction) that made you feel carefree or free from worry. Describe your experience. What thoughts come to mind? Draw one mind-picture you remember.
3. Can reading books give you courage? Why or why not?
4. Has a TV show reminded you of a book or story you read? What show? What book? What was the connection? Did the connection increase your understanding and appreciation of the book? Explain.
5. Which is scarier: a movie or a book? Why?
6. How do feelings experienced at the end of a book compare to those felt at the end of a movie? Explain your answer.
7. Can fairy tales, fables, myths, or tall tales start fantasies in your mind? Explain your answer. Give an example. How did it start the fantasy?
8. Has a "character" from a memoir (autobiography) triggered an imaginary adventure in your mind? What character? Why? What adventure did you go on?
9. Recall an early book you read that featured an animal as a main character. What book? What animal? Did you like the story? Why? Draw a mind-picture you can still see of the animal. What feelings and thoughts come back to you now? Why?

10. Recall a book, story, or reading that was about a warm, friendly, happy person. Describe this character's behavior. How did he or she perceive or see the world? What did the character make you think about?

11. Recall a book that had a violent scene in it, like a fight. Visualize a mind-picture from the episode. What do you see, feel, and think?

12. How does book violence compare to movie/TV/video game violence? Why? Give an example to show the comparison.

13. Why read poetry?

14. Do you have a poetry reading life? Why or why not?

15. Recall a book that made you laugh and cry. What happened in the book to make you feel this way? What thoughts were triggered? What images come to mind?

16. What kind of book or reading makes you think about your life? Why?

17. What book injected you with an overdose of feelings (positive, negative, or both)? Describe the "overdose."

18. Is there a poem you enjoy reading again and again? What is it about? Why do you like coming back to it? When do you return to it?

19. What book has opened your heart? Explain your answer.

20. How important is the first page of a book (fiction or nonfiction) to you? Recall a good opening to a book and describe it.

21. Recall a boring school book that you read. What was boring about it? How did you handle reading it? What did you get out of the book?

22. Do you read books or newspaper/magazine articles on health, nutrition, medicine, exercise, or fitness? Why or why not? Which of these subjects would you like to read about? Why?

23. What is a "how-to" book or article? Have you read one? Why? What did you learn?

24. If you have not read a "how-to" book or article, what "how-to" subject would you like to read about? List an area of interest and describe what you would expect to get out of it.

25. What is the key to a good "how-to" book or article? Explain your answer.

26. Is reading nonfiction different from reading fiction? Why?

27. Recall a nonfiction book you read on history. What do you remember? Do the same for a TV show on history. What do you remember from the show? Which of the two experiences really lit up and stayed in your mind? Why?

28. Does history *come to life* when you read a history textbook? Why or why not?

29. Describe a good nonfiction "real-life" story you read. What made it good?

30. Do you like reading realistic fiction (novels and short stories)? Why or why not?

31. Recall a realistic novel or short story you read. What did you take away from it? Did the reading get you into other realistic fiction? Explain.

32. Describe a book that made you more sensitive to the world around you. What increased your sensitivity? What were you thinking after finishing the entire book? Why?

33. Why do many books, stories, and newspaper/magazine pieces deal with the negative side of life? Give an example from your reading life. Did, or can you, get something positive out of books, stories, or articles about the negative side of life? Describe your experience.

34. Think about this: *Aesop's Fables*. Do you remember one? What mind-picture can you see? What moral or lesson was the fable trying to teach? Have you used it in your life? Explain.

35. What book or story from your reading life could be renamed *A Book of Fools*? Why?

36. Recall a book you were determined to finish even though you hated it. Why did you dislike it so much? How were you able to finish the book? Did you get anything out of it despite your feelings? Explain.

37. Recall a book or story where the main character hated or disliked the world. Which character? Why the hate? Did the character's feelings change by the end of the book? Did the character change? Explain your answers.

38. Do you read magazine or newspaper articles about movies? Why or why not? If you have an example, describe what you learned about movies from your reading.

39. How can books improve your knowledge of technology? Explain your answer.

40. How much have you read about computers and technology on your own? Has your reading helped you? Explain your answer.

41. What are the differences between magazine and book reading?

42. What are the differences between reading magazines and newspapers?

43. Describe a book or an article you read about nature. Was it a good read? Explain.

44. Which do you like better: watching a TV show on nature or reading a book on nature? Why?

45. Did you ever see the movie version of a book you read? Which was better: the book or the movie? Why?

46. Can a movie improve your understanding of a book you read (where movie and book are the same)? Why? (*Optional*: Can a movie improve your understanding of a book you read where both are not the same? Why?)

47. Did you ever see the movie version of a book first, and read the book second? How did this affect your understanding and appreciation of the book? Explain your answer.

48. What mind-pictures can you still see from a favorite fairy tale? Why is the tale meaningful or important to you? (*Optional*: Pencil-sketch one image.)

49. Recall a book, story, or reading that made or almost made you cry. What caused the strong feelings? Were they tears of sadness or joy? What pictures flashed through your mind as you recalled the book?

50. Recall a book, story, or tale where the main character had no real friends. How did the character handle the situation? Did the character eventually find a real friend? What did the story make you think and feel? Have you ever felt, at times, like this character? Explain all your answers.

51. Recall a book that showed how people could be mean or cruel to each other. Describe one scene. What were you thinking, feeling, and imagining? What were your reflections at the end of the book?

52. What book (fiction or nonfiction) have you read that portrayed life as a struggle or tug-of-war? Describe what happens in the story.

53. Recall a book or reading (fiction or nonfiction) about survival. Who was trying to survive? What is meant by "survival" in the book? Did the character(s) survive? Why?

54. Recall a book, story, tale, biography, or autobiography where a character or a (real) person had a lively, creative imagination. Describe it and where it took the character. How did it affect the person's life: for better or worse? Why? Compare your imagination to the character's or person's imagination.

55. Recall something you read where a character was treated unfairly. Describe the unfairness. How did he or she handle the circumstances? Was he or she successful in the end? How would you have dealt with the situation? Why?

56. Recall a book (fiction or nonfiction) you read about fear. What did you learn from it? What did you realize about fear that you did not know before? Explain. Draw one mind-picture from the book.

57. Recall a book or reading about losing or failing. What was the author's message? Did you agree? Did the book help you in any way? Explain your answers.

58. Do you enjoy books or stories about fantasy worlds? Why? Describe a fantasy world from one of your readings. Find details with your inner eye.

59. Compare reading fantasy books or stories to watching Harry Potter movies: their differences and similarities. Do you like reading science fantasy or science fiction? Explain your answer(s). (*Optional*: Give an example by describing and drawing one mind-picture from the story.)

60. What book has taken you on the longest voyage through your mind, imagination, and self? Describe the journey.

61. Why read sad poems?

62. Why read angry poems? What's in it for you? What does this poetry trigger inside you? Explain your answer by giving an example.

63. Recall a book that grew on you until you really liked it. Why did your feelings and opinion of the book change?

64. Recall a book (fiction or nonfiction) that created negative thoughts. What were you thinking? Why? What mind-pictures can you still remember?

65. Describe a good newspaper article or story you read. Give its main idea. Explain why the piece held your interest.

66. Describe a good magazine article or story you read. Give its main idea. Explain why the piece held your interest.

67. Recall a photography book or a book with many photographs that helped you see and understand the world better. Describe one photograph you liked. Did it affect the way you see things? Why or why not?

68. Do you read Native American tales or Greek myths? Why? Give an example. What keeps you engaged in these stories? If you don't like them, give your reasons.

69. Do you read stories from other lands and peoples? Why or why not? (*Optional*: Give an example.)

70. Do you think young people should read books and newspaper/magazine articles about the environment? Have you? Explain your answers.

71. Do you read books on science or mathematics on your own? Why or why not?

72. Would you ever read a book on psychology (science of the mind and behavior)? Why or why not? Give an example—if you have one—of something you learned about psychology from reading. Was it helpful in your own life? Explain.

73. Have you ever read a book on philosophy (a system of ideas and principles for conducting your life)? Why or why not? How would reading about philosophy help you in your own life? (*Hint*: Look up "philosophy" or "philosopher" in a dictionary or thesaurus for definitions and synonyms before answering.)

74. Do you like to read plays? Why or why not? What insights can you get from them? Give an example.

75. Do you read sports stories (novels, short stories, newspaper and magazine articles, nonfiction books)? Why or why not? Can these stories help you in playing sports, your everyday life, or whatever it may be? Explain.

76. Is reading sports books (stories or articles) different from reading other books? Explain your answer.

77. What character from a sports book (fiction or nonfiction) would you like to model yourself after? Why?

78. What character from a novel would you like to model yourself after? Why?

79. What person from a biography, autobiography, memoir, diary, or journal would you like to model yourself after? Why?

80. Has a book character (fiction or nonfiction) reminded you of a person you know in real life? Who was the character and the real life person? How are they alike?

81. Have you read a book (fiction or nonfiction) that is a mirror image (almost an exact copy) of your own life? What are the similarities?

82. How important is the ending of a book (fiction)? Why? Recall a good ending to a book you read. What was so good about it?

83. Recall a bad ending to a book (fiction) you read. What was so bad about it? How would you change the ending?

84. Do books with animal characters affect you differently than books with human characters? Explain your answer.

85. Recall a book that made you sad. What was it about? Why did it lead to these feelings? Is a book bad because it makes you feel down? Did you learn something despite the sadness? Explain your answers.

86. What have you read that caused you to stop, think, and reflect? Explain.

87. Can poetry open your eyes to the world? Explain your answer. Give an example.

88. Have you ever read an art book filled with drawings, paintings, and sketches? Explain whether or not it affected the way you view the world. Describe or sketch one image you still can see.

89. What mysteries of nature or the natural world can you read about in a library? Brainstorm a list of five mysteries.

90. Have you ever read an anthology or collection of short stories by one writer or many different writers? What insights come from reading short story collections? (*Optional*: Have you ever read a series of novels from one writer? What insights did you get?)

91. Have you ever read an anthology or collection of poems by one poet or many different poets? What insights and knowledge come from reading poetry anthologies?

92. Why doesn't a novelist tell you everything in his or her book? Why would an author of a nonfiction book want to tell you everything or as much as possible?

93. Do you like to listen to poetry read out loud? Or, do you like to read it silently by yourself? Explain your answer.

94. Recall a time when reading inspired you to write a story, an essay, or poem. What did you read? How did it motivate you to write? Briefly describe what you wrote.

95. Recall a novel or short story where you felt sorry for a character. Why did you feel sorry? What did you think about after reading it?

96. Recall a book, story, tale, or reading where music was important. What kind of music did you hear? How was it connected to the story? What did you think about after reading it?

97. Recall a book, story, or tale where food was the main ingredient. Describe the story's tasty delights and their connection to the characters. What is fun and entertaining about reading a book where food plays a key role? Visualize an image from the food story and draw a picture.

98. Describe an amazing conversation you listened to in a story, novel, or tale. What did you overhear? What were you thinking and imagining during the characters' exchanges?

99. Can you still enjoy a poem you do not understand completely? Explain. Give an example.

100. Has a poem or poetry helped you see things in the outside or real world you never really noticed before? Explain. Give an example from your poetry reading life.

101. Has a poem or poetry helped you see things in nature or the natural world you never noticed before? Explain. Give an example from your poetry reading life.

102. Has a poem or poetry helped you become more sensitive to other people? Explain. Give an example from your poetry reading life.

103. Do you read poetry if you're down? Why or why not? Give an example. (*Hint*: If you don't, imagine how reading poetry when you're blue might affect you.)

104. Recall a poem you enjoyed reading or listening to in your early grades. Describe whatever you remember: feelings, thoughts, and images. Why did the poem have such a strong effect on you?

105. Can reading poetry hurt? Explain.

Reading Experiences: Common (Everyday), Past (Early), and Hypothetical

106. How is a book an invitation?

107. Did your reading life and real life change once you learned how to read on your own? Explain your answer.

108. Why should you learn to calm your mind before and during reading?

109. Can you read and read and forget about everything else? Why or why not?

110. Who communicated the power of reading to you as a child? When? How? Where?

111. What is a lullaby? Can you recall a line from one? Why does a lullaby put a baby to sleep? How does it work? If you have a lullaby memory, describe it.

112. Can you keep reading a book or story even though it scares you a lot? Why or why not? Describe the experience.

113. Why does it take forever to finish reading certain books and others you breeze through?

114. Can you read and watch TV at the same time? Explain.

115. Do you have to fight yourself to read at times? Why?

116. Are there connections between reading and coolness? Explain.

117. Recall a time you chose to be alone with a book and away from your friends. Why did you choose reading over your friends? Was it a good choice? Explain your answers.

118. Has reading ever left you completely happy afterward? Explain.
119. How can you double your reading fun?
120. Has school reading inspired you to read more in your free time? Why or why not?
121. Can TV programs motivate reading? Why or why not?
122. Has a TV program motivated you to read? Which program? Which book or reading? What was the connection between the show and the book?
123. Where do you learn more from: books or movies? Why?
124. As best as you can, recall when you first switched from picture books to chapter books: Was the change hard or easy to make? Why?
125. Were you rewarded for reading when you were much younger? Explain. Give an example. Did the reward motivate you to read or to like reading more? Why or why not?
126. Recall a bad or difficult experience you had when first learning how to read. Describe the feelings, thoughts, and images from the memory.
127. Recall a word game you played in school or at home. How was it played? What did you learn? Did you enjoy playing? Explain your answers.
128. Recall a picture from a book you especially liked in your early years. Describe what you remember. When you visualize the picture, what thoughts and feelings are triggered? (*Optional*: Use an illustration you really like from later years or a current one.)
129. Did anyone push or pressure you to become a reader or a better reader? Who? Did it help or hurt you? Explain.
130. Do you read books more than once? Why or why not?
131. How can reading a book a second time be different for you?
132. What is the longest you have read at one time? What kept you going? Why?
133. How do you get yourself to read if you're not in the mood? Does it work? Explain.
134. How do you know if you really like a book you're reading? Give an example.
135. Movies use soundtracks to get you to enjoy them more. Would, or does, music get you to enjoy reading more? Explain.
136. Can music get you into reading if you feel tired or out of it? Explain.
137. Can you read in any place or situation no matter what the distractions may be? Why or why not?
138. What weather makes the best reading weather for you? Why?
139. Where do you feel more comfortable reading: home, school, or library? Why?
140. Do you read to kill or pass time? Why? When? Where? What do you like to read in this situation? Does it help to pass the time? Explain.
141. Does reading leave you drained or exhausted at times? Why? Give an example.

142. Recall a time you enjoyed sitting, reading, and relaxing—and nothing bothered you at all. Describe where you were reading, what you read, and your experience. Does this happen a lot in your reading life? Why or why not?

143. What goes through your mind when you enter a library now?

144. What was the first grownup or adult book you read? How was it different from other books you read? Could you understand and appreciate it? Explain your answers.

145. What does the expression "bury your nose in a book" mean? Have you done this lately? Why or why not?

146. Picture yourself reading on the beach: What do you see, think, and feel? What are you reading? Why?

147. Can travel books or magazines motivate reading? Give an example.

148. Do you like reading mysteries or thrillers? Why or why not?

149. Give an example of leisure-time reading you have done in math or science. What ideas or facts can you still recall? Did your outside reading inspire learning about the subject(s) in school? Why or why not?

150. Can reading one book lead you to reading your next book? Explain your answer by giving an example from your reading life.

151. Do you read graphic novels (books featuring pictures plus words)? Why or why not?

152. What is a serious reader? Are you? Explain.

153. Where do you learn more: from books or life? Why?

154. How important is curiosity to reading and reading life? Why?

155. What is a bad book (bad = lousy)? Give an example. How bad was or is it?

156. Can books help you to become more open and honest with your friends, parents, siblings, and teachers? Why or why not?

157. What has your reading taught you about school life? Could it help you deal with your real school life? Explain.

158. Has your reading taught you about competing and sportsmanship? What have you learned? Can you use it in your real sports life? Why or why not?

159. What has reading taught you about families and your own family? Give an example. Can you use it in your real life? Explain your answer.

160. My teacher once told us that she always carried a "pet book" around with her. She never wanted to be away from it—that's how much she loved her "pet." Imagine carrying your own "pet book" around with you all the time. What book would you choose? Why?

161. Describe an unforgettable reading lesson you had in or out of school.

162. Describe a reader's worst nightmare.

163. In school you have to read what is assigned. At home you can read whatever you want. Does this freedom at home motivate you to read more? Why or why not?

164. Recall a song you enjoyed singing or listening to in your early grades. What words or lines do you remember? What feelings, thoughts, and pictures did they trigger?
165. Can a book make you feel bad? Explain.
166. What are the pleasures of reading? Brainstorm five examples from your reading life.
167. Do you look for special books to help you chill out? Explain. Which books?

Reading Process

168. Reading can get you lost in a world of thought. Recall a time when your reading got you "lost in a world of thought." What were you reading? What were you thinking? Where did your thoughts take you? Was it worth the trip? Why
169. How can stories that are read aloud seem like movies in your mind?
170. What is the connection between reading and feeling? Give an example.
171. What senses come into play while you read? Give examples of how the senses affect your reading. (*Hint*: Think of sight, hearing, taste, smell, and touch.)
172. How does the outside world fade away so quickly once you begin to read? Is it easy or hard to make the switch from the outside to the inside? Why?
173. Compare thinking when reading a book to thinking when watching a movie.
174. Can reading change boredom? Explain. Give an example of how reading may or can change these feelings.
175. Can reading help drive away an anxious night? Why? How? Have an example? Describe what happened.
176. Did you ever "get lost in a crowd of words" while reading? Describe what happened. How, or did you, find your way out? Explain your answer.
177. Are there books you read more slowly? Why? Does slowing down reading speed improve your understanding? Why? Give an example.
178. Recall a time you were reading too fast. How did you know it was too fast? What was going on inside you? How do you correct or change your reading speed? What do you say to yourself when reading too quickly?
179. Describe the solitude you create when reading. (*Hint*: Look up "solitude" in a thesaurus or a dictionary for synonyms and definitions before answering.)
180. Is reading work? Explain.
181. Why do certain books (fiction and nonfiction) need more time to sink in?
182. What happens in your mind if you don't understand what you are reading?

183. Can you get through a book without totally understanding it? Explain your answer.
184. Can you recall a hard book that you finally understood by the end? How did you do it?
185. Are you aware of time passing when you read? Why or why not?
186. Recall a reading experience when time flew by. Describe what happened.
187. Do you sometimes find it hard to remember what you are reading? Why? Give an example of reading and forgetting.
188. Describe a book that lit up your mind with its awesome ideas. Name one idea communicated and explain why it meant a lot to you.
189. Recall a book that verified or supported one of your ideas. What was your idea? How did the book validate it?
190. Can books get you uptight? Why? Is that a good or bad thing? Why?
191. Can books lighten up your world? Give an example from your reading. How did the book work on you? Describe the process.
192. Do you pause for a moment to think about or reflect on what you read? Why?
193. Has a poem made you reflect on something you never really thought about? Explain. Give an example of a poem that got you to pause and think: about what?
194. What does it mean to vanish, disappear, or fade away into a book? Did it ever happen to you? Where did you go?
195. Do you have good control over your thoughts and thinking while you read? Explain your answer.
196. Recall a time you had less control over your thoughts/thinking while reading. Describe this experience. Did you gain control again? Explain.
197. She has such great concentration when she reads. But how can you tell, dear friend? What do you see? Visualize what the girl's concentration might look like and then describe what you see.
198. How do you know your concentration is breaking down while you read? What are the warning signs?
199. You're trying to read but feel distracted. You find yourself sitting there lost in confusion. How do you get back to the words on the page? How do you get back to the present moment? What will you do? Explain your answer.
200. How do you handle reading a difficult book you have to read? Give an example.
201. Is there a connection between reading and patience? Why? Give an example.
202. How is reading on a reading test different from other reading experiences?
203. Do you daydream, at times, while you read? Why? Give an example.

204. Can reading bring back memories? Explain your answer. Give an example. How did the book or reading trigger the memory? If this has not happened to you, imagine how reading might uncover a hidden memory.

205. Sentences have power, muscles, strength, force, and pep. They give off energy picked up by your concentration. To enjoy reading sentences, your concentration must meet their energy. When both energies meet, you have greater understanding and appreciation of the sentence. Concentration pumps up the imagination to work hard to create and find images. Put your energy into this sentence and see what happens: While his mother spoke to the doctor, Paul, a shy, sensitive young boy, felt embarrassed and made believe he dropped his watch on the floor, as tears came to his eyes.

   • Describe the sentence's power using images, thoughts, ideas, and feelings.
   • Describe how strong your concentration was while you read the sentence.
   • What have you discovered about reading and the reading process?
   • Can you keep up this concentration throughout an entire book? Why or why not?

206. What happens inside you if you do not see mind-pictures when reading? Why?

207. Recall a sad poem you read by describing your feelings, thoughts, ideas, images, memories, reflections, and/or dreams.

208. Do you always have to think when you read? Are there times when you hardly think at all when reading? Explain your answers.

209. Do the feelings experienced when you begin a novel differ from those felt at its end? Are there any similarities? Explain your answers.

210. Do you read poetry differently from prose (novels, stories, essays)? Why?

211. Recall a mystery or thriller you read. Can you recall a mind-picture from the book or story? Draw one image from it. What comes to mind after you finish drawing?

212. Does a book stay in your mind after you read it, or does it just fade away quickly into nothing? Describe what usually happens.

213. Recall a book where you got stuck on one feeling throughout it. Which feeling? Why did you get stuck? How did this affect your reading?

214. You play sports with passion. You do the same with video and computer games. But, do you read with passion? Isn't reading with passion the same as playing games with passion? Explain your answers.

215. Compare reading comic books to reading books.

216. Is comic book reading really reading? Does reading comic books help or hurt your reading and reading life? Explain your answers.

217. Did you ever read a food recipe? Did you understand it completely? What can be tricky about reading a food recipe? What reading skills are needed to understand it? Explain your answers.
218. Is reading searching? Explain your answer.
219. Can books and reading help you release or vent negative feelings? Why? Give an example of how this works.
220. Do reading and books teach you to think for yourself? Why?
221. Can reading motivate you to write? Why?
222. Recall a time when reading inspired you to write a story, an essay, or poem. What did you read? How did it motivate you to write? Briefly describe what you wrote.
223. What kind of book or reading takes all your energy to read? Why? What energy do you need and how do you use it?
224. Do you read to understand yourself (self-understanding)? Why or why not? Has a book (fiction or nonfiction) helped you to know yourself better? Explain.
225. Do you read poetry to understand yourself (self-understanding)? Why or why not? Has a poem or poetry helped you to know yourself better? Explain. Give an example.
226. Is there such a thing as "painless reading"? Why or why not? Give an example.
227. Poetry reading: hooked on feelings. Explain.

Words and Word Activities

228. When did you first realize that words make pictures in the mind? Do you remember an early mind-picture you visualized? Describe what you can recall.
229. What happens when words collide? For example, what happens if watermelons collide with tomatoes? Describe the collision, and then draw what you see.
230. Do certain words strike you like lightning strikes a tree? Give an example of how a word struck you like lightning. Describe what happened.
231. No: After you hear this word, what runs through your mind? Why?
232. Yes: After you hear this word, what runs through your mind? Why?
233. Read, visualize, and describe two of the following words: (a) desk; (b) swim; (c) onion; and (d) thunder. Write a short description of what you see or experience in your mind. Connect feelings and thoughts to the chosen words.

   • *word* _____
   • *word* _____

234. Are there words that bring you peace? List three words. Next to each word, describe how it brings you peace.
235. Boring: Put yourself in the middle of it and what do you find?
236. Think about it: Are there words that creep and crawl in your mind giving you goose bumps? List two examples. Describe their movements and how they give you goose bumps.
237. List three words that you live, breathe, and think about every day. Pick one word and describe how it affects you.
238. What word echoes in your mind the second you hear or read it? What echoes do you hear?
239. "I dare you": What does the expression mean? How powerful are these words? Why?
240. What two words, if you think about them at the same time, cause conflict or confusion? Describe what happens if they are together in your mind.
241. Teachers/reading: Reflect on both words. What comes to mind: pictures, feelings, thoughts, ideas, experiences, memories, and dreams?
242. Work triggers what words in your mind? Word-storm ten words.
243. Just for fun: Pick a word—a noun. Change it into a mind-picture. What thoughts are triggered by the image? (*Hint*: Brainstorm thoughts and ideas from what you visualize.)
244. List three annoying words. Pick one and describe how it annoys you.
245. What word makes you laugh or smile? Why? What power does it have?
246. Get close up to what you read by zooming in on real two-word sentences. Describe the images, thoughts, and feelings created by:

Ducks swim.

- image
- thought
- feeling

Juan jumps.

- image
- thought
- feeling

Crows fly.

- image
- thought
- feeling

247. What words come to mind when you think of "poetry"? Word-storm ten words.

248. "You can do it!" What does this popular expression get you to think, feel, and imagine? Can these words help you or someone who needs motivation? How would they work on and in you?

249. What are teasing words? Give an example of a word or words used to tease. Describe how they affect people. How do you deal with teasing words in the real world?

250. Pretend you are a camera with a close-up lens. Go right up to a word and look deeply into it. For example, zoom in on the word "gray" with your big lens. What do you see, experience, think, feel, and imagine? Describe your "gray" journey.

251. What word do you think about a lot? Why? What does it trigger in your mind?

252. Victim: What words can be connected to it? Make a list of ten words by word-storming.

253. Have the words (lyrics) of a song or songs helped you to see things in the real world you never noticed or understood before? Explain. Give examples from your "music life."

254. How does listening to a song's words make you happy or feel good? Give an example. Do the words create pictures in your mind? If this happens to you, draw one image triggered by the song's lyrics.

255. What song lyrics bring you peace? How? Describe the peace you feel.

Writing, Drawing, and Creative Thinking

256. Pretend you're looking through a camera with a powerful zoom lens that gets close up to a person reading. Focus on the eyes of the reader. Draw a pencil-sketch of these "reading eyes." What does your picture make you wonder about reading and readers? Why?

257. Picture and sketch: Read the following two-word sentences and visualize them in your mind. Pencil-sketch the mind-pictures you see from: (a) willows weep; (b) seagulls fly; (c) boys fight. Pick the silliest image (one you like and can draw) and pencil-sketch it. Your drawing can be a cartoon with a short caption.

258. Pencil-sketch—with details—an old book that you love, but is now falling apart. Focus totally on the mind-picture of the book and sketch it. (*Hint:* If you don't have an "old book" in your memory, imagine or visualize one in your mind.)

259. Visualize and draw a cartoon showing many readers in an imaginary place where you would not think of finding them. Look at your finished drawing carefully and write whatever thoughts come to mind.

260. If a six-month old (human) baby could read, what books would he or she take out of the "infant library"? Brainstorm some possible titles. Feel free to make up original silly or serious titles.

261. If giraffes could read, what books would they take out of the "zoo library"? Brainstorm some possible titles. Feel free to make up original silly or serious titles.

262. If parakeets could read, what books would they take out of the "budgie library"? Brainstorm some possible titles. Feel free to make up original silly or serious titles.

263. If ants could read, what books would they take out of the "hilly library"? List some titles by brainstorming.

264. Read, visualize, and pencil-sketch cartoon images for these absurd, silly, ridiculous two-word sentences:

   • Children float.
   • Fish ski.
   • Books sweat.
   • Balloons surf.

265. Do you like reading horror stories or books? Why or why not? Give an example by sketching one mind-picture you still remember.

266. Recall a sports book (fiction or nonfiction) you read. What or who was it about? Are there any mind-pictures you remember? Draw an image: What comes up?

267. Make up a scary sentence completely from your imagination.

   • Read it back to yourself silently and out loud.
   • Visualize the sentence in your mind and draw it.
   • What comes to mind after you finish the entire activity?

268. Make up a scary sentence using a scene from a movie you saw.

   • Read it back to yourself silently and out loud.
   • Visualize the sentence in your mind and draw it.
   • What comes to mind after you finish the activity?

269. Make up a ridiculously absurd sentence completely from your imagination.

   • Read it back to yourself silently and out loud.
   • Visualize the sentence in your mind and draw it.
   • What comes to mind after you finish the activity

270. Which is easier: writing from your own imagination or writing from images you see in movies, video games, computer games, or on television? Why?

271. Who is "Bookman"? Create this imaginary reading being. Draw a portrait or cartoon of "Bookman." Write a fifty-word story (or longer) on this imaginary reading being's life. (*Hint*: You can also use "Bookwoman" to answer the question.)

272. Draw a self-portrait of you reading. Visualize your favorite place and position to read. Add your own personal details to create a clear picture of your reading experience. Explain what can be learned about you and your reading life from the self-portrait.
273. Visualize an island of readers in the middle of the ocean. Describe this imaginary reading world you see with your mind's eye in twenty-five to fifty words.
274. You lie down on a couch with a book in your hands. An overhead lamp sprays a yellow light on the book's pages. This scene has happened many times in your reading life. Visualize the image and put yourself right in it. Examine it carefully with your mind's eye. Describe what comes to mind about your reading life in twenty-five to fifty words after viewing the image.

One-Line Statements and Opinions

275. Always read as if it is your first time. Explain.
276. Warning: I read and think at the same time. Explain.
277. What book do you think would make a good movie? Why?
278. Caution: I brake for good writing. Explain.
279. Think about it: Why bother reading books about games, hobbies, music, sports, or pets if you can find out about them on the Internet?
280. Reading and books teach you about your own survival. Agree? Disagree? Why?
281. Read, visualize, feel, and think—Got it! Got what? Explain the statement's meaning.
282. What books should kids read nowadays? List three books or subject areas. Pick one book or subject and explain why it's vital for them to know.
283. Should books with a lot of violence be read? What purpose can they serve? Recall a particularly violent book you read. Was it helpful or positive in any way? Why?
284. Reading turns your head in every direction. What does the statement mean or suggest? What do you think: agree or disagree? Why?
285. Say "yes" to yourself when you read. What does the statement mean or suggest? Do you say "yes" to yourself when you read? Why or why not?
286. Word rescuers: dictionaries and thesauri. What does the statement mean or suggest? Do you agree or disagree? Explain.
287. Do you consider reading a bad book a total waste of time? Why or why not?
288. All books and reading about food are usually fun, entertaining, and educational. Agree? Disagree? What do you think? Why?
289. A passionate reader makes a good book better. Explain.

290. Caution: Reading slippery when misunderstood. Explain.
291. Don't worry, read poetry, and be happy. What do you think? Do you agree or disagree? Why? What kind of poetry might work?
292. Reading gives you something for nothing . . . and the best things in life are freebees. What does the statement mean or suggest? What do you think about it? Explain.
293. Books bend your mind. Explain. (*Hint*: Look up "bend" in a dictionary or thesaurus for definitions and synonyms before answering.)
294. Your reading life, world, and experiences are secret gardens. Explain.

Ratings and Quotations

295. "There should be a little voice in your head like the storyteller is saying it. And if there's not, then you're just looking at words" (Lakeisha, ninth-grader in San Francisco). What is the statement saying in your own words? Is this true for your reading experience? Explain.
296. "The words loved me and I loved them in return" (Sonia Sanchez). How important are words according to the quotation? What does the phrase "the words loved me" mean? How do you "love" words? What does the phrase mean? Explain your answers.
297. How often do you reread books? Rate your frequency of rereading books on a scale from 0 to 10, where 0 = never, and 10 = a lot or as often as possible. Give a reason for your rating.
298. How powerful is your concentration when reading? Rate your level from 0 to 10, where 0 = no concentration, and 10 = total concentration. Give reasons for your rating.
299. Rate your ability to think about or reflect on what you read on a scale from 0 to 10, where 0 = giving no thought, and 10 = giving a lot of thought. Give a reason for your rating.
300. "I am not a speed-reader. I am a speed-understander" (Issac Asimov). Why does Asimov choose "speed-understanding" over "speed-reading"? Do you? Explain.
301. Rate how fast you understand what you read (consider all kinds of reading) on a scale from 0 to 10, where 0 = slow, and 10 = quick to understand. Give reasons for your rating.
302. How much energy do you put into your reading? Rate it on a scale from 0 to 10, where 0 = no energy, and 10 = a great amount of energy put into reading. Give reasons for your rating.
303. "The ability to read awoke inside me some long dormant craving to be mentally alive" (Malcolm X, *The Autobiography of Malcolm X*). According to the quotation, the "ability to read" triggered a desire "to be mentally alive." What does this phrase mean? How would the experience help you in daily life? What does the "ability to read" wake up inside you?

Explain your answers. (Look up "mentally" in a dictionary or thesaurus for definitions and synonyms before answering.)

304. "Each book was a world onto itself, and in it I took refuge" (Alberto Manguel, *A History of Reading*). How is a book "a world onto itself"? How is a book "a world"? Why would the author "take refuge" in a book's world? Why would it become like a shelter? Are books a "refuge" or safe place for you? Explain your answers.

HOW TO USE BOOK 2

One Suggested Sample Survey Approach for Presenting Questions with Notes

Here is one of many possible survey approaches to use in Book 2/Round 2: Continue exploring common, everyday reading experiences. The questions make kids feel good about responding because they form a direct pipeline to the heart of their reading lives. *Examples*: (a) What is the longest you have read at one time? What kept you going? Why? (b) Has reading ever left you completely happy afterward? Explain. Choose ten and divide them up in your questioning.

Dig deeper into how they read with reading process questions: Greater awareness of their private reading worlds can improve their reading and response to literature by showing them a broader range of pleasures. Increased insight into the mind's magic theater of reading, to see it as an imaginary stage or TV screen where numerous performances take place and where the inner eye views the shows, will amp up enjoyment and understanding of the reading process.

Example: Are there books you read more slowly? Why? Does slowing down your reading speed improve your understanding? Why? Give an example. Pick ten and blend them into your questioning.

Now that the kids have started to motivate themselves—call it *self-motivation*—by moving inside their imagination, go further into the reading process by asking slightly more advanced word questions on changing words and sentences into mind-pictures. Continue developing the creativity in words and reading with this *example*: Boring—put yourself in the middle of it and what do you find? *Remember:* One purpose for reading and changing words into pleasing and not-so-pleasing images is to inspire students to write words coming from 3-D pictures visualized in their imagination. Split up five- to ten-word questions amongst the others.

Poetry reading-life questions help them to think more about poetry as a viable subject to study, and also to expand their experiences in it. Poetry questions heighten kids' awareness of the reading process because they begin to realize the effects/affects of words/lines in a poem: one line or word will illuminate and emotionally rev up the mind's magic reading theater. *Picture shows* created by poetry spark feelings, thoughts, ideas, memories, and experiences, enhancing preteen/teen responses to literature.

Poetry questions and poetry reading enable adolescents to enjoy reading prose (fiction and nonfiction) by building, deepening, and clarifying the reading process. *Example*: Has a poem made you reflect on something you never really thought about? Explain. Give an example of a poem that got you to pause and think: about what? Select three questions and use them throughout your questions.

Resume asking one-line statement and opinion questions. In raps and discussions emphasize that they should not jump the gun with quick answers to them. One-liners stir up emotions and thoughts, so the first response may or may not be the best. More searching for reading experiences will make kids *think twice* before answering automatically. *Examples*: (a) Always read as if it is your first time. Explain. (b) Where do you learn more from: books or movies? Why? Intersperse five to ten one-liners and opinions throughout your questioning.

Similar to Book 1/Round 1 of thirty to seventy-five questions, ask lighter, creative questions if things get too serious. Go to (a) drawing; (b) creative-thinking/absurd; and (c) hypothetical reading situation questions. *Examples are*: (a) Visualize and draw a cartoon showing many readers in an imaginary place where you would not think of finding them. Look at your finished drawing carefully and write whatever thoughts come to mind. (b) If a six-month-old (human) baby could read, what books would he or she take out of the "infant library"? Brainstorm some titles. (c) Picture yourself reading on the beach: What do you see, think, and feel? What are you reading? Why? Throw in about five to ten so your class/child will see reading and reading life through their drawings, creative thinking, as well as their imaginative and/or realistic responses to hypothetical reading scenes. In your raps, remind them that "masterpieces" are not necessary for a good answer to drawing questions. Kids enjoy responding to questions by drawing.

An absurd creative-thinking question such as "If a six-month-old baby could read" and "If an ant could read" have a purpose to their silliness. It's all about choosing books to read: How does a child choose a book? Why did she choose *that* book to read? What is student's/child's connection to the books she reads? Absurdity in school makes adolescent hearts grow fonder.

Also, many kids are clueless when it comes to selecting books to read. They opt for the easiest book on the library shelf just to complete the assignment for their book lists (although there's nothing wrong with this method every so often to mix things up). Choosing often becomes mindless, uninspiring, a random act that gets dumb and dumber. Add two to four silly questions to your list and ask them when the time is right for a fun, meaningful question to motivate thoughtfulness when picking a book to read.

Book 2 has many book recall questions. Your selection, which depends on the genres of books your class/child reads, helps them explore what their book reading lives are about. *Example*: Recall a book (fiction or nonfiction) you read about fear. What did you learn from it? What did you realize about fear that you did not know before? Explain. Draw one mind-picture from the book. Ask the class five to ten book recalls, but give them choices of questions to answer so they don't come up empty. These are not test questions requiring grades; they're about remembering book experiences and realizing the phenomenal worlds of reading: the parallel universes and virtual realities that inhabit their imaginations.

Written responses to book recalls answer key questions about their motivation to read: How do kids respond to literature? What remains from the books they read: images, feelings, thoughts, ideas, words, lines, dialogues, characters, settings, scenes, events, and themes? How good, bad, clear, and understandable are the *shows* visualized in the mind's magic reading theater? How involved are they in their reading? Can they connect reading life to real life? What are their attitudes toward their present—and past—reading lives?

Ask more nonfiction reading questions to further investigate students' experiences in the genre. Book 2/Round 2 expands the nonfiction genre with survey-type questions on how-to books/articles, history, science, math, nature, biography, autobiography, memoirs, sports, photography, art, psychology, philosophy, and travel (books, newspapers, and magazines).

Nonfiction reading is key to student success from elementary school through college. Think about these facts: (a) Fifty percent of kids that enter college today have trouble reading required textbooks. (b) The majority of classroom reading is nonfiction. (c) Standardized tests have mostly nonfiction passages to read and interpret. Consider the importance of reading-in-the-content-area in your classroom reading program and this question category will gain momentum in your selections.

Nonfiction questions clarify their preferences in, and attitudes toward, the genre: why they are motivated or unmotivated by it. *Examples*: (a) Describe a good nonfiction real-life story you read. What made it so good? (b) Does history *come to life* when you read a history textbook? Why or why not? Choose five to ten and incorporate in your questioning strategy.

Which questions would conclude Book 2/Round 2 of thirty to seventy-five questions? *Closers* should leave students/child looking forward to the next set of questions. The upcoming choices are the author's hypothetical strategy for asking closing questions. Your selections may be different, and that's the beauty of *Motivating Teen and Preteen Readers*. Each teacher and parent shapes his own approach according to a particular class/child. Question selection is subjective. Discussion leaders can go through Books 1, 2, 3, and 4 and randomly pick questions as they see fit. *Experiment* with various questions and categories. Have fun with the questions and your kids will, too. The book of questions is an *open book* for all to see reading and reading life.

To finish Book 2, discussion leaders can go to past (early) reading experience questions and writing questions. The former sets up more emotional involvement with reading/reading-life experiences; *for example*: Who communicated the power of reading to you as a child? When? How? Where? Let your students/

child feel a sense of nostalgia for their early reading lives, to see how enjoyable it was—or wasn't—with all that magic wrapped up in those memories of reading. If kids discover a small part of an event, scene, or memory, it should initiate a thoughtful written response. They can take that piece further by inner-eye scanning, reflecting, and contemplating until more things come into view on the imaginary TV screen in the mind. (See figures 2 and 3, "Describe Your Experience" and "Inner-Eye Scan for Book Memories.")

The latter questions on writing, such as "creating scary sentences from the imagination and the movies," teach students that writing can also be entertaining. Writing one sentence at a time makes it basic and fun. Take nothing for granted about their writing abilities in these activities. Even more quirky is "creating an absurd sentence totally from the imagination." Expect some crazy-sounding winners here. Pick five questions on past reading experiences and writing as closers for Book 2 or Round 2 of questions.

But how do kids create silly sentences from the imagination? One answer is picture-storming. *Explain in a teacher/parent rap:* "To picture-storm images—trigger one image after another nonstop—until you find one you like. Look at the image with the inner eye; watch it on the imaginary TV screen inside your head; and let the eye beam its searchlight on that image to see it clearly. Keep looking at it and write your ridiculous sentence from the image. Write and include the details from your silly image in a complete sentence on your paper."

Model the picture-storming technique for your class/child; or have creative students show others how to do it via oral picture-storming. Demonstrate how to make things up (pictures) in their minds via the trigger method of creativity. Explain how the imagination or inner space is infinite and that unlimited possibilities and choices—images—lie inside them.

Discussion leaders can end their questioning by asking a *combination* drawing, absurd, and longer writing question: Who is "Bookman"? Create this imaginary reading being. Draw a portrait or cartoon of "Bookman." Write a fifty-word story on this imaginary reading being's life. After responding to many questions on reading and reading life, preteens/teens will enjoy the self-amusement park called the *mind's magic writing theater*, despite the tough cerebral workout.

Keep the idea of a reading-writing connection going throughout your questioning and let it lead the students/child into the creative-writing questions in the next round. "Bookman" could be a final choice for the closing question. But what about your choices: What would be your closers as discussion leader?

KEY INFORMATION AND PROCEDURES FOR ASKING AND ANSWERING QUESTION CATEGORIES

Feel free to select your questions from over three hundred in Book 2, except for questions on words, sentences, and writing. Check out the developmental sequence, starting from visualizing: (a) single words; (b) two-word sentences; (c) longer sentences; and ending with (d) longer writing responses (stories) involving creative thinking and writing. The sequence teaches and motivates adolescents to see words as pictures, thoughts, ideas, meanings, and feelings, not just black on white.

Generally, Book 2's questions are tougher than Book 1's; *for example*: How is a book an invitation? "Tougher" means: deeper thinking on a subject; more scanning for reading experiences; and greater visualization, concentration, and reflection. The questions ask for more, challenging students to stop, search, and think about a response that is there and not impossible to answer.

If enthusiasm for responding to questions wanes at times, use teacher/parent raps (quick two-minute talks) to rejuvenate your kids/child. Mini-discussions can jumpstart attitudes toward reading and reading life. Also, use the class website for developing and improving weaker responses and for showing stronger responses (all done anonymously). Pump them up! (Go to "Implementing Workable Schedules/Strategies for Presenting Questions in Book 2" for more information on class websites in *Motivating Teen and Preteen Readers*.)

Book 2 has many questions on common, everyday reading experiences and the reading process. Use a *series* of five questions on everyday reading experiences or the reading process in a forty-five-minute period to see which questions trigger the strongest responses and passion in a student's/child's reading life: Question choices and the number presented will vary from teacher to teacher and parent to parent.

These analytical questions ask kids, at times, to face their reading problems. If they respond in an open, honest, genuine, and direct way, adolescents gain insight into their current reading situations and can change them. *Motivating Teen and Preteen Readers* wants young people to question themselves about their reading and reading lives—call it *self-questioning*.

To spark greater interest in nonfiction, experiment with a week-long series of nonfiction questions on various books and reading. Try one question a day for several days: See how much your students/child can handle, and, more importantly, how much the questions help them think about and grow passionate in this genre.

Opinion questions challenge kids to come up with thoughtful and emotional responses. *Emphasize in raps*: "Before you answer an opinion question, make sure you know, first, what it asks or states, and then search your memory for different experiences connected to the question. Add them up in your mind and write your opinion. Your responses express your attitude toward reading. They show how motivated you are." (Go to figure 2, "Describe Your Experience," for a technique to search for "different experiences.")

Recall questions can be used: to supplement a novel or nonfiction work read in class; for outside reading projects or reports; and/or just-for-fun for leisure-time/outside reading. The idea behind book recalls is to bring back positive memories—feelings, thoughts, images—from past and current books to remind them of the beauty of reading and books. The questions help expand a response to literature: the emotional, psychological, and intellectual experience of a book or reading.

Stress key points about answering book recalls in raps/talks: "Recalling books you've read in the past can be tricky because we forget important facts, details, and events, whether they were fiction or nonfiction books. Before answering a recall question, find a book memory; look at the mind-pictures; think of the main idea of the book; concentrate on it and whatever else comes to mind and respond. For a book you're reading now or recently finished, answering a recall question should be easier because it's fresh in your memory. However, you still need to recall, visualize, think, reflect, and concentrate to find answers." (See figure 3, "Inner-Eye Scan for Book Memories.")

A question that may give students difficulty is "to recall an ending to a book they read." If they can't remember one, allow them Internet access to look up a summary of a book which can spark the ending. Websites to check out are: www.allreaders.com; www.kidsreads.com; www.ask.com; www.amazon.com; and www.google.com. Internet book summaries and reviews as triggers to revive memories are acceptable in *Motivating Teen and Preteen Readers*. They can also wait for the discussion to restimulate forgotten book memories; and go to the school, public, or their home library to find the book and skim it for the answer.

Some book recalls genuinely require more effort; *for example*: Can you recall a book that is a mirror image of your life? They have to understand the expression "mirror image" before responding. When kids grasp the concept, after the discussion leader explains it, they search their memory for a book reminding them of their own lives and back it with comparisons. Recalling, visualizing, and reflection are needed. Define, describe, explain, and reinforce these skills in raps and discussions.

Word, word-activity, and sentence-visualization questions advance those in Book 1. Students enjoy absurd word questions such as: What happens when watermelons collide with tomatoes? Reading and visualizing word questions connect real-life experiences with words—what words: bring you peace, echo in your mind, and give you goose bumps?

Book 2's questions go from visualizing single words (nouns, adjectives, verbs) to visualizing and drawing two-word sentences (both real and surreal): from "Boys fight" to "Children float." Longer sentence questions test students' powers of visualization and make them work harder to find details in mind-pictures. For instance, they're asked to zoom in on sentences to see the triggered images close up. This strategy improves the inner eye's capacity to see what's happening inside the mind's magic reading theater. The questions push kids to further explore the skill of changing words into images and have fun inside the imagination. Use the sample two-word sentence questions as models to make up your own real and surreal/absurd sentences for class work and homework.

Emphasize in raps: "Sentences, whether they are real or silly, no matter how long they are, become quick flicks in the mind's magic reading theater." Describe reading sentences as energy from the reader's thoughts, feelings, and imagination meeting the energy, power, and lives of words—their images, thoughts, feelings, and meanings—which leads to reading pleasure.

Follow up word questions with basic writing questions like these mentioned previously: (a) Make up a scary sentence from your imagination; and (b) Make up a ridiculously absurd sentence totally from your imagination. Juxtaposing word and sentence-writing questions creates a new appreciation for reading and writing. In *Motivating Teen and Preteen Readers*, reading means changing words into images, feelings, and thoughts, while writing means changing 3-D images from the mind, imagination, and memory into words and sentences. Kids are inspired to write when they see the inside world lit up with images created and visualized in the mind's magic writing theater.

Poetry questions continue examining adolescent poetry reading lives and experiences. *Examples are*: (a) Can you still enjoy a poem you do not understand completely? Explain. Give an example. (b) Has a poem or poetry helped you see things in the outside or real world you never really noticed before? Explain. Give an example.

Use the questions to lead your class/child into Book 3 or Round 3 of questions on a positive note about poetry reading. Let the questions demonstrate how poetry can motivate their real lives. Stress connections between poetry reading life and everyday life.

Mix poetry questions with word and writing questions. Together they form a powerful combination to boost interest in reading, reading life, and the real world because there are lots of pictures, feelings, thoughts, memories, and reflections wrapped up in words, sentences, and poetry lines. This approach helps kids to: read and visualize; visualize and write; heighten the reading-writing and writing-reading connections; and link reading life and poetry reading life to daily life. The books of questions affect both reading and writing.

Common, everyday reading experiences comparing reading books versus watching a TV show on nature illuminate major differences between the mediums. Or, another *example*: Can watching the movie of a book you read improve your understanding of the same book? Here students have a chance to express their ideas and beliefs about reading a book versus watching a movie of the same book. Inject combined everyday reading experience and opinion questions to trigger emotion, motivation, and to keep opening up adolescent reading life.

Book 2 also has questions on science fiction, science fantasy, mysteries, thrillers, and horror stories. Expose them to different genres they might not consider for school reading lists or leisure-time reading. Preteens and teens should *experiment* with and keep an open mind to various reading genres to see if they can expand their preferences and enjoyment.

Use a survey approach in Book 2 or Round 2 of questions if it works with your students or child. However, stick with particular question categories if that fits the class's/child's needs at the time. Discussion leaders should use the *trial-and-error* technique with different approaches to and sequences for asking questions. Create your own strategy and see how it affects their motivation to respond and read.

Continue to ask rating questions about their reading experiences. Insert "Rate your ability to think about and reflect on what you read on a scale from 0 to 10, where 0 = giving no thought, and 10 = giving a lot of thought" after they complete a bunch of book recall questions on fiction or nonfiction. Use rating questions at opportune times.

One-line statement questions can be great closers. *Example*: A passionate reader makes a good book better. Explain. It's one way to end Book 2/Round 2 of questions and get them primed for the next set of thirty to seventy-five questions in Book 3/Round 3.

Book 2's final questions may come from an assortment of questions: opinion, creative writing, common everyday reading experiences, quotations, and original one-line statements from the author. Choose questions that summarize, balance, and complete the class's/child's written and oral responses from Book 2/Round 2.

Implementing Workable Schedules/Strategies for Presenting Questions in Book 2

- After skimming and reviewing Book 2's or the other books' questions (for a random selection of questions), continue the schedule used in Book 1, if that works. Variations for presenting the questions remain the same as Book 1. (See "Implementing Workable Schedules/Strategies for Presenting Questions in Book 1.")
- Elementary school teachers for grades 4 to 6 can try this previously suggested approach described in Book 1 for middle/high school teachers: One forty-five-minute period a week with three to five questions prefaced by teacher raps and followed up by a discussion. Allow twenty to thirty minutes for responding to the questions and fifteen to twenty-five minutes for discussion. *Experiment* to find the right number of questions to ask and time limits for responding. Each class and set of questions will require varying amounts of time. Play with implementing this longer period to see what works best for a particular group of students.
- As an *option* to asking several questions in a forty-five-minute period, try a thirty-minute lesson and present only one question that is timely and relevant to a particular class's needs and wants. Spend the extra time discussing the kids' responses to it. Appropriate fifteen minutes for responding "thoughtfully" to the question. The remainder of the period (fifteen minutes, max) is spent on students reading their answers out loud and discussing them.

Parents can also try this approach with their kids. (Allow ten minutes for a written response and ten minutes, max, for talking about it.) Sample question categories for this option are: "Ratings and Quotations," "Drawing, Writing, and Creative Thinking," and "Word and Word Activity."
- Scheduling of mini-lessons also remains the same as Book 1.

Here are *new key strategies* for presenting questions (grades 4 through 10):

- Set up a bonus box with additional questions from Books 2 or 1 on three-inch by five-inch index cards (one question per card), which kids respond to during their free time in school or at home. (Parents can do the same by setting up a bonus box for their child.) They search through the box for a question on reading/reading life, pick ones they like, answer it in their notebook, writing the book number and question. The bonus box can be plain (shoe box or small cardboard box) or decorated.
- The bonus box works from elementary through high school and can be used for extra practice in answering questions. Students may take a question to do at home and enter it in their reading notebooks. The bonus box works in the same way for middle to high school kids. Call it "extra credit," and yes, extrinsic rewards are possible in *Motivating Teen and Preteen Readers*.
- Bonus boxes are great ways to introduce many good questions that teachers and parents will have no or little time to present. It becomes a subtle way to assess motivation and passion for reading and reading life. The bonus box is also a way of presenting struggling learners with important questions that might interest them and help improve attitude and ability in reading. Make sure all questions are written in their notebooks. Remind students to return index cards to the bonus box when finished so their classmates can respond to them.
- *Try exchange programs*: For any mini-fifteen-, thirty-, or forty-five-minute lesson, have kids share their written responses with each other. They keep exchanging their notebooks for classmates to read. The total time limit for this mini-lesson is: five minutes each for writing, sharing, and discussing written responses orally with the entire class. In this approach, students get to read responses they might not have heard in a class discussion.
- A *second exchange program* follows the same principle; however, in this approach, entire notebooks are shared between classmates for review. Allow fifteen minutes for these informal, fun readings kids will appreciate. They can choose buddies, but should not keep the same person for every exchange. If a student doesn't want others to see his or her notebook, that's fine. Some kids might feel embarrassed because of their writing skills. Add a five- to ten-minute whole-class discussion. *Initiate the dialogue with*: "What did you learn about your friend's reading life experiences? Did you learn anything new about reading? How can reading your classmates' notebooks help you in your reading?" The notebook exchange is used after they complete the

questionnaires/chats and approximately thirty questions from Book 2 (or later on with Books 3 and 4).

• Another fun strategy is the *music hour* (See "Additional Strategies for Implementing the Books of Questions" for more information on this technique): Teacher/parent presents typical mini-lesson or extended time lesson and plays light, upbeat, preferably instrumental, background music while students/child respond(s) to the question. The objective is to use music to soothe kids into thinking, reflecting, and writing. The question then becomes: Does the music focus or distract them? In this author's experience, music helps kids in writing and reading, and besides, many listen to music when doing homework. Teachers might open the door for listening to music while responding to homework questions from Books 2, 3, and/or 4 if students feel it helps them get into their reading lives. (Recommended for grades 4 through 10.)

• In the *early question/late response* approach, the teacher gives a question early in the morning and kids respond later in the day, for example, late morning, after lunch, or before dismissal. The purpose of the delay is to see if an "incubation period" has any effects/affects on the later response: Can it enhance their answers to the question? Students have five minutes to answer, which is followed up by a five to ten minute discussion. Parents can employ the same approach by presenting the question after school and having their child respond later in the early evening. (Recommended for grades 4 through 6.)

• A second type of delay tactic is called *relax-and-respond*. This works for a mini-lesson, extended-time lesson, and bonus box or homework questions. Kids receive a question, read it, take a one-minute "relaxation break," and then answer the question. This approach allows students to deliberate and think in peace before answering a question. Does a "break" help or hurt the quality and effectiveness of a student's response? This is a typical mini-lesson where a class/child has five minutes to relax-and-respond and five to ten minutes for discussion. (Recommended for grades 4 through 10.)

Notes for all discussion leaders when implementing Book 2:

• Skim, review, and choose thirty questions or more ("extras" go in bonus box).
• To expedite class lessons in grades 4 through 10, type up the longer questions that will take up too much class time to copy from the board. Make photocopies for each student. Kids cut off and tape questions as they come up in the various mini-lessons. (The book number is included for easy and quick reference when they evaluate their progress in *Motivating Teen and Preteen Readers*.)
• All teachers can extend discussions (time/schedule permitting) when students are enthusiastic about what their classmates express, and also if they believe the oral/written responses would initiate greater motivation to read and future raps about reading lives. As discussion leaders, take advantage of these opportunities when they present themselves. Parents can extend and

expand one-to-one discussions with their child when she is really tuned in to what's being said and when it can grow a passion for reading.

- Aim to complete one hundred to two hundred questions max in the year. By the time Book 2's questions are completed, teacher and parent discussion leaders should have a good idea as to how many questions they can get in until the end of the year (Books 3 and 4). Middle and high school teachers should adjust the number of questions asked according to class schedules and teaching realities.

- By asking approximately 120 questions in a year (three questions per week for forty weeks) and having motivating raps and discussions, elementary-school teachers and parents will help kids help themselves to make a difference in their reading and reading lives. The short blasts of mini-lessons add up: They have a cumulative effect/affect and will create the changes sought. If middle and high school teachers ask sixty questions in a school year, it would benefit the kids and be a realistic goal for *Motivating Teen and Preteen Readers* in grades 6 through 10.

Refer to the "Not-for-Parents-Only Guide for *Motivating Teen and Preteen Readers*," "Why Won't Michael Read? One Solution," and the upcoming "Evaluation Questions for Book 2" for more information on presenting and scheduling student questionnaire 2 and student-teacher/parent chat 2.

USING TECHNOLOGY TO IMPLEMENT THE BOOKS OF QUESTIONS

Motivating Teen and Preteen Readers can be enriched through a class/section website. Google offers a free service for setting it up: Go to sites.google.com for procedures on the classroom site template that contains the following items that would expand the project:

- Homework/extra credit assignments
- Reminders/announcements (teacher blog posts)
- Class calendar
- Word of the week
- Forms and documents for parent-teacher contact
- Reading list
- Useful links
- Template tips for teachers to create and work with the website

A class/section website saves a lot of class time, and benefits *Motivating Teen and Preteen Readers* (and any other core subject) by posting:

- Homework/extra credit/bonus box questions on reading/reading life
- Examples of stronger versus weaker written responses

- How to improve written responses by asking questions about them
- Motivating teacher raps about reading, reading life, and the questions
- Follow-up, expanded, and continued discussions about in-class question/ dialogue
- Advice for parents trying to implement and extend the project at home with kids

Notes: Educators who have difficulty setting up a class website can go to the school computer teacher, tech-savvy teachers in the school, or the district tech/ computer expert to assist them in its creation. The website would be great for elementary school teachers in grades 4 to 6; it would be even more valuable for middle to high school teachers who have less time and more scheduling constraints to implement the books of questions. All teachers can recommend *Motivating Teen and Preteen Readers* to concerned parents as a motivational reading project for kids that they can do at home. The technology is a great way for educators and parents to connect. Another website that will help discussion leaders set up their own website and blog post for free is www.weebly.com.

EVALUATION QUESTIONS FOR BOOK 2

Evaluations: Student Questionnaire 2 and Student-Teacher/Parent Chat 2

Student questionnaire 2 follows the completion of thirty to seventy-five questions from Book 2 or a random selection of questions from the different books (considered Round 2). Kids reread all written responses (from Books 2 and 1) and answer questionnaire 2, followed up by a teacher/parent review of their notebooks and class/one-to-one discussion of their responses. Students will feel inspired after the rereading and answering the questionnaire: It's a natural consequence of the overall assessment process. Self-evaluations enhance their feelings of self-efficacy, and yes, it really works, according to this educator.

Student-teacher/parent chat 2 follows student questionnaire 2. Before chatting, skim students'/child's reading notebooks. Meetings are optional for classroom teachers (time permitting), but not for parents.

Suggested Questions for Student Questionnaire 2

Note: Before responding to questionnaire 2, students reread all their answers from Books 2 and 1 or Rounds 2 and 1, where questions were selected randomly from all four books.

1. What feelings and thoughts come up after rereading all your responses?
2. Was your experience answering these questions different from the first time? Why?

3. Did you have any new insights into reading and reading life? Explain your answer. Give an example if new things were revealed.
4. Which question stuck in your mind? Why?
5. Which question was hard to answer? Why?
6. Which question triggered many reading life experiences? Why?
7. Which question made you think the most? Why?
8. Did you have fun answering the drawing questions connected to reading? Explain.
9. Which picture from the drawing questions did you enjoy more: The one visualized in your mind or the one you drew? Explain your answer.
10. Does your inner eye see more the more you practice using it? Explain.
11. What does it mean to read and visualize? Describe what happens.
12. Do you see words more creatively after answering the word questions? Explain.
13. Have discussions improved your written responses to the questions? Explain.
14. Were your written responses detailed? Explain.
15. Describe a side trip taken in reading that was unrelated to the question.
16. What would you change or improve in the books of questions? Why?
17. Have your reading and reading life changed after completing the questions? Explain.
18. Did the chat change your attitude toward the books of questions? Explain.
19. Brainstorm three questions about reading and reading life to use in the books of questions.
20. What are your thoughts about reading, reading life, and the books of questions?

Suggested Questions for Student-Teacher/Parent Chat 2

Note: Student-teacher/parent chat 2 questions can also be used in student questionnaire 2. If working with a random approach to question selection (asking questions from Books 1, 2, 3, and 4), make sure to choose evaluation questions covered in class lessons, discussions, and from the appropriate suggested questions for chats 1, 2, and 3.

1. Are you having fun with *Motivating Teen and Preteen Readers* after completing the questions?
2. Would you call yourself a reader?
3. Have the books of questions made you a more confident reader?
4. Have the questions made you feel good or better about reading?
5. Describe what your reading life is like now.
6. Are you more aware of what goes on inside yourself while reading?
7. When you think of the word "reading," what other words come to mind?
8. How much thought and reflection go into your responses before you write?

9. Have the books of questions made you more of a thinker?
10. Are you more aware of the power of words since starting the books of questions?
11. Is it easy or hard to dig up past reading memories and experiences?
12. What would you add to my comments made about your responses?
13. Has a question helped you with your reading or reading life?
14. Do you think the books of questions can build positive reading habits?
15. Which technique or thinking skill works best to answer the questions?
16. Brainstorm three thoughts you have about reading and reading life.
17. Name three feelings you have about reading and reading life.
18. Are you more aware of your reading life now?
19. Have the books of questions helped you to see your reading world in a new way?
20. Are you looking forward to the next round of questions?

Book 3

Every truth has four corners: As a teacher I give you one corner, and it is for you to find the other three.

—Confucius

ABOUT BOOK 3

Continuity, Progression, Surveying, Skimming, Perusing, and Question Categories

Book 3 continues the inquiry- and passion-based strategy into reading and reading life started in Books 1 and 2 or Rounds 1 and 2. There is continuity, progression, and advancement in the questions. Book 3's questions are tougher because students must use more skills, effort, and thought in writing answers. Your selections as discussion leader challenge kids with mini-mental-emotional workouts, pushing them deeper into reading and reading-life experiences.

The 348 questions provide many choices for teachers, parents, and kids. Whether using a survey or random-selection approach in Book 3, *ask*: reading-process, word and word-activity, writing, drawing, hypothetical reading situation, one-line statement, opinion, rating, and quotation questions. *Emphasize* clusters of word and word-activity questions to motivate creativity inherent in words, something that should be included in the curriculum and taught in connection with reading and writing.

To advance a class/child further into the art of reading *and* writing, feature this selection: reading-process, words and word-activity, writing, and drawing questions. And don't omit other question categories such as common, everyday reading experiences; book recalls; and past reading experiences. When picking (any) questions, avoid jumping to the easiest ones: Provoke the class or child with some toughies.

Book 3's categories, appearing in order from the most to the least frequently asked questions in each, are:

- Reading Experiences: Common (Everyday), Past (Early), and Hypothetical
- Reading Process
- One-Line Statements and Opinions
- Writing, Drawing, and Creative Thinking
- Words and Word Activities
- Reading Reflections: Book Recalls, Nonfiction, and Poetry
- Ratings and Quotations

BOOK 3 QUESTIONS

Reading Experiences: Common (Everyday), Past (Early), and Hypothetical

1. What does reading do for you?
2. What are you reading on your own or in your free time now? Why?
3. What has reading taught you about yourself?
4. Do you read books your friends read? Why or why not?
5. How can reading be "the great escape"? Recall a time when reading helped you to escape. Where did the great escape take you? Did you enjoy it? Why or why not?
6. Fill-in-the-blank: As I lay reading I _____
7. Why do you keep reading a book? What drives you to finish it?
8. What does it mean to read under pressure? Give an example.
9. Did a teacher ever challenge you to become a better reader? How? Why? Did the challenge work? Explain. (Who else challenged you if it wasn't a teacher?)
10. Can other people help you create a passion for reading? Explain.
11. How can *you* create a passion for reading?
12. Is your family a family of readers? Explain.
13. What was the first or an early book you read that had a lot of pages? Did you like reading it? Why or why not?
14. Is reading books an experiment of some sort? Why? What is this experiment about? (*Hint*: Look up "experiment" in a dictionary for definitions before answering.)
15. Reading is a meeting or an encounter. Explain. What are you encountering while reading? Give examples. (*Hint*: Look up "encounter" in a thesaurus or dictionary for synonyms and definitions before answering.)
16. Imagine a clear day in reading. Record your thoughts, feelings, and experience. What does, or would, such a day look like?

17. Imagine this: How would you, as the super duper reading doctor, create a program to develop perfect concentration in reading for kids? Brainstorm ideas for the different steps in your program. List three steps that would help students reach perfect concentration in reading.
18. What do you, the reader, expect from the writer of a book you're reading? Why?
19. When does reading become boring? Explain.
20. Can a great adventure story change a boring life or bored reader? Why or why not?
21. Imagine turning into a giant mind's eye. How would this fantasy eye change your reading experience? Give an example of how it would work and its effects on your reading life.
22. Books can transport you to worlds totally unrelated to what you are reading at the moment. Has this ever been your experience? Explain. Give an example.
23. Did someone's words heal or make you feel better? Give an example.
24. What is your idea of a good book? Use an example from your reading life.
25. What secrets can novels reveal about life and living? Give an example. Did a secret from a novel help you in real life? Explain.
26. Have you ever given a friend a book (you read) that you thought was very good? What book? What was so good about it? Why share it?
27. Recall when you broke a bad reading habit. What bad habit? How did you stop it? How did your reading change afterward?
28. Recall a time you kept reading even though you were really tired. Could you understand what you read? Describe what happened.
29. Describe two great mind-pictures you remember from your reading life.
30. What challenge in your life was similar to one you read in a book? Did you handle your challenge the same way as the book character? Explain.
31. Can reading books teach you self-guidance: how to manage and direct your own life? Explain by giving an example from your reading and real life.
32. Can books help you make difficult decisions or choices? Has a book influenced a choice you made? Did it help you out? Explain your answers.
33. What have reading and books taught you about "X" the unknown? Give an example of one unknown that has become known to you through your reading and reading life.
34. Can a book make you aware of something about yourself that you did not realize? Explain your answer by giving an example from your reading life.
35. What are the connections between reading, books, and values such as honesty, trustworthiness, and tolerance? (*Hint*: Look up "values" in a thesaurus or dictionary for synonyms and definitions before answering.)
36. How does reading motivate you to think about your life? Give an example.

37. What is the one thing you really know about reading? How does it help your reading life? Would it help others in reading? Why or why not?
38. Imagine having a problem with reading and your reading life: You just don't want to read; you don't like it because it's boring; and you can do a million other things. So you decide to call the reading doctor for help. What might be her remedy for your reading woes? What do you think she would prescribe for your conflict? Why?
39. Has a book made you feel better when you were sick? Why or why not? Give an example if you have experienced this. If not, imagine how this could happen.
40. How are the books you read like a history of your life?
41. How are books like parachutes? (*Hint*: Look up "parachute" in a dictionary for definitions before answering.)
42. Can your reading life change your everyday life? Why or why not?
43. Recall a time reading helped you solve a problem. Describe what happened.
44. Would you recommend reading books as a problem-solver to friends? Why or why not?
45. Did you ever experience a positive change in your reading and reading life that seemed to come out of nowhere? What do you think caused the change? Describe your reading after the change.
46. Can reading and books help you if you are scared or have fears? Has a book inspired you to action and change when you were afraid of something? Explain your answers.
47. Can reading make your world crystal clear? Why or why not?
48. Can reading books (fiction or nonfiction) about jealousy help you if you have a jealousy problem? Why or why not?
49. What are the connections between reading and writing?
50. What line from a novel, story, play, poem, or any reading will you always remember? Why?
51. How does a reading journal connect reading to writing?
52. Why would other kids be interested in your blog or reading journal you kept on the Internet?
53. Can books, stories, or poems scare you away if they get too close to your real life? Or, can this same book, story, or poem motivate greater interest even though it gets too real for you? Explain your answer. Give an example.
54. Do you forget about what you read immediately after you finish reading it? Why or why not?
55. Do you remember a time when you lost interest in reading? When? Why? How did you get past those feelings? Or, did you? Explain your answer.
56. Can you exist without reading and books? Why or why not?
57. Can the world exist without reading and books? Why or why not?

58. Has reading made you take a closer look at your family, friends, and life? Did it make you see things in a brighter or darker light? Explain your answer.
59. Can reading and books defrost a cold heart? Explain.
60. Have reading and books made you a happier person? Explain your answer.
61. What are the connections between reading and rewards?
62. Can anything prevent you from enjoying a great reading life? Explain.
63. How can you expand your reading life?
64. Energetic, focused, relaxed reading leads to . . .
65. What are the connections between reading and change? Explain.
66. Which is more fun for you: class, small-group, or independent reading? Why?
67. Is there a secret way to make reading more fun, pleasurable, and entertaining? Why or why not?
68. What is your number-one reason for reading? Explain your answer.
69. My latest inspiration from reading books is _____
70. Do you have to read? Explain your answer.
71. Is it possible to know your friends better by what they like to read? How would it help you get a read on or understand them? Explain your answers.
72. You are what you eat, but, are you what you read? Explain.
73. What do you take away from reading every time you read? Explain your answer.
74. What can you miss if you read very little? Why?
75. When does reading become too much for you? What happens? Give an example. Describe your reading limits.
76. Is reading to get away from a nasty world a bad way to deal with reality? Aren't you avoiding things? Explain your answer.
77. Do you think it is important and necessary to read aloud to a one-year-old child? Why? What could he get out of your reading orally? What would you get?
78. If you were teaching a young child how to read, what idea would you communicate about reading? Why?
79. How would you motivate a friend to read if she hates to read?
80. How would you motivate a poor reader to improve his reading? How would you develop, reinvent, and change his reading life? Describe your remedial reading program to save his reading and reading life from going under.
81. Do you think that unhappy readers—readers who don't like or hate reading—need to be healed, and from what? Why or why not?
82. What have books taught you about the world outside your neighborhood? Brainstorm five or more insights you have realized through your readings.
83. Do you qualify for the 4-D Readers' Club: *determined, daring, dedicated, demanding*? Prove you have the qualifications by describing yourself in

each of the "d" categories. How do you fit into each? (*Hint*: Look up the "d" words in a dictionary or thesaurus for definitions and synonyms before answering.)

84. What do you think is a crucial time in a reader's life? What was, is, or will be your crucial time? Explain your answers.
85. Does self-knowledge or the desire to know yourself better motivate you to read? Explain your answer.
86. Brainstorm ten things that come to mind when you think about your reading life.
87. Do reading and books make the world simpler or harder to live in? Why?

Reading Process

88. Describe the reality or world reading puts you inside of: What does it look like?
89. Reading is in the mind's eye of the reader. Explain.
90. Reading connects you to what? Explain your answer.
91. Can you read without feeling? Why or why not?
92. Discover yourself—read! Explain.
93. What are you best at in reading? Give an example and how you use it.
94. What is the hardest part of reading for you? Why?
95. How can you improve your ability to read?
96. How are you living a story when you read it? How is this possible?
97. Why bother getting inside a character's mind from a play that you're reading?
98. Which needs more concentration: reading silently or listening to someone read orally to you? Why?
99. How are you, the reader, an artist?
100. Reading is a workout in the mind—mentally, emotionally, and physically. Explain.
101. Recall a wacky mind-picture that jumped out at you while you read and totally stopped you. Describe what you saw. Then look closely at the image and contemplate it (examine it carefully and continuously) for a few seconds. What else comes to mind?
102. What do you think a writer expects from you, the reader? Why?
103. In what ways can you, the reader, connect with the writer of a book?
104. Should you be aware of what you feel before, during, and after reading? Is it necessary? Explain your answers.
105. When does time slow down in reading? How does it happen? Give an example.
106. Read a passage from a novel or lines from a poem. Find one exciting mind-picture from the story or poem. Contemplate the image—stay with it—for fifteen seconds. What does your contemplation reveal?

107. Is your mind's eye wide open when you read? Describe this ideal reading state.
108. Project the following sentence on the mind's imaginary TV screen:

The students looked at their reflections in the pond.

- What mind-pictures do you see?
- Can you put yourself in the scene? Why or why not?
- How would you put yourself in the sentence and become a participant?
- What are the students thinking and feeling while looking at their reflections?

109. How do your feelings and mind's eye work together in reading? What is their connection? Do you need both to be a successful and passionate reader?
110. How are the mind-pictures you see in reading different from the images you see on a TV, movie, or computer screen?
111. What holds your attention in this sentence? *The father teaches his little daughter how to ride a bicycle.* What parts of the image pop out on the TV screen in your mind? What feelings and thoughts does the picture trigger?
112. How would you describe a: (a) thoughtful reader and (b) thoughtless reader. Where do you belong in these categories? Why? How do the thinking styles affect reading and reading life?
113. How are your feelings connected to your inner reading voice (the voice silently reading words from a page)? Why is this connection important in reading?
114. How does your head (brain) work together with your heart (feelings) in reading? What does this combination produce? Give an example of how they connect with each other while you read.
115. Finish-me-off: When I read I listen to me, too, and this is what I hear . . .
116. How do your life experiences affect your reading and reading life? Do they have positive, negative, or no effects? Why?
117. Why do books make you think a lot?
118. Would you call thinking a lot a lot of fun? Explain.
119. Can reading and thinking be made entertaining and pleasurable? How would it work? Make up an imaginary program or method to do this.
120. Do you believe everything you read? Why or why not?
121. Do you ask questions about what you read? Explain.
122. Anxiousness, uneasiness, and worries can hurt reading. Explain.
123. How can you instantly increase your concentration when reading?
124. What is perfect concentration? Have you experienced it? If you have, describe it.
125. Can you practice concentrating? Would practicing help you reach a higher level or even perfect concentration in reading? Is this possible? Explain your answers.

126. Are there connections between reading and confidence? Why or why not?
127. Can reading books boost your confidence? Why or why not?
128. Should you forget about yourself and your life when you read? Explain.
129. Does reading make you more aware or unaware of your everyday life? Explain.
130. Can identifying with a book character make you more self-aware? Explain. Give an example. (*Hint*: If you don't have one, try to imagine how identifying with a character can change or affect your self-awareness.)
131. How does a creative imagination help you appreciate characters in a novel or real people in biographies and memoirs?
132. How many lives do you lead when reading a novel? Explain your answer.
133. How many lives do you lead when reading a play? Explain your answer.
134. How many lives do you lead when writing a story? Explain your answer.
135. How can reading books prove or verify your own beliefs? Give an example. Which belief was validated by a book? Describe the connection between the two.
136. You are never alone when you read a book. Explain.
137. How is reading like telepathy? (*Hint*: Look up "telepathy" in a dictionary before answering.)
138. Can reading books help you with conflicts you have with other kids? Or, is it something that has little use in your world? Explain your answer.
139. Reading can make your head feel lighter. Explain.
140. Reading can make your head feel heavier. Explain.
141. Can a reading idea trigger a writing idea? How? Make up or give an example of how you can go from a reading idea to a writing idea.
142. Do you think about what you read after you finish reading? Why or why not? Give an example.
143. Do you reread and reflect on your responses to the questions after writing them? Why or why not?
144. Can rereading and reflecting on your responses to the questions motivate you to read and write more? Why or why not?
145. How does reading develop contemplation skills? (*Hint*: Look up "contemplation" in a dictionary or thesaurus for definitions and synonyms before answering.)
146. Write one thought you have about something you are reading right now. Reflect on that thought for thirty seconds. What comes to mind?
147. How can you deepen your reading experience?
148. What is reading without mind-pictures? Explain.
149. What words describe your inside world while you read? List ten words. Pick two key words and explain why you chose them. (*Hint*: Brainstorm ideas and picture-storm images to find the words that describe your inside reading world.)

150. Athletes say they are playing "in the zone" when they are at their best. Describe your reading when you read "in the zone."

151. Reading means moving inward. Explain the statement's meaning. How important is this process in your reading life? Is that why reading is called a "lonely pleasure"? Explain your answers.

152. Reading = self-communication. Explain the statement's meaning. How important is this in the reading process?

One-Line Statements and Opinions

153. Reading: your ticket to ride. . . . Explain.

154. Read if you believe in magic. Explain.

155. Be yourself—read! Explain.

156. Life-savers for children—books. Think about this statement and then visualize an image in your mind. Create a cartoon poster to communicate the idea. Use the statement as a caption for your illustration. (*Hint*: Picture-storm images before drawing, and pick one you really like and can draw.)

157. Starvation diet: five minutes of leisure time reading a day. Explain what the statement suggests about leisure-time reading.

158. The English poet William Wordsworth called reading a book a "lonely pleasure." What did he mean? Do you think it's something negative? What was he getting at? Explain your answers.

159. Words do not stop on a page. What does the statement mean or suggest? What do you think about it? Why?

160. Read as if your life depended on it. Do you? Explain what the statement means and suggests to readers.

161. Keep an open mind to what you read. Explain the statement's meaning. What do you think: agree or disagree? Why?

162. The pictures imagined when reading are only as powerful as your mind's eye. What do you think: agree or disagree? Why?

163. Read—relief is just a word away. What does the statement suggest? What do you think about it? Agree? Disagree? Why?

164. Writing is a figment of your imagination. What does the statement mean? Agree? Disagree? Why?

165. Reading's cool miracle = _____

166. Words can heal a sick person. What do you think? How would words help?

167. Your life is really a life of words. Explain the statement's meaning. What do you think: agree or disagree? Why?

168. What do you enjoy more: fiction or nonfiction? Explain your answer.

169. Is the writer always right? Are you always in agreement with him or her? Should you be? Why is this a key factor in your reading? Explain your answers.

170. Get into this: The more you read, the more you ask questions. What does the statement mean? Is it true in your reading life? Why or why not?

171. Reading and books can help you get rid of the negatives from yourself. Explain. What do you think: agree or disagree? Why? Give an example, if you have one.

172. The more you read the greater your sensitivity becomes to yourself, others, and the world. What do you think? Why?

173. Frequent reflection about what you read motivates a passion for reading. What does the statement mean or suggest? What do you think? Why?

174. Reading and books can stop you from thinking for yourself. Explain the statement's meaning. Do you agree? Why or why not?

175. Read for power. Explain. (*Hint*: Look up "power" in a dictionary or thesaurus for definitions and synonyms before answering.)

176. Hooked on books? Are you? Why or why not?

177. What books do you think students should be reading in school? Brainstorm a list of five books. Pick one book and explain its importance: Why should it be read in school?

178. Reading can ruffle your feathers. Explain the statement's meaning. Do you agree? Why or why not?

179. Reading is all in the mind. Explain the statement's meaning. Is that a problem for many?

180. All reading is educational. What do you think: agree or disagree? Why?

181. Books and reading give you all the questions and the answers. Explain the statement's meaning. Do you agree or disagree? Why?

182. Powerful concentration creates powerful reading. Rewrite the statement in your own words (without changing its meaning). Is the statement true for your reading experience? Explain by giving an example.

183. Troubled reader: no pictures in the mind. Explain the statement's meaning. Has it happened to you? How do you overcome this situation? Explain your answers.

184. The more you read, the smarter you get. Agree? Disagree? Why?

185. The less you read, the dumber you get. Agree? Disagree? Why?

186. Read and move to the beat of the world. Agree? Disagree? Why?

187. Reading keeps your mind active, running, working, open, magical, powerful, and alive. Agree? Disagree? Why? How could reading perform this amazing feat?

188. Reading = communication. Explain. (*Hint*: Look up "communication" in a thesaurus or dictionary for synonyms and definitions before answering.)

189. Check, test, and prove your ideas: Read! Explain the statement's meaning.

190. Good books make good readers. What do you think: agree or disagree? Why?

191. Reading every day improves your memory. Do you agree? Why or why not?
192. Reading books = self-education. Explain.
193. Read more books, harder books, challenge yourself to move on, to keep going forward and not backward in your reading and reading life. Explain the statement's meaning. Do you agree? Why or why not?
194. Reading = practice, practice, practice, and then more practice. . . . Do you think this is true or is it just hype for improving reading? Explain.
195. My mind's eye
sees all that I read
in quick little flashes.

What does the statement mean?
196. Reading books = self-maintenance. Explain the statement's meaning. How well have you maintained yourself through reading books? Describe your experience.
197. Fight for yourself and your life: Read! Explain.
198. A calm, peaceful mind is one step to overcoming a reading problem. Explain.
199. Reading and books can be challenges to your everyday life. What does the statement mean? Do you agree? Why or why not? Give an example from your reading and real life.
200. Warning label: Don't read too much, there are bad side effects. What do you think: agree or disagree? Why?
201. Reading every day quietly and gently changes your world. Explain.
202. You find more truth in books than the outside or real world. What do you think? Why?
203. He who loves to read enjoys himself in thought. Explain.
204. Read to dream. . . . Explain.
205. Do books and reading give hope? Why or why not?
206. Reading life grows happiness. Explain. What do you think? Why?
207. EXIT: reading solitude. Explain the statement's meaning.

Writing, Drawing, and Creative Thinking

Note: Many of the writing questions are crossover questions and can easily fit into the word/word-activities question category (e.g., 240, 241, 245, 246, 247, 248). Extra time should be allotted to the longer writing questions (e.g., 249, 250, 251).

208. Describe reading and books as adventure.
209. Draw a cartoon of an imaginary machine that improves reading skills and ability. How would it work? How would readers use it?

210. Create a new instrument that increases reading fun. Give it a name. What does your invention look like? Visualize and draw a pencil-sketch of it. How would it work? How would it create greater reading enjoyment? (*Hint*: Use brainstorming and picture-storming to search for ideas and images of the original invention.)

211. Picture this: It was on a starry summer night when a young boy's eyes grew bigger and bigger as he focused on the book he was reading. Draw the picture you see and contemplate it. What do you think is running through his mind: thoughts, feelings, reflections, ideas, and memories? (*Hint*: Think of a fantasy or dream world when searching with your mind's eye for pictures of this scene.)

212. Imagine books in a place where you would not normally find them. Visualize this image and draw it. Next, contemplate the picture: What are you thinking? (*Hint*: Picture-storm images of the most ridiculous places where you would never think to find books.)

213. Reading begins in your real eyes and ends in your mind's eye. Visualize this idea and image. Draw a cartoon or dreamlike picture of the statement.

214. Describe and pencil-sketch the image this sentence creates in your mind: The two dogs, one big and one small, ran in circles chasing after each other's tails. What thoughts and feelings does the sentence trigger?

215. Create a sentence that really gets your heart beating or pounding. Visualize and then draw a picture of the sentence.

216. Reading puts those "snow-capped mountains" right in the middle of your mind's eye. Can you see them? Visualize this scene. Focus on your image and draw it. Make it into a poster promoting reading and reading life. What does it all mean? What feelings, thoughts, and ideas are you communicating through your poster? Write a caption at the bottom of your finished work.

217. Visualize this dream or fantasy scene: *Words explode like fireworks across sunny blue skies.* Imagine, describe, and draw the mind-picture you see. What are some of these exploding words in the sky?

218. Make up three ridiculously silly sentences.

- Use sentence-storming (trigger one sentence after another) to find your answers.
- Visualize each sentence and briefly describe what you see.
- How can creating silly sentences help you become a better writer?

219. Make up an absurd (ridiculous) paragraph of four to eight sentences.

- Visualize the paragraph and pencil-sketch the pictures you see.
- Creating, writing, reading, visualizing, and drawing a silly passage: What connects all these processes used in the exercise? Explain.

Hint: Use storming techniques to build your paragraph.

220. You just walked into a room full of books. The books call out to you. You hear their voices coming through the pages. What are they trying to say to you? Make up an imaginary conversation (like a play dialogue) between the books and you. Your conversation should be one hundred words or more.

221. Draw a cartoon of a reader changing words into pictures, feelings, and thoughts.

222. Draw a dreamlike, fantasy, or surreal cartoon picture of yourself wrapped up in a book. Picture-storm images first, and then illustrate one you like.

223. How do you make reading a habit? Create a five-step program that would do this.

224. Describe a book's character (fiction) or a real life person's cool, hip world (nonfiction) in twenty-five to fifty words.

225. Visualize "paradise": Picture-storm images of the word. Pick one image and contemplate it for sixty seconds. Describe what happened during your contemplation in fifty words.

226. Visualize an imaginary "book garden." What are you looking at with your inner eye? Keep searching for more and more images in your mind by picture-storming. Now draw what you see—your imaginary "book garden."

227. Imagine reading a book on a mountaintop. Visualize this scene—with you in it. Picture-storm images. Pick one and pencil-sketch a poster promoting reading. Include a one-line caption at the bottom. When you finish the poster, contemplate it and write whatever comes to mind.

228. Caution: Don't leave your mind in another place when reading. Think about the statement's meaning and find an image to illustrate it. Draw a cartoon: Write a one-word caption to sum it up. What is a key to the reading process according to your cartoon? Why?

229. If a snowman could read, what books would it take out of the "frosty library"? Brainstorm five titles.

230. Readin' & breezin': What thoughts come up? What mind-pictures are triggered? Picture-storm images and illustrate one in a cartoon, fantasy, or dreamlike drawing. (*Hint*: Visualize first, draw second.)

231. Imagine yourself deep in thought while reading. Pencil-sketch this mind-picture: What one thing pops out immediately when you visualize the image? Why is this detail so important? (*Hint*: Make sure you create that "pop-out" in your drawing.)

232. Imagine that: What happened to the child who never stopped reading? Write an imaginary tale in one hundred words or more. Illustrate the story with one or more sketches. (*Hint*: Picture-storm images and brainstorm ideas before starting your story.)

233. Imagine your reading life as a series of newspaper headlines. Brainstorm five to ten headlines that show important events or times in your reading life.

234. Describe a character's (fiction) or real person's (nonfiction/biography/ autobiography) unique, special, private, solo world that he or she lives in. View things totally from this person's eyes and write about what you experience in fifty words.

235. Imagine you are given a big shopping cart and let loose in a bookstore. What would you put in your cart for your reading pleasure? List ten books and items you would take. What would they say about your reading, reading life, and your life? Write your answer in twenty-five to fifty words.

236. Imagine that: She's reading her favorite book, the one where golden streams of light burst from the words on the pages. Picture it. Draw it. Contemplate it. Write the story behind the reader's fantasy in twenty-five to fifty words. What is going on?

237. Reading: the stress-buster. Picture-storm images for this statement. Pick one image: sketch or draw it. (*Hint*: Use a cartoon, fantasy, or dreamlike drawing.)

238. Describe your experience of reading aloud to others: images, feelings, thoughts, memories, and reflections. Write a fifty-word narrative, anecdote, or account of your oral reading.

239. What is your favorite word at the moment? Contemplate it for thirty seconds. Describe what happened during your contemplation in twenty-five words or more.

240. Try this experiment: Say your favorite word over and over to yourself for thirty seconds and then describe your experience in twenty-five words or more. You can say the word silently or out loud.

241. "Yeah, that's right pal, there are words that make you boil under the skin." Think about a word that makes you feel this way and write the story behind it in twenty-five words or more.

242. Recall words said to you that brought joy. Give an example and describe their power in twenty-five words. (*Optional*: Recall words that you read or imagined that created joy. Write their stories in twenty-five words.)

243. What words race through your mind every day? Give some examples. Pick one and describe the effects of its daily trip in twenty-five words.

244. Picture-storm—trigger one image after another—the word "lake." Describe one mind-picture you see. Contemplate it for thirty seconds. Write about your contemplation in twenty-five words or more. What thoughts come to mind about "lake" at the end? What have you realized?

245. There are words that jumpstart streams of ideas, thoughts, beliefs, and opinions whenever you read, hear, imagine, or say them. The word should send your mind flying. Search for a word that does this to you. When you find one, contemplate it. Describe the "flight of the word" in twenty-five words or more.

246. What journey does "Blueberries explode" take you on? Read the sentence three times. Imagine it. Concentrate on the picture. What do you

see? What is your inner eye viewing on the TV screen in your mind? Now put it all together with thoughts and feelings brought up by the image. Write about your journey in fifty words. (*Optional*: Substitute other fruits and vegetables for blueberries such as bananas, oranges, lettuces, or lemons. Picture-storm images for "Bananas explode" and use colored markers or crayons to draw what you visualize. Or, you can do it mentally and write a description of what you see.)

247. Words are little worlds teeming with life. Explain. Search for a word—noun, adjective, verb—that demonstrates this statement. Describe this word-world in twenty-five words or more.

248. Words = short, short stories. Prove it by writing a short, short story about a "word."

 • Create a list of nouns, adjectives, and/or verbs.
 • Pick one word for your short, short story.
 • Word-storm words, brainstorm ideas, and picture-storm images to start a story.
 • Write a story about the chosen word in fifty words.

249. A new store opened up in your neighborhood called WORDS 'R US:

 • Visualize this imaginary place for thirty seconds.
 • Picture-storm images of the store, from the inside and the outside.
 • Pick one image and illustrate (pencil-sketch) it.
 • When you finish the drawing, reflect on it.
 • Write whatever comes to mind in twenty-five words or more.

 Hint: What is this store all about? What is it selling to the people?

250. Imagine that: Write a fantasy, myth, tall tale, fable, fairy tale, or dream about a perfect imaginary reading life in one hundred words or more. Brainstorm ideas and picture-storm images to jumpstart your story. (*Hint*: What would make this reading life so extraordinary?)

251. Imagine a room with enough space for only one single bed, and where the curtains covering an open window fly up from the wind, letting in a blaze of sunlight for an instant, and there you are, lying down—reading ...Visualize this scene and then contemplate it for a minute. Write a story of fifty words or more using this image as the starting point. Just for fun, draw or sketch the mind-picture of this scene.

252. Imagine extreme horror stories about reading and reading life:

 • Picture-storm images of their scary scenes.
 • Pencil-sketch your favorite ones.
 • Reflect on one of the finished sketches.
 • Write what comes to mind for the sketch.
 • Have you experienced an extreme reading or reading-life horror story? Give an example if you have gone through one. What made it extreme?

253. Pencil-a-story: Write a very, very, tiny story about reading. Write it on a pencil. Draw an outline of the pencil first and write your story inside it in twenty-five words. Get it all inside your pencil: an itsy-bitsy story about reading.

254. Every night you like to read fantasy tales to your seven cats. They all sit around on soft cushions and listen attentively to the stories. Make up your own fantasy tale of fifty to one hundred words that would be a cat favorite.

255. Fantasize that: Instead of putting a model sailing ship inside a bottle, they squeezed in Superbaby and Superbaby's favorite books, corked it, and sent it out to sea. . . .Visualize yourself as Superbaby and describe your reading voyage on the open seas in one hundred words.

256. Use your inner eye to zoom in on a memory. Find the mind-picture(s) and describe what you see in twenty-five to fifty words. Read your work silently and out loud. Do the words in your description bring back your memory accurately and clearly? Why or why not?

Words and Word Activities

257. Write one thought for each word:

- tricked
- sweat
- puppy

258. Words trigger pictures, thoughts, and feelings. In this sense they are three-dimensional. View the following words with your inner eye on the imaginary TV screen in your mind. Describe the images, thoughts, and feelings brought up by each word:

library

- image
- thought
- feeling

bicycle

- image
- thought
- feeling

parrot

- image
- thought
- feeling

bully

- image
- thought
- feeling

259. You just tasted words sweet as candy. What are some of those sweet tastin' words? Word-storm a list of ten words. Roll 'em around in your mind: Describe your little tasting trip in twenty-five words or more.
260. Game over: What *word-echoes* do you hear in your mind? Word-storm or brainstorm a list of five answers.
261. I promise: Promises, promises . . . _____.
262. ME ME ME ME me me me me me me me . . . and what does "me" get you thinking? Why?
263. What do you visualize when beauty meets sadness? Describe a mind-picture you see and draw it.
264. What happens if pigeons collide with sneakers? Describe the image you visualize; pencil-sketch it; and write a caption for your sketch.
265. What happens if tulips collide with cats? Visualize the resulting image and then sketch it in pencil.
266. What happens if dumb collides with dumber? Draw what you imagine or see. Describe your picture in twenty-five words and write an original caption for it.
267. Words can make you want something really badly. Explain the statement's meaning. Give an example of a word that made you feel this way. Describe what happened.
268. What word puzzles you? Why?
269. *A little peace gives you a chance.* Where does this sentence take you? What place? Explain.
270. Think of a word that means a lot to you. Write it and then contemplate the word for a minute. What comes to mind? Why is it so important to you?
271. Imagine that: What word, if you keep repeating it in your mind, gains more power, energy, and life? Describe what happens as you repeat it silently to yourself in twenty-five words or more. (*Hint*: Use nouns, adjectives, or verbs as your repeating word.)
272. Where does the word "know" take you? Contemplate "know" and describe its journey in your mind in twenty-five words or more.
273. Experiment: Unscramble the jumbled words to form a complete, absurd sentence:

rolling path wild hiking where was started
down green giant the mountain I peas

- How did you combine the jumbled words to form a sentence? What was the key?
- Visualize, describe, and draw the sentence-image you see.
- What does the jumbled sentence exercise show you about writing sentences?

274. Words can be releases, openings, and even rescuers. What does the statement mean and suggest? Give an example to prove it.
275. What words, phrases, or self-commands have saved the day for you? How do they work?
276. What words can make you drift away from the real world? List three examples. For each word, describe where you drift off to. What do they get you to experience?
277. Can a word or words make you more aware, alert, or conscious? Why or why not? Give an example of how a word created greater awareness in you. If it has not happened to you, imagine how a word can do this.
278. What are "fighting words"? Give an example of "fighting words" you have said to someone—friend, classmate, enemy—or have been said to you. What can be the short- and long-term consequences? Describe what may or did happen.
279. Just for fun: Use your inner eye to zoom in for close-ups of: pizza; shark; ignorance; and garbage. Visualize two of the words and describe what you see, feel, and think.

    word _____
    - image
    - feeling
    - thought

    word _____
    - image
    - feeling
    - thought

280. *What if:* Fill in the blanks with five silly and/or serious "what-ifs":

    1. _____
    2. _____
    3. _____
    4. _____
    5. _____

281. "Positive words" are words that bring you up and say "yes" to you. Make a list of three positive words. Pick one word and contemplate it for sixty seconds. What pictures, feelings, and thoughts are triggered by the contemplation?

282. Contemplation words: List three words (nouns, adjectives, verbs) that would be fun words for you to contemplate. Pick one and contemplate it for sixty seconds. Write about what you experienced in twenty-five to fifty words.
283. Word-storm ten words that make you hungry. Pick one word and contemplate it for thirty seconds (give it careful and continued attention). Where did the contemplation take you?
284. Try this experiment: Take the word "shout" around an imaginary roller rink as fast as you can and find twenty connected and/or unconnected words to it. When you finish, read over your word list. What thoughts, ideas, and feelings come up? Where does "shout" take you? Any surprises? Did you learn things about words or word life? Explain your answers.
285. Try this experiment: Take the word "safe" around an imaginary roller rink as fast as you can and find twenty connected and/or unconnected words to it. When you finish, read over your word list. What thoughts, ideas, and feelings come up? Where does "safe" take you? Any surprises? Did you learn things about words or word life? Explain your answers.
286. Warning: Word-storming "violence" makes you hostile. Explain the statement's meaning by first word-storming "violence." List ten words or more and then answer the question. Is the statement true? Why or why not?
287. What are the softest, gentlest words you know? List three words. Why is each so gentle or soft? Describe the feelings and thoughts each word creates. (*Optional*: Using the three words, create three soft and gentle sentences, visualize each, and illustrate them.)
288. Have you ever read a word that suddenly took you off the page and into another world? What word? Where did you go? Why did it take you off the page? Was it a fun journey? Why or why not?
289. Words collect many thoughts to feed your mind. Explain. Give an example.
290. We live in a world of words: some we like, others we dislike. Reflect for a minute on words that affect your life. Make two lists of words: "goodies" and "badies." Pick one word from each list and give reasons why it's a "goodie" or "badie" for you.
291. What words do you hear in your self-talk or conversations with yourself? Give an example. Why do the words come up? Are they positive, negative, or both? Explain your answers. (*Optional*: While reading, what words do you hear in your self-talk? Why do they come up? Do they help or hurt your reading? Explain.
292. How powerful are words? Explain your answer by giving examples.
293. Recall words said to you that still cause hurt and pain if you think about them. Give one example and describe their power.

294. How deep can some words go? List two words—nouns, adjectives, verbs—that run deep if you read, hear, or imagine them. Pick one and describe how far it can go inside you. (*Hint*: Use contemplation, reflection, picture-storming, word-storming, or brainstorming to find the answer or depth of the word.)
295. Can you remember when you "had words" with a friend? What were these "words"? How did they make you feel and think? Why? Was peace made afterward? What were the "words of peace"? Were they effective? Why?
296. What are you thinking right now? What thoughts are going through your mind? Write your thoughts and then read them to yourself. Do your words express your thoughts accurately and clearly? Why or why not?
297. What are you feeling right now? What feelings are you experiencing? Describe them and then read what you wrote. Do your words express your feelings accurately and clearly? Why or why not?
298. How important are words to you as a reader? Explain.
299. How important are words to you as a writer? Explain.

Reading Reflections: Book Recalls, Nonfiction, and Poetry

300. Why is a poem like a jigsaw puzzle?
301. How often do you read poetry in your free time? Why?
302. Recall a book, play, tale, fable, fairy tale, or myth where a character wanted something badly. What was it? Did the character get it? Was the struggle worthwhile? Did you identify with or connect with the character in any way? Explain your answers.
303. What magazine article gave you new ideas about anything? List one new idea and how a magazine article triggered it.
304. Recall a magazine article where you found out something new on almost every page. Give an example.
305. What nonfiction book made you really appreciate nonfiction? Why?
306. What nonfiction book would you like to read next? Why?
307. Did you ever start reading a sad book and stop? Why? If you stopped, did you return to it at another time like a week, month, or year later? Did you finish it the second time around? What was different about this reading? Explain your answers.
308. Imagine that: Poetry slows you down. What does it mean? Give an example.
309. What lines of a poem speak directly to you, your life, and experiences? What is the poem saying?
310. What secrets can poetry reveal about living your life? Give an example from poems you have read. Did a secret help you in your everyday life? Why or why not?

311. What secrets can myths reveal about living your life? Give an example from a myth you read or you heard read aloud. Did a secret help you out in your everyday life? Explain.

312. What is a self-help book? Have you read one? Why? What did you want to find out? Did it help you? Why or why not?

313. What self-help books would you like to read? Why?

314. Has a book (fiction or nonfiction) removed any misconceptions or illusions you had about the real world? Explain your answer by giving an example.

315. Recall a book (fiction or nonfiction) that clarified a misunderstanding you had about the way people behaved or acted. What was your misunderstanding? How did the book help you to undo it?

316. Recall a book character (fiction) who was searching for some kind of truth. What truth was the character searching for? Was it found? Did the truth help or hurt? What did you think and feel at the end of the book? Explain your answers.

317. Recall a book where jealousy was a theme. Who was jealous of whom? Why? What were the consequences? Was it resolved? Why or why not? How would you have handled the jealousy if you were the book character?

318. Did you ever feel like a book was talking directly to you? Why? What was its message and connection to you?

319. Do you enjoy reading books or stories that are journals or diaries of other people's lives like *The Diary of Anne Frank*? Why or why not?

320. Can journals of writers, artists, athletes, or entertainers help you in your life? Why? Give an example. If you do not have one, imagine how reading other people's journals could help you out.

321. Have you ever thought about a book many years after reading it? Did you have any new insights? Did your appreciation for the book change? Explain your answers.

322. Has a book ever triggered a thought you could not get out of your mind? What was the thought? Why did you keep thinking it? What was its connection to the book and your life? Explain your answers.

323. Describe a practical or useful book you read. What important ideas were communicated? Did you put any into action? Did it work? Why or why not? How strong was the connection between the book and real or everyday life?

324. Poets are teachers. Explain. Give an example of what a poet has taught you.

Ratings and Quotations

325. "Take up and read, take up and read" (Saint Augustine). What does the quote mean? What does it suggest? Why does he repeat the lines? Is the quote important to you? Explain your answers.

326. Rate how much you feel when you read on a scale from 0 to 10, where 0 = nothing at all and 10 = everything. Give a reason(s) for your rating.

327. How good are you at reading under pressure? Rate your ability to read under pressure on a scale from 0 to 10, where 0 = poor and 10 = excellent. Give reasons for your rating.

328. "You know you've read a good book when you turn the last page and feel a little as if you lost a friend" (Paul Sweeney). Can you recall a time when you finished a book and felt the same as the quote? Describe what you experienced.

329. How good are you at changing words into mind-pictures (images)? Rate yourself on a scale from 0 to 10, where 0 = poor ability and 10 = excellent ability. Give reasons for your rating.

330. How good are you at changing mind-pictures (images) into words? Rate yourself on a scale from 0 to 10, where 0 = poor ability and 10 = excellent ability. Give reasons for your rating.

331. "Reading means borrowing" (G. C. Lichtenberg). What do you borrow when you read? What have you borrowed recently?

332. What does the following quote mean? "Never judge a book by its movie" (J. W. Eagan). Do you agree or disagree? Why? Give an example. (*Optional*: Compare the Harry Potter books to the Harry Potter movies. Are the movies better or worse than the books? Why?)

333. "I read my eyes out and can't read half enough. . . . The more one reads the more one sees we have to read" (John Adams). What does the quote mean? Has this been your experience? Explain by giving an example from your reading life.

334. "The poet can only write the poems: It takes the reader to complete the meaning" (Nikki Giovanni). What is the quotation saying? How does a reader "complete the meaning" of a poem? Is it easy or hard to do this? Explain your answers. (*Optional*: Find a poem you read in class or on your own. Describe what the poem said and expressed. Discuss how you, the reader, "completed the meaning" of the poem.)

335. "I did realize, as do you, how blessed I was to know bookjoy, the private pleasure of savoring text" (Pat Mora). "Bookjoy," according to the quotation, is the "private pleasure of savoring (feeling or experiencing) text (the author's words). What is "bookjoy" to you? Describe this experience. Give an example of it from your reading life.

336. Rate how seriously you take reading on a scale from 0 to 10, where 0 = not seriously and 10 = very seriously. Give reasons for your rating.

337. What does the following quote mean? "We read to know that we are not alone" (C. S. Lewis). Is this true for you? Why or why not? Give an example.

338. How much do you really believe in reading and books? Rate your belief on a scale from 0 to 10, where 0 = none and 10 = great or total. Give reasons for your rating.

339. How clear is your mind when you read? Rate your clarity on a scale from 0 to 10, where 0 = totally cloudy and 10 = totally clear. Give reasons for your rating.

340. How much do you like to read? Rate your desire to read on a scale from 0 to 10, where 0 = hating reading and 10 = loving reading. Give reasons for your rating.

341. Explain whether or not the quotation is good advice to improve your reading, reading test scores, and reading life: "Resolve to edge in a little reading every day, if it is but a single sentence. If you gain fifteen minutes a day, it will make itself felt at the end of the year" (Horace Mann).

342. Do you believe in and feel confident about your reading abilities? Why or why not?

343. "Sticks and stones may break my bones, but words will make me go in a corner and cry by myself for hours" (Eric Idle). How powerful are words according to the quote? Why? Is the quote true for you? Are you sensitive to spoken words? Explain.

344. Your presence in reading is required, that is, you need to be there when you read. Rate your presence in reading when you read on a scale from 0 to 10, where 0 = none (you're not there), and 10 = total or complete (you're all there). Explain the reasons for your rating.

345. How well do you communicate with yourself while reading? Rate your ability on a scale from 0 to 10, where 0 = poor and 10 = powerful self-communication. Give reasons for your rating.

346. "Children are made readers on the laps of their parents" (Emilie Buchwald). Explain the quotation's meaning. What do you think? Agree? Disagree? Why?

347. "Not to know is bad: Not to wish to know is worse" (African proverb). What is the quotation saying? What is the quotation's connection to reading? Do you want to know or would you rather not know more about reading and reading life? Explain your answers.

348. "Read in order to live" (Gustave Flaubert). Explain the quote's meaning. Write an essay about the quote in one hundred words or more. (*Optional*: Instead of an essay, write a fairy tale, fable, or myth about the quotation in one hundred words or more.)

HOW TO USE BOOK 3

One Suggested Sample Survey Approach for Presenting Questions with Notes

Check out this survey approach for Book 3: Skim the questions first to choose an eclectic range of openers to excite and challenge them. Continue to stress thinking things through before responding and the students will be surprised by and rewarded for their efforts.

Examples of openers from Book 3's questions: (a) Read if you believe in magic. Explain. (b) What has reading taught you about yourself? (c) Reading connects you to what? Explain your answer. Ask whatever question categories you think will trigger the imagination. Pick five to ten openers and ask them on consecutive days.

Book 3's reading process questions are tougher and take kids deeper into what happens inside when they read, helping them to unravel reading's magic and mystery. *Example*: How many lives do you lead when reading a novel? Explain your answer. Answer the question yourself: It requires more recollection, reflection, and visualization. Select ten and mix them up in your questions.

There are many word and word activity questions in Book 3. Words when experienced, ideally, as three-dimensional, virtual, holographic worlds, can motivate kids to find greater meaning and value in them and pump up interest in reading. If words are seen more creatively, they become gateways to writing, and the reading-writing connection—a secondary purpose to *Motivating Teen and Preteen Readers*. The degree of difficulty gets rougher for the word questions. *Examples are*:

- You just tasted words sweet as candy. What are some of those sweet tastin' words? Word-storm a list of ten words. Roll 'em around in your mind: Describe your little tasting trip in twenty-five words or more.
- ME ME ME ME me me me me me me me . . . and what does "me" get you thinking? Why?
- "Positive words" are words that bring you up and say "yes" to you. Make a list of three positive words. Pick one word and contemplate it for sixty seconds. What pictures, feelings, and thoughts are triggered by the contemplation?

Combine ten word and word-activity questions and divide them up in your survey approach; or ask a series of five questions from this category, one each day for a week to inspire creative fun and play with words.

Book 3's many writing questions are important. If kids' reading lives can be rejuvenated with fresh looks at and insight to the power of words, it will, in turn, motivate new connections to their writing lives.

For example, start off with an absurd, creative-thinking question: (a) Make up three ridiculously silly sentences. (b) Use sentence-storming (trigger one sentence after another) to find your answers. (c) Visualize each sentence and briefly describe what you see. (d) How can creating silly sentences help you become a better writer?

Go to paragraph writing next: (a) Make up an absurd (ridiculous) paragraph of four to eight sentences. (b) Visualize the paragraph and pencil-sketch the pictures you see. (c) Creating, writing, reading, visualizing, and drawing a silly passage: What connects all these processes? Explain. (d) *Hint*: Use storming techniques to build your paragraph.

Introductory writing questions lead to advanced ones requiring more imagination:

- What happened to the child who never stopped reading? Write an imaginary tale in one hundred words or more. Illustrate the story with one or more sketches. (*Hint*: Picture-storm images and brainstorm ideas before starting your story.)
- Write a fantasy, myth, tall tale, fable, fairy tale, or dream about a perfect imaginary reading life in one hundred words or more. Brainstorm ideas and picture-storm images to jumpstart your story. (*Hint*: What would make this reading life so extraordinary?)

Use a developmental approach when asking writing questions: (1) begin with an introduction to words with word and word activity questions, the foundation for both reading and writing; (2) build writing skills and motivation starting with single sentence activities; (3) follow it up with questions asking for written responses of twenty-five to fifty words; and, (4) at the end of Book 3, ask the longer creative-writing questions requiring responses of one hundred words or more. Pick five writing questions and blend them with your other questions.

Let drawing questions elicit students' phenomenal reading worlds. Bring them right in front of their *eyes* in a fun way. By visualizing what reading universes look like from the *inside out* and then drawing the images, kids develop greater awareness, understanding, and appreciation of what it is they're actually doing in their own and very real reading lives.

Example: Draw a dreamlike, fantasy, or surreal cartoon picture of yourself "wrapped up in a book" you're reading. Picture-storm images first, and then illustrate one you like. Illustrating reading life shows kids' that it can be serious and entertaining simultaneously. Choose five drawing questions and intersperse them amongst your other questions.

Hypothetical reading situation questions allow students to present their ideas about reading and reading life via fictitious scenarios. These set-up events make them controlling agents and empower them to create and direct a course in reading. Similar to drawing questions, hypothetical questions provide adolescents with alternative perspectives of looking at reading in an enjoyable, meaningful, and challenging way.

Examples:

- Imagine a clear day in reading. Record your thoughts, feelings, and experience. What does, or would, such a day look like?
- Imagine this: How would you, as the super duper reading doctor, create a program to develop perfect concentration in reading for kids? Brainstorm ideas for the different steps in your program. List three steps that would help students reach perfect concentration in reading.

Choose five hypothetical reading situation questions.

One-line statement and opinion questions, and there are many in Book 3, give students more chances to voice their ideas, attitudes, and feelings on reading and reading life. *Examples*:

- You are what you eat, but, are you what you read? Explain.
- Reading = self-communication. Explain the statement's meaning. How important is this in the reading process?
- Can you exist without reading and books? Why or why not?

Pick five to ten one-liners and opinion questions.

Use rating questions to switch from the more subjective responses of one-line statement and opinion questions to the more objective responses about their reading and reading lives. Students change gears to describe how things really are when they read. *Examples are*:

- How good are you at reading under pressure? Rate your ability to read under pressure on a scale from 0 to 10, where 0 = poor and 10 = excellent. Give reasons for your rating.
- How clear is your mind when you read? Rate your clarity on a scale from 0 to 10, where 0 = totally cloudy and 10 = totally clear. Give reasons for your rating.

Choose three to five rating questions.

Go to potential closers, quotation questions, to finish off Book 3 or Round 3. By this time your class/child has answered over ninety questions (whether sequentially from Book 1 to 3, or randomly selected from all four books), so their insight to reading has grown and they should be ready to wrap things up with some quotes.

Check out these wrapper-upper quotations:

- "I read my eyes out and can't read half enough. . . . The more one reads the more one sees we have to read" (John Adams). What does the statement mean? Has this been your experience? Explain by giving an example from your reading life.
- "Read in order to live" (Gustave Flaubert). Explain the quote's meaning. Write an essay about the quote in one hundred words or more. (*Optional*: Instead of an essay, write a fairy tale, fable, or myth about the quotation in one hundred words or more.)

The positive quotes require students to synthesize many reading experiences. As discussion leader, conclude Book 3/Round 3 with a series of quotations. Ask one every other day of the week. Select three quotes to complete Book 3/Round 3.

A survey approach covers most reading areas and genres. But keep in mind the other question categories, the "forget-me-nots": (a) Common, everyday reading experience questions keep kids up to date with what happens in their daily reading lives. (b) Book recalls can always be asked in conjunction with books read in class, for reports and homework, student book lists, as well as leisure-time reading. (c) Past reading experience questions inspire kids to reflect more on early reading life and recall events that made them readers. (d) Poetry questions heighten their connections to words, images, feelings, thoughts, experiences, observations, perceptions, and the affective side to reading and everyday life. (e) Nonfiction reading and book questions make up the bulk of school reading and should be addressed in each of the four books of questions. Ask five to ten "forget-me-nots" and blend them in with your other questions.

KEY INFORMATION AND PROCEDURES FOR ASKING AND ANSWERING QUESTION CATEGORIES

Motivating Teen and Preteen Readers was arranged in order of the easiest to the toughest questions (in the author's opinion). Expect to find many provocative questions from Book 1 to 4.

Some differences in Book 3: more parts to each question; more skills needed to respond to questions; questions are a little tougher but do-able, cerebral workouts; and questions push students to take extended, deeper looks at reading and reading life.

If the class/child struggles at the beginning, let discussions, raps, and website posts fill in the missing pieces of difficult questions. *Example*:

- Visualize an imaginary "book garden." What are you looking at with your inner eye? Keep searching for more and more images in your mind by picture-storming. Now draw what you see—your imaginary "book garden."

Students respond to this combined creative-thinking (hypothetical imaginary reading situation) and drawing question: First, they visualize the "book garden" by picture-storming, and second, from the images created and viewed by the inner eye, select one to draw. And remind them it's the idea brought out by the drawing that counts, not necessarily its beauty.

- There are words that jumpstart streams of ideas, thoughts, beliefs, and opinions whenever you read, hear, imagine, or say them. The word should send your mind flying. Search for a word that does this to you. When you find one, contemplate it. Describe the "flight of the word" in twenty-five words or more.

First, students search for the word via an inner-eye scan; second, contemplate the found word; and third, describe the "flight of the word" in a short written response.

Another example is:

- Imagine a room with enough space for only one single bed, and where the curtains covering an open window fly up from the wind, letting in a blaze of sunlight for an instant, and there you are, lying down—reading. . . . Visualize this scene and then contemplate it for a minute. Write a story of fifty words or more using this image as the starting point. Just for fun, draw or sketch the mind-picture of this scene. (*Note*: This writing-and-drawing question and others require thirty to forty-five minutes for kids to complete their responses. When asking questions that involve writing, contemplating, and drawing, you should leave extra time for responding. Also, kids can finish their drawings at home for homework.)

The four skills needed to answer the aforementioned question are:

- Visualizing the hypothetical reading scene.
- Contemplating the imagined scene.
- Writing a story using the given mind-picture as a starting point.
- Drawing the mind-picture visualized and seen.

This cognitive, visual, emotional, creative workout question becomes a *see-cruise* through the self-amusement park of the imagination.

Besides the harder multiple-skills questions, Book 3 has other difficult questions:

- How are books like parachutes? (*Hint*: Look up "parachute" in a dictionary before answering.)
- How is reading like telepathy? (*Hint*: Look up "telepathy" in a dictionary before answering.)
- How can you deepen your reading experience?

Students look up key words in the first two questions to understand what they're asking: Even with the definitions, they will need to think creatively and analyze the meanings, functions, and processes of "parachutes" and "telepathy" to find answers.

The last question pushes kids to search for answers. It is open-ended and has many potential responses that can affect adolescents' motivation to read. How much recall, reflecting, critical thinking, and visualizing will they put into this wide-ranging question? Can they apply the trigger method of creativity to brainstorm ideas about "deepening the reading experience"? When responding to tougher questions, *tell kids*: "Relax, they aren't test questions."

Question categories are not absolute. *Crossover questions* fit into more than one category, sometimes two, three, or four, making them slightly harder to answer. *Example*: Can reading life change your real life? Why or why not? Category areas according to the author include: book recalls, past reading experiences, reading-process, and opinion questions.

The question requires students to:

- Recall a book that affected or changed their real lives.
- Search past reading experiences and connect them with real life events to see if reading (books) caused any change.
- Reflect on the reading process to see if it has the power to connect them to personal and everyday life situations and/or problems.
- Express their opinions because it might be the kids themselves who created the change in the first place and not a book they read.

The question is: Who or what creates the change—the student, book, reading, or a combination of all three? This question should ignite great discussions with teens and preteens.

There is greater emphasis in Book 3 on the reading process and writing questions, as well as the reading-writing and writing-reading connections, where motivation to read evolves naturally, organically, and creatively from the art of writing.

Check out the following reading process questions to see if they connect kids to their reading lives. Think about how heavier reading process questions might lead to a reading-writing connection:

- Reading is in the mind's eye of the reader. Explain.
- Discover yourself—read! Explain.
- Why bother getting inside a character's mind from a play you're reading?
- How are you, the reader, an artist?
- Do you think about what you read after you finish reading it? Why or why not? Give an example.

Are there any connections between reading and writing? Here's what the author found for each of the five questions, respectively:

Writing is also in the mind's eye of the reader-writer. Can the students/child make that connection and use the reading process framework—the mind's magic reading theater—for writing and find the *mind's magic writing theater*?

If you can "find yourself" in reading, it may spark the idea in adolescents that they can "find themselves" and their voices through writing or self-expression.

Getting into any character's head, whether in a play, novel, or memoir, can be highly contagious: It can become a catalyst for writing about fictional characters or real people from the kids' lives. As characters' stories play out in the mind's magic reading theater, their acts may stimulate ideas for the students' own writing in the mind's magic writing theater.

Kids don't think of themselves as "reader-artists," but they are when changing words into holographic images and virtual realities. Why can't they reverse the process and make themselves "writer-artists"? Why can't they take the many images, memories, dreams, experiences, and reflections from their real and imagined lives and change them into words, sentences, and stories (fiction or nonfiction)? Will they see connections to the writing process?

When children get into the habit of reflecting after they read, it triggers ideas, insights, feelings, and perceptions about themselves, other people, and the world, which can turn into prompts or story starters for their own fiction and nonfiction pieces.

There are *combination questions* in Book 3 where multiple skills are required to respond to the different parts. Check out the upcoming *combination question*, which is also a *crossover* word, word-activity, and writing question. Think how it connects adolescents to reading/reading life and makes the writing-reading connection. Also, figure out the various skills kids need to answer this question: Visualize "paradise": Picture-storm images of the word. Pick one image and contemplate it for sixty seconds. Describe what happened during your contemplation in fifty words. (Multiple skills are: visualization, picture-storming, inner-eye scanning, contemplation, thinking, and writing.)

Look at this *combination question* requiring reading, visualizing/inner-eye scanning, thinking, feeling, and writing skills to see if it can trigger a writing-reading connection: What journey does "Blueberries explode" take you on? Read the sentence three times. Imagine it. Concentrate on the picture. What do you see? What is your inner eye viewing on the TV screen in your mind? Now put it all together with thoughts and feelings brought up by the image. Write about your journey in fifty words. (Although not listed as an option to the questions, kids can draw the mind-picture visualized and contemplated.)

Can writing questions become *catalysts* for boosting kids' motivation to read? Get students into words like "paradise"—the depth—and how it evokes images, feelings, thoughts, worlds, experiences, and memories. If kids can write about words and see them in a fresh light (that words do not live alone, are three-dimensional and virtual), they get a better feel for and insight to them and can be motivated to read via a writing-reading connection.

The latter question shows preteens/teens the absurd, entertaining, visual, emotional trips they can take in both the mind's magic reading and writing theaters by changing silly two-word sentences into funny mental images and writing about the experience in a short, short story. They use their writing journeys as an inspiration to read and make the writing-reading connection. As discussion leader, work backward from writing to reading (or reversing the reading-writing connection) to see if the joy of writing can lead to the joy of reading.

Prepare your class/child for Book 4/Round 4 with Book 3's writing questions. But remember *teacher/parent choice*: Stick with reading questions mainly, if that's where your students'/child's needs are. Teachers may be happy with their instructional programs in writing and not want more lessons in this area.

Emphasize word/word-activity questions and writing questions to jumpstart the creative imagination: What do the following questions conjure up in *you*, discussion leader?

- What happens if dumb collides with dumber? Draw what you imagine. Describe your picture in twenty-five words and write an original caption for it.
- What are the softest, gentlest words you know? List three words. Why is each so gentle and soft? Describe the feelings and thoughts each word creates (*Optional*: Using the three words, create three soft and gentle sentences; visualize each; and illustrate them.)
- What is your favorite word at the moment? Contemplate it for thirty seconds. Describe what happened during your contemplation in twenty-five words or more.
- Just-for-fun: Use your inner eye to zoom in for close-ups of: pizza; shark; ignorance; and garbage. Visualize two of the words and describe what you see, feel, and think.

Discussion leaders: Stop, contemplate, and respond. . . .

Several toughies were given to demonstrate the creative levels and skills involved in responding, and also to show that many word and word-activity questions are multiple-skills questions. Some observations and thoughts about the above questions are, respectively:

This absurd question drops kids in the heart of their imaginations to come up with a "collision" of words, or *creating something from nothing*. It requires several skills to respond: visualizing, creative thinking, describing, drawing, and writing. It is a tough question, yet silly, serious fun for kids and adults alike.

Difficult question: Key strategies for answering are by an inner-eye scan for words; word-storming words; brainstorming ideas; picture-storming images; visualizing images created by these gentle words; and describing the thoughts and feelings triggered by the words. Lots of cerebration and emoting here because the responses are about thinking, feeling, reflecting, and deliberating: stopping to look at and experience the gentle and soft words.

Contemplating provides a creative and more intense way of looking at words: It triggers many unusual responses, showing kids incredible universes words inhabit if they give them continued attention. This is also a toughie because they have to contemplate, recall, and then write about the experience.

In Book 3 students take a closer look at words they visualize by zooming in on them. How would this influence visualizing "pizza"? When they take a closer look (with the inner eye), will it create a greater passion and appreciation for words? Will the idea of close-ups work their way into the reading process and motivate reading as well as writing? The question tests the power of the inner eye to see things. Will the new visualization technique amplify their feelings and thoughts about what they see and strengthen a response to literature and writing? (Think about the close-ups used in TV food commercials: pizza really pops out of the screen.)

Many questions in Book 3 make reading real by connecting reading life to everyday life. A goal of *Motivating Teen and Preteen Readers* is developing connections between reading and: writing, reflecting, thinking, feeling, imagining, concentrating, contemplating, creating, communicating, recalling (memory), drawing (art), fantasizing, escaping, problem-solving, self-discovery, self-awareness, self-understanding, self-knowledge, self-communication, self-education, self-motivation, self-efficacy, responsibility, empowerment, values, power, stress, rewards, change, sensitivity, dreaming, venting, challenges, confidence, solitude, healing, magic, mystery, curiosity, and wonder.

Examples of questions connecting reading life with real or everyday life are:

- Reading: your ticket to ride. . . . Explain.
- Be yourself—read! Explain.
- Can reading and books teach you self-guidance: how to manage and direct your own life? Explain by giving an example from your reading and real life.

What are these questions' connections between reading life and real life?
Discussion leaders: Pause, reflect, ponder, and respond. . . .
Possible answers are, respectively:

Reading takes kids many places: It's their passport to a better life. Reflect for two minutes on the history of *your* reading life to see its effects/affects on your real or everyday life and discover this truth.

Reading is a process where adolescents experience and feel themselves: It's just a kid and a book hanging out and enjoying each other's company together.

Is there a good self-help book out there on how to reduce stress? A book can guide, direct, and improve your life and lifestyle. It can help young people and adults make decisions and choices via the expertise of professionals in their respective fields. And it doesn't have to be a self-help book: It could be a novel, poem, play, or short story that educates or guides people on how to deal with and handle hassles, conflicts, problems, and everyday life.

As students build greater awareness of reading life from Books 1 and 2 or the first sixty to one hundred questions, they'll become more open and motivated to answer the numerous one-line statement and opinion questions in Book 3 or Round 3 of questioning. Let kids express themselves by releasing feelings they have about reading, which they don't usually get a chance to do in classroom situations. They empower themselves through their written and oral responses. Extend raps and discussions if the timing is right and schedule permitting. Venting goes a long way to increase interest in reading, reading life, and life.

Review the following sample questions: Picture yourself as discussion leader fielding a multitude of responses to them. Think about whether they will ignite discussions in your classroom or at home:

- Reading and books can stop you from thinking for yourself. Explain the statement's meaning. Do you agree? Why or why not?
- Frequent reflection about what you read motivates a passion for reading. What does the statement mean or suggest? What do you think? Why?
- Reading keeps your mind active, running, working, open, magical, powerful, and alive. Agree? Disagree? Why? How could reading perform such an amazing feat?
- Reading and books can be challenges to your real life. What does the statement mean? Do you agree? Why or why not? Give an example from your reading and real life.

How would you, as discussion leader, answer the questions? Are you stopping to reflect, to use an inner-eye scan to find different viewpoints, concepts, memories, thoughts, feelings, beliefs, and experiences (their pluses and minuses) needed to respond in an open, honest, objective way?

The questions in *Motivating Teen and Preteen Readers* trigger many potential discussion questions about reading and reading life in a natural manner:

Do young people let books and authors do the talking and thinking for them?
Do kids actually reflect on what they read?
Do students question what they read or accept everything automatically?
What would happen if kids reflected more about what they read?
Would reflection engage them more in reading and the reading process?
Can reading keep the mind energized like computer or video games?
What is the actual impact of reading on adolescent lives?
How can reading challenge real life?
What would be the challenges reading presents to everyday life?
How powerful is reading really?
Does reading take an active or passive role in most teens' and preteens' lives?

Think about this: Can these questions stir up class and one-to-one discussions?

Hypothetical reading situation questions motivate discussions and teacher/ parent raps:

- If you were teaching a young child how to read, what idea would you communicate about reading? Why?

- How would you motivate a friend to read if he hates to read?
- How would you motivate a poor reader to improve his or her reading? How would you develop, reinvent, and change his/her reading life? Describe your remedial program to save his or her reading and reading life from going under.

Once kids get into hypothetical reading situations — the theoretical, abstract, and ideal — they can open their minds and stimulate creative and critical thinking, reflecting, wonder, curiosity, and engagement: Call it inspired concentration. The skills give adolescents room to move in their imaginations and resolve fictitious reading events. Maybe the written responses, reflecting their attitudes, opinions, and prejudices about reading, would provide feedback and insight to help their reading lives. Can students take their own and/or their friends' advice and use it on themselves? That is a question to be answered through the four books of questions.

Drawing questions add to Book 3's ambiance of seriousness, fun, play, and diversion by building artistic/creative skills. For example, they use picture-storming, a form of visualization, to trigger creative thinking. They ask students to explore the imagination by visualizing and then drawing their reading lives. The questions become problem-solving situations, which define and describe reading experiences. Their drawings *mirror back* what reading and reading life are about (hopefully with a fresh perspective), and also, put a little love back in their reading hearts.

Discussion leaders: See if this drawing question triggers your creative imagination: Reading puts those snow-capped mountains right in the middle of the mind's eye. Can you see them? Visualize this scene. Focus in on your image and draw it. Make it into a poster promoting reading and reading life. What does it all mean? What feelings, thoughts, and ideas are you communicating through your poster? Write a caption at the bottom of your finished work.

To create and visualize the expression "snow-capped mountains," picture-storm images, brainstorm ideas, word-storm words, and sentence-storm sentences/captions. What is conjured up? The combination question involves multiple skills: creative/critical thinking, visualizing, drawing, and writing.

Rating questions can be asked toward the end of Book 3 or Round 3. After so many questions on reading and reading life, students have a chance evaluate their reading skills and knowledge and should be ready with numerical responses and the reasons for them.

Will they be prepared for this question? How good are you at changing words into mind-pictures (images)? Rate yourself on a scale from 0 to 10, where 0 = poor ability and 10 = excellent ability. Give reasons for your rating.

Rating questions bring teens and preteens closer to the reality of their reading lives. Once they grade themselves with the self-monitoring questions, they get a *read* on their reading, and the answers leave their "marks" or impressions, that is, give them something to think about. . . .

Quotations are words students can live by; they enable them to see, via self-discovery, what the reading world embraces. Their realizations will lead to increased self-motivation, self-determination, self-reliance, and self-efficacy. (The author's original one-liners are also considered quotations.) Discussion leaders might also adopt these sayings for themselves. . . .

How would *you* respond to these quotes? Would they be good catalysts for discussions?

- "You know you've read a good book when you turn the last page and feel a little as if you have lost a friend" (Paul Sweeney). Can you recall a time when you finished a book and felt the same way? Describe what you experienced.
- "Reading means borrowing" (G. C. Lichtenberg). What do you "borrow" when you read? What have you "borrowed" recently?
- "Sticks and stones may break my bones, but words will make me go in a corner and cry by myself for hours" (Eric Idle). How powerful are words according to the quote? Why? Is the quote true for you? Are you sensitive to spoken words? Explain.

Lots of experiences; unique, private events; those hardly expressed by kids, will come out in class or one-to-one dialogues. *For example*: Books that have been kids' "friends" should trigger some fascinating answers for discussion. And what about the things students borrow from books? Where will that conversation lead? Rock star Eric Idle's quote about his sensitivity to words will draw a myriad of student examples showing the power of words, ones they would not reveal unless provoked. And what about *your* experiences with words? Would kids be interested in what teacher and parent discussion leaders have to say? This teacher thinks so. . . .

Discussion leaders: Try out the author's one-line statement questions to see where they take you:

- Words do not stop on the page. What does the statement mean or suggest? What do you think about it? Why?
- Read as if your life depended on it. Do you? Explain what the statement means and suggests to readers.
- Keep an open mind to what you read. Explain the statement's meaning. What do you think: agree or disagree? Why?

One-liners emphasize a key concept of *Motivating Teen and Preteen Readers*: Words do not live alone once they enter the mind's magic reading and writing theaters. The statements advise students about how to read and the art of reading: that is, the ways to make reading more energizing, absorbing, and expansive, for example, by heightening their intensity and passion levels ("Read as if your life depended on it"), as well as "keeping an open mind" to what they read. The one-liners or quotes, from famous authors to not-so-famous teacher-authors, can also be *closers* to summarize reading and reading life experiences from Book 3/ Round 3 of questions.

An alternate way to close Book 3 is to ask a variety of questions. The finale should include ideas and experiences brought out by earlier questions. Create a smooth transition to Book 4/Round 4 using your closers.

Examples to conclude a survey or eclectic approach are:

- My mind's eye sees all that I read in quick little flashes. Explain.
- Brainstorm ten things that come to mind when you think about your reading life.
- Do reading and books make the world simpler or harder to live in? Why?

Ideas brought out by these *closers* are, respectively:

- The mind's eye rapid seeing of what a reader reads.
- Pictures, impressions, and visions of reading life.
- Effects and affects of reading and books on readers' lives.

Open-ended questions have many possible responses. So when asking this type of question, discussion leaders should also keep an open mind to the kids' written/oral responses. (Accept answers supported by specific examples and past/ present experiences.)

Discussion leaders: How open-minded can you be to these open-ended questions? How many responses can be brainstormed, picture-stormed, or word-stormed for each of the following questions?

a. What does reading do for you?
b. How can you create a passion for reading?
c. Words can make you want something really bad. Explain the statement's meaning. Give an example of a word that made you feel this way. Describe what happened.
d. Describe two great mind-pictures you remember from your reading life. Can you appreciate these questions' open-endedness? *For example*:

  1. Reading can do many things for you: make you more observant, informed, intelligent, aware, thoughtful, sensitive, empathetic, and peaceful.
  2. How *you* create a passion for reading is *the* question of the books of questions: find different genres you're interested in; learn/know what books you like/dislike; choose books carefully; demand a lot from yourself when reading; learn to see what you read as a holographic, virtual reality; use reading as an instant escape/refuge from the real world; read

for fun; feel what you read; reflect on what you're reading; concentrate on what you read; and make books/reading part of your life experiences and daily life: "I am part of everything that I have read" (Theodore Roosevelt).

3. Words can make you want something really badly: recess, lunch, puppy, beach, pool, summer, chocolate, bicycle, mountains, lake, woods, hot fudge sundae, McDonald's, baseball, basketball, playground, and gym. Get the idea?

4. A fun discussion starter: recalling two great mind-pictures from past reading experiences. What comes up immediately? This is a good class or one-to-one (parent/teacher-child) conversation that can go on and on. By Book 3/Round 3 of questions, kids have visualized so much via book recalls, for example, that their descriptions should be detailed enough and appealing to keep the other students and discussion leader interested.

Open up the class/child with open-ended questions: Let kids pump themselves up to read, so they can recreate the paradise lost to test-mania.

IMPLEMENTING WORKABLE SCHEDULES/STRATEGIES FOR PRESENTING QUESTIONS IN BOOK 3

- Procedures for implementing workable schedules used in Books 1 and 2 remain the same for Book 3, with a few upcoming exceptions.
- Before starting Book 3, skim, review, reread, and select thirty questions or more based on the students'/child's needs, wants, and previous written/oral responses.
- Experiment with assigning questions for homework via a class website to supplement and further develop questions done in class. This strategy would work from elementary through high school.
- Give two questions every other day or continue with one if that works best. Extend time limit to twenty minutes (max) for two-question mini-lessons. If kids can't finish their responses in the allotted time, let them work on answers whenever they have free time during the school day or at home. Try one question daily if your schedule permits it and kids are highly motivated. Use one forty-five-minute period with up to five questions as a suggested alternative approach. Also, at an opportune time, present one important question related to the students' needs in a thirty-minute lesson and have an extended discussion on their written responses (ten-minute max for written responses followed up by a twenty-minute talk).
- Writing questions asking for fifty to one hundred words require extra time (approximately thirty to forty-five minutes max, that is, if teacher discussion

leaders decide to advance *Motivating Teen and Preteen Readers* to the content area of writing and the writing-reading connection.

- Longer questions involving writing, drawing, and contemplating, or another type of combination question requiring more time (beyond twenty minutes), should be taken into consideration before attempting. Extra time has to be made available when choosing these types of questions for lessons. The mini-lessons in Book 3 are not always "mini."

- Continue experimenting, not only with the best times to present the questions and the strongest ones, but with making up your own original questions and even expanding some questions from Book 3. All teacher and parent discussion leaders should experiment, experiment, experiment to find the creativity in themselves and the students/child.

- Select thirty to seventy-five questions from Book 3 for the mini- and longer lessons. If thirty are given in class or at home (one-to-one situations), use the additional questions for homework and/or bonus box questions. Find new ways to apply the many diverse questions in Book 3; don't let the "good ones," in your estimation, go to waste.

- Keep "promoting" the bonus box in raps as a way for kids to increase what this author calls their "Reading Passion Quotient" (RPQ). How engaged and involved students are in reading/reading life can be measured by answering extra questions in school or at home. It shows initiative, drive, and commitment.

- Continue working with the "exchange programs," where kids share their written responses to the questions with classmates before discussion begins. Allow them to make several exchanges before they read their answers aloud. Also, after the student and teacher evaluations for Book 3, allow them to share their notebooks with each other to cross-fertilize ideas and experiences about reading/reading life.

- Using *duets* is another way of varying the routine whole class mini-lesson. Students pick and work with a partner to answer a question. Allow five minutes to respond and then partners take turns reading, discussing, and questioning each other's answers. Teachers can present the strategy in two ways: All duets answer the same question; or, they respond to different questions. Discussion leaders should pick those questions they feel would inspire strong written responses, and also, ignite an enthusiastic one-to-one dialogue between two students.

- *Sample duet questions* are: (1) Hooked on books? Are you? Why or why not? (2) What is the hardest part of reading for you? Why? (3) Reading connects you to what? Explain your answer. Questions are written on three-inch by five-inch index cards; teachers redistribute the cards to different partners in the next round of duets. Time limit is fifteen minutes, max, for writing and discussion. (Recommended for grades 6 through 10.)

- A method for varying the class lesson is the *three-student brainstorming session*. All students choose classmates for quickie brainstorming sessions. Each three-student group brainstorms answers orally to the same or different questions handed out by the teacher. Brainstorming is followed by a three-way discussion on the ideas and experiences that came out about reading/ reading life. Discussion leaders should pick questions they believe would initiate many strong oral responses, as well as a lively follow-up discussion amongst the three students.
- *Sample three-student brainstorming questions* are: (1) What does reading do for you? (2) How can you instantly increase your concentration when reading? (3) What self-help books would you like to read? Why? Allow ten to fifteen minutes, max, for brainstorming and discussion. The strategy's purpose is to see what fresh, innovative insights about reading result from the brainstorming sessions. Can their answers potentially inspire positive attitudes and renewed interest in reading? (Recommended for grades 6 through 10.)
- *Notes for duets and three-student brainstorming sessions*: Careful selection of questions by discussion leaders is crucial to make things work in the alternative approaches to whole class mini-lessons. Trial and error and the kids' maturity (or EIQ, emotional intelligence quotients) are all factors in both strategies.
- After answering questions from Books 1, 2, and half of Book 3, kids are asked to create their own original questions about reading/reading life. The responses evaluate how much thought they give to reading life, as well as their passion for reading, after answering fifty or more questions. If an original student question "passes" either a panel of student judges, the entire class, and/or the teacher, the student is given a blank three-inch by five-inch index card to write the question (questions can be put on both sides of the card). The cards are put in the bonus box. Allow five to ten minutes to make up questions. In the follow-up discussion, students read their questions aloud to classmates and analyze their value and utility for five to ten minutes. Student and/or teacher judges decide later which questions will be used. Creating your own questions can also be done for homework to avoid using class time. It has been this teacher-author's experience that students from grades 4 through 6 will respond to this difficult activity with surprisingly strong answers/questions. (Recommended for grades 4 through 10.)
- Continue giving inspiring raps prior to the questions, especially at times when the overall written responses lack effort and thought. A quickie rap always makes sense and a difference.
- Spot-check struggling students' reading notebooks from time to time. Have informal talks to get them thinking, involved, and back on track.
- Avoid overloading the class/child with extra questions at inopportune times, for example, when workloads and stress levels are high, and before standard-

ized tests. But push more work on the kids when their motivation to answer the plethora of questions on reading and reading life is strong.

- Refer to "Evaluation Questions for Book 3" and "Not-for-Parents-Only Guide to *Motivating Teen and Preteen Readers*" for more information on presenting questions, procedures, and scheduling student questionnaire 3 and student-teacher/parent chat 3.

Notes for middle and high school teachers:

- Make the necessary adjustments for the number of questions asked and how often presented (how many lessons per week).
- The forty-five-minute extended-time lesson will fit in with most middle and high school schedules. Perhaps one or two whole-period lessons each month might be the best way to go for presenting *Motivating Teen and Preteen Readers* at these levels. Also, teachers can post three to five questions on the class/section website to do for homework and have five- to ten-minute follow-up discussions the next day in class (time/schedule permitting).
- The longer writing lessons and other combination questions from Book 3 (writing, contemplating, drawing) requiring a full forty-five-minute period can fit into teachers' schedules in grades 6 through 10. These lessons offer a fun change of pace to the normal routines teens and preteens experience during the school year.

EVALUATION QUESTIONS FOR BOOK 3

Evaluation Procedures: Student Questionnaire 3 and Student-Teacher/Parent Chat 3

Student questionnaire 3 follows the same procedures previously used:

- Student questionnaire 3 comes after completing thirty to seventy-five questions.
- Students reread all their written responses.
- Students answer questionnaire.
- Teacher reviews, comments on, and discusses responses with class.

Student-teacher/parent chat 3 follows student questionnaire:

- Teacher skims and reviews students' reading notebooks.
- Optional teacher chats with kids are based on written responses.
- Student-parent chats are not optional.

Suggested Questions for Student Questionnaire 3

Note: Kids can reread and review their written responses at home or in school.

1. What thoughts came to mind after rereading your responses?
2. Describe how much effort you put into your written responses.
3. Were these questions tougher to answer than the earlier ones? Explain.
4. Which questions gave you the most trouble? Why?
5. Did the questions challenge you enough? Why or why not? Give an example.
6. Do you read your responses after you write them? Why or why not?
7. What was the most fun about Book 3 or Round 3 of questions?
8. Which question was fun to answer? Why?
9. Were you looking forward to answering these questions? Explain.
10. Have the questions through Book 3/Round 3 ever been boring? Explain.
11. Were these questions a mental workout for your mind? Explain your answer.
12. What have you learned about reading or reading life by answering the questions?
13. Were you thinking more before responding to the questions? Explain.
14. How good was your memory when answering recall questions? Explain.
15. Is your memory improving as you answer more and more recall questions? Explain.
16. Have you become aware of new worlds through the questions? Explain your answer.
17. What have you learned about any of your bad reading habits?
18. What have you discovered about words?
19. What does the word-storming technique show you about words?
20. Can word-storming be used in real or everyday life? Explain.
21. What was your favorite question on words? Why?
22. What have the questions shown you about reading and thinking? Explain.
23. What have you learned about reading and visualizing? Explain.
24. Describe one new insight you uncovered about the reading process.
25. Has answering many questions helped you with your writing? Why or why not?
26. Did you enjoy responding to the questions using drawing? Why or why not?
27. What drawing questions did you like? Why?
28. Did the absurd (silly) drawing questions reveal things about reading and reading life you did not know? Explain.
29. What silly question did you like? Why?
30. Have the poetry questions inspired your poetry reading life? Why or why not?
31. Describe what you learned about concentration after answering the questions.

32. What question helped you realize reading's surprises and mysteries? Explain.
33. What is the connection between reading and writing?
34. Did the questions affect how you see reading and reading life? Explain.
35. Have you become a believer in reading through the questions? Why or why not?
36. Do you now look at reading and reading life in a more open way? Why or why not?
37. Has your ability to visualize what you read improved? Why or why not?
38. What storming techniques did you use to answer questions? Give an example.
39. Describe a side trip you took in reading unrelated to the daily question.
40. Have these responses improved compared to your previous responses? Explain.
41. How honest were you in answering the questions? Explain.
42. Did the discussions help to improve your written responses? Why or why not?
43. What have you learned about your attitude toward reading and reading life?
44. Did the discussions affect your attitude toward reading and reading life?
45. Have you taught yourself something about reading? Explain your answer.
46. Do you appreciate the solitude, quietness, and peace of reading? Explain.
47. What have you learned about real or everyday life after answering the questions?
48. What have you realized about negative reading experiences?
49. Describe the connections between reading life and real life.
50. Do you believe that you can motivate yourself to read? Why or why not?
51. Where does motivation to read come from: the outside or inside? Why?
52. Do you find yourself approaching reading differently now? Explain your answer.
53. Did the questions on words motivate you to write? Why or why not?
54. Would you make any changes in the books of questions? Why or why not?
55. What, if anything, has changed in your reading life? Explain your answer.
56. Brainstorm three questions about the reading process.
57. What are your thoughts about reading and reading life after finishing the questionnaire?

For student questionnaire 3, select twenty to twenty-five questions according to the overall questions asked up until then. These can also work in the final questionnaire of *Motivating Teen and Preteen Readers*. Questions from student questionnaires may be used *interchangeably* with student-teacher/parent chats, as well as in the earlier questionnaires/chats where suitable.

Suggested Questions for Student-Teacher/Parent Chat 3

Note: These questions will work as a final chat for Motivating Teen and Preteen Readers. *Discussion leaders can also use them in the student questionnaires as they see fit.*

1. Is the thrill gone or are you still having fun answering the questions?
2. Are you finding reading to be more fun?
3. The first thought that comes to mind when you hear "reading life" is:
   _____.
4. Does the questioning become too much or annoying at times?
5. What's new in your reading world?
6. Rate yourself as a "reader": not serious, half serious, serious, or, very serious.
7. Which of your written responses really amazed you?
8. How much self-communication goes on inside you when reading?
9. Do you like the creative-writing questions?
10. Do you like writing about words?
11. Have you discovered new things about "words" when writing about words?
12. Brainstorm three ideas or thoughts you have about "words."
13. Do you use classroom or your own techniques to answer the questions?
14. Describe one of your techniques for answering the questions.
15. Were your responses automatic or do you think them through before writing?
16. Name one thing you learned in the discussions or raps.
17. What did you learn from your friends' reading experiences during the discussions?
18. Which classmate's written response(s) did you like a lot?
19. What have you realized about the connection between reading and feelings?
20. Can the books of questions motivate a student to overcome a reading problem?
21. Describe three feelings you have about *Motivating Teen and Preteen Readers.*
22. Have you accomplished any of the goals of *Motivating Teen and Preteen Readers?*
23. Have you learned to help yourself in reading through the many questions?
24. Do reading and reading life make more sense to you now?
25. Are you mad, sad, or glad about your reading and reading life?
26. Do you know more about the reading process since starting the books of questions?
27. Has your imagination improved after answering the questions?
28. Do you think there is a secret to becoming a successful or good reader?

29. What do you think is the magic of reading?
30. Where do you get your motivation, desire, or enthusiasm to read?
31. How would you describe the book of questions to a friend who knows nothing about it?
32. How important is *Motivating Teen and Preteen Readers* in your reading life?
33. Do the chats help your reading and reading life in any way?
34. Name one thing you learned about your reading life since the questions began.
35. Do you see yourself reading more in your free time and the future?
36. Do you see yourself becoming a lifelong reader?
37. Can the questions make an unhappy reader into a happy reader?
38. How can a child change a dull reading life to a bright reading life?
39. How would you get more kids to read or enjoy reading?
40. How would you improve your written responses?
41. If you were the teacher, what comments would you make about your responses?
42. Are you looking forward to the next book or series of questions?
43. Have you been inspired to read more since *Motivating Teen and Preteen Readers* began?

Book 4

The teacher who is indeed wise does not bid you to enter the house of wisdom but rather leads you to the threshold of the mind.

—Kahlil Gibran

ABOUT BOOK 4

Continuity, Advanced Placement Questions, Survey Approach, and Question Categories

Book 4 is the advanced placement book. Questions are tough, serious, and fun because they push kids' limits for getting into this magical process of reading. The purpose of Book 4's questions is to challenge students to see what they've learned: It's an indirect evaluation of their growth and progress in Books 1, 2, and 3 or the first three rounds of ninety or more questions. There is continuity between the questions of Books 3 and 4 (question categories stay the same) and expansion by the latter book on previous questions.

Advanced placement questions (APQs) are crossover and/or combination questions involving several category areas and multiple skills that trigger entertaining mental and emotional workouts. One-line statement questions about the reading process extend thinking about the act of reading and develop fresh ways to look at and appreciate it. New AP word questions, such as "imaginary word encounters," are extreme creative problem-solving situations using words—more fun in the self-amusement park of imagination. Although not new, the "fill-ins" or "finish-me-off" questions on reading and reading life are open-ended questions requiring several skills to respond.

Keep using a survey approach in Book 4/Round 4, stressing certain categories, starting with openers or introductory questions such as: one-line statement, reading process, word and word activity, writing, drawing, hypothetical reading situation, opinion, book recall, and quotation questions. At the same time, blend in the "forget-me-not" questions: common, everyday reading experiences; past reading experiences; creative thinking/absurd; poetry reading life; nonfiction reading/books; and rating. Try an assortment of questions to keep things moving and interesting.

Before starting Book 4/Round 4, experiment with APQs: Answer them yourself to find out the do-able and inspirational questions, as well as to get an understanding of where this writer is coming from with a creative and progressive approach. APQs are indicated by number before each category.

Book 4's categories, in order from most to least frequently asked questions in each are:

- Reading Experiences: Common (Everyday), Past (Early), and Hypothetical
- Writing, Drawing, and Creative Thinking
- One-Line Statements and Opinions
- Reading Process
- Words and Word Activities
- Ratings and Quotations
- Reading Reflections: Book Recalls, Nonfiction, and Poetry

BOOK 4 QUESTIONS

Reading Experiences: Common (Everyday), Past (Early), and Hypothetical

(APQs in this category are numbers: 16, 24, 25, 26, 38, 44, 51, 53, 54, 55, 56, 57, 58, 64, 65, 67, 69, 75, 76, 79, 80, and 86.)

1. Did you think reading was fun when you first learned how to read? Do you think reading is fun now? Explain your answers.
2. What does the phrase "story time" bring to mind?
3. Did you ever think reading was easy? Why or why not?
4. What do you think of reading tests? Why?
5. Is reading every day stressful to you? Why or why not?
6. Do you think that giving away free pumpkins to five-year-olds is a good way to encourage them to go to the library and read? Why or why not?
7. Can an older child help a younger child in reading? Would it work? Is it possible for the tutor to improve his or her reading while helping someone else to read? Explain your answers.
8. Have you ever shared a sad day with your friend—a book? Describe what happened using an example from your reading life. (*Hint*: If you have no real-life experience with this situation, imagine and visualize what it would be like.)

9. Can reading become a substitute for living? Explain.
10. Can your feelings interfere with reading? Explain your answer by giving an example.
11. Imagine that: Saved by the book. Has it happened to you? Explain.
12. When does reading totally absorb you? Describe what happens.
13. When does reading totally turn you off? Describe what happens.
14. How are readers like thrill-seekers? Give an example.
15. Did your mind ever *explode* or *erupt* when reading? Describe what happened.
16. In what ways is reading about silence?
17. What unexpected insights have you discovered through reading? Give one example.
18. Some great ideas I got from reading and books are _____.
19. Why should you read the best books you can find first?
20. What is your biggest hassle in reading right now? Why? Give a possible solution.
21. Is reading all about *you*? Why or why not?
22. Think about this: What possibilities lie ahead of you when you begin reading a new book? Give two or more examples and explain why each is a possibility.
23. Think about this: From this moment on you cannot read anything for the rest of your life. Describe what came to mind immediately. Then, write what else you thought.
24. In what way is reading an "entrance"? (*Hint*: Look up "entrance" in a thesaurus or dictionary for synonyms and definitions before answering.)
25. In what way is reading a "passage"? (*Hint*: Look up "passage" in a thesaurus or dictionary for synonyms and definitions before answering.)
26. "You can communicate with a book? You gotta be kiddin' me! It's only a book; I can't hear it because it don't talk." What doesn't this person understand about books and reading? How would you explain "communicating with a book"? What would you say?
27. Is there a connection between reading and open-mindedness? Explain.
28. Have reading and books opened up your mind? Why or why not? If your mind has been opened, what has it been opened up to?
29. What does it mean to "read between the lines"? How does this ability affect your reading and reading life? Give an example of it from your reading life.
30. Think about this: The silent communicator—a book. What comes to mind when you reflect on this statement?
31. Did your mind (or brain) ever crash like a computer when reading? Describe what happened. Did it come back to life? Did you resume reading? Why or why not? If you did not, imagine how you might revive yourself in this situation and continue reading.

32. How important is self-discipline in your reading and reading life? Why?

33. Have you ever had a reading experience of the strangest kind? Recall, visualize, and write about what happened. Draw a mind-picture you remember.

34. What was the most incomprehensible book, story, myth, tale, essay, or poem you read? What made it so hard? Did you try rereading it? Did you understand it the second time around? Explain your answers.

35. Reading expands your world, but in what way(s) can it shrink your world? Explain.

36. Do you have to pump yourself up to read? Why or why not?

37. How do you pump yourself up to read?

38. Think about this: Mary was confused about reading; some days she liked it, and other days she disliked it. How would you, as the reading guidance counselor, help Mary to end her confusion and make a decision about reading? What would be your rap to her? Why?

39. Imagine that: A friend of mine said he loved to read the dictionary for fun. Why would you want to do that—even if it's for fun? Was I missing something about dictionaries that my friend knew? How can you explain this fascination with reading the dictionary for fun?

40. Where are your feelings when you read?

41. Try this experiment: Find a paragraph you like from a book you're reading. Read it three times. Has anything changed after rereading it? Explain your answer.

42. Do you ever feel that you are constantly talking to a book while you are reading it? Explain your answer.

43. Recall a time when you were reading and listening to music at the same time. Describe this reading solitude.

44. Have you ever felt like you were traveling in the dark while reading a novel? Give an example. Did you eventually end up in the light? Describe what happened.

45. What does it mean to "skim" a book you're reading? How do you understand what you read if you "skim"? Can skimming help your reading? When should you use this technique? (*Hint*: Look up "skim" in a dictionary for definitions before answering.)

46. Why should you question the things you read?

47. She started to read a novel and just took off on the first flight in her imagination. *Where* did she go? Why? (*Hint*: Imagine, yeah, imagine . . .)

48. Which medium gets you more inside a character's mind: books or movies? Explain.

49. Imagine that: What is "book abuse"? Visualize and describe it.

50. How can a book become a reality check for your own life? Give an example.

51. Can a book make you feel vulnerable? Why or why not? If it has, explain how this feeling or thought was triggered? (*Hints*: If it hasn't, try to imagine how a book or reading can do this. Look up "vulnerable" in a dictionary or thesaurus for definitions and synonyms before answering.)

52. Fear, reading, and books: are there connections between them? Explain.

53. How does reading connect with rising, soaring, or climbing?

54. Is there any connection between reading and rebelling? Explain.

55. Try this experiment: Read aloud a page from a novel (or any piece of fiction) to yourself and then read it to another person (parent, friend, sibling). Write about both oral reading experiences. How are they the same and different?

56. Think about it: One day, while looking into a mirror, you see yourself as the author of an autobiography you're reading. You feel good because you think you know who you are. Everything about you and your life comes together in the mirror's reflection. The world makes sense now. . . .

    • What does this suggest about reading and self-knowledge or knowing yourself?
    • How could this experience affect your everyday life?
    • Would it help or hurt? Why?

57. Can reading and books inspire you to search for and find out more about yourself? Why? If you have experienced this in your reading life, give an example. If you have not, imagine, and then describe, how reading and books would motivate you to find out about and know yourself.

58. Why does your reading and reading life constantly change?

59. Describe the ways reading and books connect you to everyday life.

60. Imagine that: I read to escape from and forget about myself. What does the statement mean? Is it true for you at times? Why or why not?

61. Think about this: If you were given a year off from school with the condition that you read two hours every day, what would you read and why? Brainstorm a list of books or whatever reading you might do. What would be your daily reading schedule? Could you read two hours a day in everyday life? Why or why not?

62. What is your secret to living a good reading life? How does it work for you? Would it work for others? Why or why not?

63. What steps would you take to change your present reading life? List three steps.

64. How are reading and books a test or trial of your world or reality?

65. Imagine that: Joseph loved history books. He enjoyed going back in time: time-traveling to wherever he wanted to go, from five hundred years to five years ago. His journeys into the past and discoveries of other worlds made him feel like a thousand years old. How could this be if he was only

thirteen? What has Joseph realized about the magic of reading history books? Can you appreciate history the same way he does? Explain your answers.

66. Do you read historical novels? Why or why not? How would you describe your "history reading life" both in and out of school?

67. Can you make yourself over or reinvent yourself through reading and books? How could such a change happen? Would it be easy or hard to do? Why?

68. Describe a private, solitary, extraordinary world you discovered through reading and books.

69. Why is a novel a small miracle or wonder?

70. Books trigger night dreams. Has it happened to you? If so, was the dream about things in the book? Or, was the dream about your life? What happened in the dream? Do you think it was telling or saying something to you? Explain your answers.

71. Think about this: Do you usually reflect for a few seconds before responding to a question from the mini-lessons? Why or why not? How can reflecting impact your reading life?

72. A motivated reader is_____

73. An unmotivated reader is _____

74. How would you create world literacy? Why is it so important for our survival?

75. Can reading and books shut down your world? Explain your answer.

76. Do you lose time or gain time when you read? Explain your answer.

77. In school there are standards you have to achieve to pass reading. But what are your reading standards? What do you want from reading to make it successful and fun in your life? Brainstorm a list of five personal standards you would like to achieve in reading.

78. With a little daily reading, you _____

79. How can reading and books create tolerance, acceptance, and respect for other people?

80. Can solitude, silence, thinking, reflecting, concentrating, imagining, and feeling make reading fun, pleasurable, and entertaining; or do they just make it into heavy-duty work? Explain your answer.

81. Is reading real life or is it something else? Explain your answer.

82. Have you ever met someone who claimed that a book changed her or his life? What did the person say about the experience and the changes that happened? What did you think? Did you believe what was said? Why or why not?

83. If a friend, teacher, parent, sister, or brother offered you a book and said "it could change your life," would you read it? Why or why not? Has this ever happened to you? Give an example—if you have one to share.

84. Reflect on and then think about your reading and reading life for two minutes. What do you see, visualize, think, feel, experience, and remember?

Do you see changes coming to your reading and reading life? Can you predict what might happen? Explain your answers.

85. Once you can taste and digest the knowledge, insight, understanding, and pleasure coming from reading and books, you become a reader. What does the statement suggest? Can you call yourself a reader in this sense? Is this your future reading life? Is it your present reading life? Explain your answers.

86. When is a reader born?

Writing, Drawing, and Creative Thinking

Note: Most questions in this category are considered APQs because of the multiple skills needed to respond to them such as creative and critical thinking. Also, their crossover nature, that is, combining several question categories, makes these more difficult.

87. Visualize and then draw a dream image of a mother reading with her child. What thoughts and feelings does your drawing trigger?

88. I read to escape from the real world. Imagine a dreamlike, surreal, absurd, or fantasy image for the statement. Picture-storm images and pencil-sketch one you like.

89. Draw or sketch an abstract picture (lines, shapes, forms, colors, designs with no people, objects, or places) of a class silently reading. Explain what you're trying to show in your abstract work. (*Optional*: Create an abstract drawing of you reading silently to yourself.)

90. Picture this: Build your ideal reading room in your imagination. What would go inside? Describe details. Sketch a picture of the room. How would your reading room—or environment—affect your reading?

91. Draw an abstract picture—lines, shapes, forms, colors, designs—of you struggling with your concentration while reading. Look at your finished drawing and record your thoughts and feelings.

92. Try this experiment: Read one page from a book (fiction or nonfiction) and let your mind wander after you finish the page. Take a little side trip for thirty seconds. Where did your mind wander? Describe the trip in twenty-five words.

93. List three of the shortest words you know—two to four letters long—that are really big or important to you. Pick one and show how a short word grows large in your world. Use twenty-five words for your explanation.

94. Search for a word (noun, adjective, verb) that triggers many mind-pictures.

- Scan the different images with your inner eye.
- Draw quick pencil-sketches of them.
- Look closely at and then reflect on your sketches.
- Describe their power in fifty words.

95. "Thought words":

   • List five words—read, spoken, written, or imagined—that trigger instant thoughts.
   • Pick one word from the list and reflect on it.
   • Write what comes to mind in twenty-five words.
   • Why does the word create an instant thought?

96. All-star: Visualize and draw or pencil-sketch one mind-picture you see.

97. Try this for fun: Whisper your favorite word and then let your mind go for thirty seconds. Write about the experience in twenty-five words or more.

98. Reading books starts "power surges" inside you, the reader. What does the statement mean and suggest? Draw a cartoon of it by picture-storming and visualizing the images. (*Hint*: Look up "surge" in a dictionary or thesaurus for definitions and synonyms before answering.)

99. Try this experiment: Artists paint pictures with oils, pastels, and watercolors. Writers paint pictures with words. Find a paragraph in a book you're reading where the writer paints a picture with words. Describe the "word-painting" you see with your inner eye in twenty-five words or more. Use fiction or nonfiction for the experiment.

100. Imaginary word-encounter #1: Imagine what would happen if mirrors met sun. What do you see with the mind's eye? Picture-storm images and pencil-sketch one.

101. Imaginary word-encounter #2: Imagine what would happen if candles met cave. What do you see with your mind's eye? Picture-storm images and pencil-sketch one.

102. Imaginary word-encounter #3: Imagine what would happen if sleepwalkers met shadows. What do you see with the mind's eye? Picture-storm images and pencil-sketch one.

103. Imaginary word-encounter #4: Imagine what would happen if kindergarteners met daisies. What do you see with the mind's eye? Picture-storm images and pencil-sketch one.

104. Imaginary word-encounter #5: Imagine what would happen if clouds met smoke. What do you see with the mind's eye? Picture-storm images and pencil-sketch one.

105. Imaginary word-encounter #6: Imagine what would happen if freedom met fireworks. What do you see with the mind's eye? Picture-storm images and pencil-sketch one.

106. Imaginary word-encounter #7: Imagine what would happen if ice met trees. What do you see with the mind's eye? Picture-storm images and pencil-sketch one.

107. Imaginary word-encounter #8: Imagine what would happen if bubbles met bubbles. What do you see with the mind's eye? Picture-storm images and pencil-sketch one.

108. Imaginary word-encounter #9: Imagine what would happen if tornado met buildings. What do you see with the mind's eye? Picture-storm images and pencil-sketch one.

109. Imaginary word-encounter #10: Imagine what would happen if rainbows met fantasies. What do you see with the mind's eye? Picture-storm images and pencil-sketch one.

110. Ponder and reflect on the word "friend" for sixty seconds. Roll it around in your mind. Let whatever happens happen without trying to control it. Write about your experience in fifty words (or more).

111. A book you're reading fires you up. Draw an abstract picture—lines, shapes, forms, colors, and designs only—of this experience. What does a "fired-up mind" look like as an abstract drawing? Explain.

112. Picture this: Reading and drifting. What do you see or visualize? Fill in the details of your mind-picture. Draw the image: What thoughts and feelings does it trigger? (*Hint*: Draw a cartoon to illustrate your image.)

113. Visualize and then describe mind-pictures from an imaginary poem titled "Blue Fog." Picture-storm or create images in your mind connected to the poem's title. What feelings and thoughts are triggered by each of your images?

114. Contemplate the phrase "alone in a book" for sixty seconds. What does your contemplation conjure up? Write a twenty-five- to fifty-word description.

115. Visualize an imaginary "book zoo." Draw a cartoon picture of it and add a caption. What books might be in the cages for people to see? (*Hint*: Brainstorm different books, book titles, or ideas and then picture-storm images.)

116. Visualize an imaginary "word jail." Draw a cartoon picture of it and add a caption. What words might be locked up? (*Hint*: Word-storm words; brainstorm ideas; and/or picture-storm images before answering.)

117. Free, loose, open, independent, liberated, freedom, released, clear, freed: Where do these words take you? What "places"? Describe the journey in twenty-five to fifty words.

118. The perfect imaginary reading buddy makes reading fun no matter the circumstances. Visualize this imaginary being: Write about your fictional friendship in one hundred words and how it makes your reading life into a wonderful life. (*Hint*: Picture-storm images and brainstorm ideas to start your story.)

119. WORDS: breakfast of reading champs. Picture-storm cartoon images for the statement. Visualize and sketch your favorite one. Explain the statement's meaning.

120. Reading: one of the longest trips you'll ever take in your life. Explain the statement's meaning and what it suggests. Draw a poster for it. Use the

statement as the poster's caption. (*Hint*: Picture-storm images; brainstorm ideas; and/or word-storm words before drawing. Think fantastically.)

121. Get into it: Imagine losing yourself so deeply in a novel or short story that you become a character and live his/her exact fictional life. Describe trading places, temporarily, with a book character in twenty-five to fifty words. Use an example from your reading life.

122. Visualize an imaginary cloud made for readers. What do you see with your mind's eye? Draw the picture you imagine. (*Hint*: Picture-storm images and pick one to draw. Think absurd, silly, and ridiculous for your illustration and have fun with it.)

123. Picture this: The teacher had a secret fantasy of a class full of happy, satisfied, and delighted readers. Create the teacher's fantasy by picture-storming images, brainstorming ideas, and word-storming words. Be the teacher and write about her ideal classroom of contented readers in one hundred words. Illustrate one scene or mind-picture you envision. (*Hint*: Think of a reading fantasyland in your classroom.)

124. "A picture is worth a thousand words." Recall a picture, painting, drawing, or photograph seen that is "worth a thousand words." Describe the artwork. Then brainstorm ideas, thoughts, images, feelings, memories, reflections, and dreams it triggers in twenty-five to fifty words. (*Optional*: Draw a quick pencil-sketch of the picture, drawing, painting, or photograph.)

125. Visualize an imaginary "word garden." Draw an image of it. (*Hint*: Picture-storm images and/or brainstorm ideas before drawing. Think surreal, dreamlike, fantasy, and illustrate your "garden.")

126. Start with the word "win" and take it for a ride in your mind; take it as far as you can. Keep moving through images, feelings, ideas, experiences, words, and memories until you can't go any further. Once you've stopped, look around. In a short story of fifty words or more, describe your journey to the last stop for "win." Where are you at the end of your ride? (*Hints*: Look up "win" in a thesaurus or dictionary for synonyms and definitions before answering. Brainstorm ideas; word-storm words; and/or picture-storm images for "win.")

127. Relaxation time: Put your head down and close your eyes for five minutes. When you finish, write about your experience. Describe whatever came to mind in fifty words or more. Do your words—or description—give an accurate account of what happened while your eyes were closed? Why or why not?

128. Think about this: Reading opens the "doors of perception" to thought, knowledge, judgment, sensation, observation, awareness, attitude, and even common sense. What are these "doors of perception"? Write a fifty-word essay explaining the statement's meaning. (*Hint*: Look up "perception" in a thesaurus and dictionary for synonyms and definitions before answering.)

129. Venus liked to read cookbooks and look at the photographs of food before bedtime so she could have tasty, delicious, yummy dreams. Imagine one dream she had: What do you see or visualize? Describe the dream in fifty words. List the words and photographs that might have triggered this chef's scrumptious dreams.

130. Imagine yourself as a lifelong reader. What do you envision, foresee, and anticipate? Write about your future reading life.

131. There are "select" or "choice" words that come from your parents that affect you in a big way—and you know what they are.

   • List three words you can depend on hearing from them.
   • Pick one and reflect on it for thirty seconds.
   • Write a comedy/play about the "word" in one hundred words.
   • Discuss and really get into the word with your parents in your little comedy.
   • Use the "word" as the main idea of, and prompt for, your play.

   Hint: Make it absurd, ridiculous—just have fun with your play. Use word-storming, brainstorming, and/or picture-storming to get your play going.

132. Visualize a daydreamer's dictionary of imaginary words that would take you out of school, take you out for a walk or stroll in your imagination, where everything comes up real nice.

   • Create a list of three words you might find in the "daydreamer's dictionary."
   • Choose one word as your story or daydream starter.
   • Expand the word by brainstorming, picture-storming, and word-storming.
   • Write a daydream of one hundred words or more that will take you on a fun flight.
   • Read your finished daydream silently and orally to yourself.
   • Does your daydream transport you into another or alternative world? Explain.

   Hints: Read and visualize your "story." Do your mind-pictures work? Are they pleasing, satisfying, and relaxing? Use an *imaginary* noun, verb, adjective, or *any* word that works as your story-daydream starter.

133. What word is a good "story starter"?

   • Create a list of five possible words to start a short story.
   • The words can be nouns, adverbs, adjectives, verbs, propositions, or pronouns.
   • Reflect on each one until you find a "story starter": the first word of your story.

- Let the word take you to the end of your short story of fifty words or more.
- Let the word go wherever it wants to go and see what happens.
- Use storming techniques to help trigger your story.

134. Think of words that make you mad or angry.

- List five to ten angry words and pick three for a story.
- Put the "angry words" into an imaginary room in your mind.
- Visualize them hanging out together: What world do the words create?
- Use your imaginary room to write a one-hundred-word story about these words.
- Title your piece "Three Angry Words," or create your own title.
- The story can be a fairy tale, fable, myth, tall tale, or fantasy.
- Draw or pencil-sketch one or more illustrations from your story.
- Did your story make you angry? Why or why not?

135. Picture this: You're lost in the woods in a bad dream.

- What words run through your mind?
- List five to ten words and think about or reflect on each one.
- Pick one that rocks you and write a story from and about it.
- Your "story-word" should be connected to the dream you had.
- Write a one-hundred-word short story describing what happened in the dream.
- Use word-storming, brainstorming, and picture-storming to jumpstart the story.
- *Optional*: Draw quick pencil-sketches of "scenes-from-a-dream."

136. There's always something about the word "hero":

- Contemplate the word for sixty seconds.
- What do you see, feel, think, and experience?
- Pick one image to start a story about hero.
- Write a one-hundred-word absurd story about hero.
- Read the finished story silently to yourself.
- What is a hero according to your story?
- Did anything about the word, story, or your writing surprise you? Explain.

137. There's always something about the word "zero":

- Contemplate the word for sixty seconds.
- How many ways are you connected to zero?
- Pick one connection to start a story about zero.
- Write a one-hundred-word absurd story about zero.
- Read your finished work silently to yourself.

- What happens to zero in your story? How is it defined? What is it?
- Were you amazed or surprised by anything in the story? Why or why not?

Hints: If you have trouble with your contemplation, try word-storming zero for connected and unconnected words. You can also visualize or picture-storm silly scenes with zero. Or, you can jumpstart your story with a pencil-sketched visualized image.

138. Imaginary tales: They say that words are already inside you when you are born. These special words reveal your life and destiny. Picture this happening to you. Can you think of any words that might have been planted in you at birth? What word or words?

- Search for a possible word you might have been born with.
- Contemplate it for sixty seconds. What comes to mind?
- Why this word? How does it affect you—your life? Why?
- Write a one-hundred-word story titled "My Birth-Word of Destiny."
- Use storming techniques to jumpstart your story.

Hint: Write a fable, myth, tall tale, or dream about your birth word.

139. Try out this experiment: Draw an abstract design for the word "confidence." Visualize the word using shapes, lines, forms, colors, and designs. Pencil-sketch your drawing. Does the word connect with your abstract drawing? Explain. (*Hint*: If you have trouble with your abstract, word-storm confidence to find connected words and then continue drawing.)

140. Try out this experiment: Draw an abstract design for the word "impatient." Visualize the word using shapes, lines, forms, colors, and designs. Pencil-sketch your drawing. Does the word connect with your abstract drawing? Explain. (*Hint*: If you have trouble with your abstract, word-storm impatient to find connected words and then continue drawing.)

141. Story time: One day Sweet Baby Jane discovered a new giant word. As she crawled around on the carpet in the living room, this colossal word, made out of six-foot block letters, stood in front of her like the Empire State Building. She glanced at it for a second, then stared at it until she hypnotized herself with the mighty word.

- What was the giant word Baby Jane encountered? Draw a picture of it.
- Pretend you are Jane: How does the word affect you? What do you experience?
- What baby thoughts and feelings come to mind?
- How will you handle the gigantic word? What will you do?
- Write a one-hundred-word fairy tale titled "Baby Jane and the Jumbo Word."

Hint: Use the questions as guides for writing the story.

142. Fantasy story time: Matilda tried to climb out of a giant bowl of spaghetti, but it wasn't really spaghetti at all, just mounds of words. Piles and piles rose to the top of the bowl. She desperately tried to get out alive, that is, without being sucked up by all the words, meanings, ideas, thoughts, feelings, and pictures that might be triggered by them in her mind. When Matilda looked out in front of her, she _____.

Finish the rest of her journey in a short story of one hundred words or more using the guide questions below to jumpstart your writing:

- What did Matilda see, think, feel, experience, and understand?
- How would she get out? Could Matilda use the words for escaping?
- Would the mounds of words prevent her escape?
- What words did she see in these giant mounds that filled up the bowl?
- Did a word take her on a side trip in her mind? What word(s)? Where did she go?
- What were the consequences of her spaghetti-word journey?
- Did she make it out alive and well—or what happened to her?

Hint: The questions are guides: you don't have to answer each one for your story.

143. Write a funny tale about bunnies for kindergarten children (age five):

- Word-storm ten words or more for bunnies.
- Brainstorm ideas and picture-storm images from the words.
- Use the stormed words, images, and ideas to help write and illustrate your tale.
- Write a short caption (one sentence long) for each illustration.
- Read your story silently and orally while checking out your drawings.
- Critique your story: What are the pluses and minuses? Give reasons.
- Describe the entire writing experience from beginning to end in twenty-five to fifty words.

Hint: For illustrations use markers, crayons, paints, pastels, or colored pencils.

Optional: Read your story to a kindergarten class to see how they respond. Did your tale make them laugh? Ask them what they liked about it.

144. Imagine that: Poor Carlos, he ran into some words that done him wrong. He couldn't believe it, but it was almost as if the words followed him into a dark alley and cornered him, leaving the boy with no exit, no place to run, no place to hide. As he stood with his back against the wall, he held up his hands and said, "No mas! No mas!" ("No more! No more!") to stop those words from invading his life. But it didn't matter, they still got to him, and suddenly Carlos . . . _____.

Fill in the one-hundred-word conclusion to Carlos's story using the guide questions below:

- What words got inside him?
- What happened to Carlos after the words became part of him?
- Did anything change in his life?
- How did he deal with himself, the world, and those words now?
- What was going through his mind?
- How powerful were the words?

Hints: Use the questions as guides; you don't have to answer each one. Use word-storming, brainstorming, and picture-storming to jumpstart the story.

Optional: Draw cartoon sketches of your conclusion to Carlos's fate.

145. Visualize this imaginary event: The Great War of Words.

- Visualize words in a battlefield fighting against each other.
- What words are in this war? What mind-pictures do you see?
- What is going on in these imaginary struggles and battles between words?
- How did the war start? When, where, and how will it end? Will it end?
- What are the consequences of "The Great War of Words" on the world?
- Search for answers by word-storming, picture-storming, and brain-storming.
- Write a one-hundred-word fable, fairy tale, fantasy, myth, or tall tale titled "The Great War of Words."

Hints: Before writing, visualize different images and scenes from this fantastic war. Use the questions as guides; you don't have to answer each question.

Optional: Draw quick pencil-sketches of word-battles in the great war.

146. Imagine: Mrs. Words:

- Who is she? What does she do? What does she look like?
- What are her connections to words? What do words mean to her?
- What words does she use? How does she use them?
- How do they affect her life and other people's lives around her?
- Where do the words take her? What places? What worlds?
- Visualize Mrs. Words and contemplate this imaginary word-being's life.
- Write a fable, fairy tale, fantasy, myth, or tall tale of one hundred words on her life.
- Draw a picture of her and add a caption.

Hints: Use the questions as guides; you don't have to answer each one. Use storming techniques to get your story started.

147. Try this experiment: Draw an abstract design for the word "effort." Visualize the word in your mind using shapes, lines, forms, colors, and designs. Sketch your abstract drawing which represents effort. Does the

word connect with your abstract sketch? Explain. (*Hint*: Your finished work defines effort without using people, places, and things—anything recognizable.)

148. Try out this artistic word experiment:

   • Visualize the words "orange," "yellow," and "green."
   • Use each word to paint mind-pictures of different-sized rectangles.
   • Place the three colored rectangles one on top of the other.
   • Contemplate the mind-picture you created for two minutes.
   • Describe what happened during the contemplation in fifty words or more.
   • Any surprises from the visualized and contemplated imaged? Explain.

149. Make up three original questions on reading and reading life based on your reading experiences. Brainstorm ideas to create the questions. Answer the questions afterward.

   • Question #1: _____
   • Answer #1: _____
   • Question #2: _____
   • Answer #2: _____
   • Question #3: _____
   • Answer #3: _____

One-Line Statements and Opinions

(APQs in this category are numbers: 150, 159, 164, 166, 170, 172, 173, 175, 176, 178, 179, 180, 183, 188, 191, 193, 196, 197, 198, 199, 200, and 202.)

150. Let your feelings breathe—read. Explain the statement's meaning. Does it have meaning for you? Why?

151. Reading and books keep away negative thoughts. What do you think? Agree? Disagree? Explain.

152. Imagine that: Only you can put fun into your reading and reading life. Agree? Disagree? Explain.

153. Think about this: Reading means freedom. Explain the statement's meaning. Give an example from your reading life.

154. Expect to exert yourself when you read and in your reading life. Why?

155. Read a book like you stole it. Explain.

156. Read though your heart is aching. Explain.

157. Reading books clears you right up. Explain.

158. A day without reading is a day without a good movie. Explain.

159. A book is a confidant who listens to your life stories—for better or worse. Agree? Disagree? Why? (*Hint*: Look up "confidant" in a dictionary or thesaurus for definitions and synonyms before answering.)

160. Reading can never hurt you. Agree? Disagree? Why?
161. Reading is about attitude. What do you think? Explain. (*Hint*: Look up "attitude" in a dictionary before answering.)
162. Mind-pictures: reading's little miracles. Explain.
163. Warning: Don't buckle up—reading lifts you higher. Explain.
164. "Ladies and gentlemen, your attention please: Watch this book disappear through the magic of reading right before your very eyes." What does the statement mean or suggest? Explain.
165. Imagine that: Wherever you read, there you are. Explain the statement's meaning.
166. Warning: Reading can make you feel "big" and reading can make you feel "small." Explain the statement's meaning or what it suggests about reading. What do you think: agree or disagree? Why?
167. Exercise your brain with words, words, words—and then more words, words, words. Explain.
168. Certain books you read never grow old. Explain. Give an example from your reading life.
169. Do you consider reading your responsibility? Why or why not? If you believe reading is, describe your responsibility.
170. I read, therefore I am aware. Explain. Agree? Disagree? Why?
171. I read, therefore I feel. Do you agree? Why or why not?
172. Reading seizes the moment. Explain.
173. Reading is living in the moment. Explain.
174. Imagine that: You're reading, you're free. . . . Explain.
175. Reading is also contemplation. Explain. What do you think? (*Hint*: Look up "contemplation" in a thesaurus or dictionary for synonyms and definitions before answering.)
176. Books give . . . and take. . . . Explain.
177. Is it better to give than receive when you read? Why or why not?
178. Meet the Thesauruses: There's Mr. Thesaurus, Mrs. Thesaurus, and all the little Thesauruses—a nice family of words with all their synonyms and antonyms, just words, words, words. What is the statement trying to communicate about the thesaurus? What is it suggesting? Why?
179. A book is "alive" when you read it. Explain what the statement suggests. Do you agree? Is this possible or not? Explain your answer.
180. Analyze this: Novels exaggerate the real world. What do you think: agree or disagree? Why? (*Hint*: Look up "exaggerate" in a dictionary or thesaurus for definitions and synonyms before answering.)
181. Think about it: Know why you read what you read. Is this idea important for you, the reader, to understand? Explain.
182. Words heal; words hurt. Explain.
183. Imagine that: Your secrets are safe in a book. Explain the statement's meaning.

184. The life in a book comes from the life in you. "Translate" the statement into your own words. Explain its meaning. What do you think about it: agree or disagree? Why?
185. Explain the statement's meaning: A moment in the mind's eye, forever in your reading life and real life. Find an example from your reading and describe it.
186. Read to live, but don't live to read. What does the statement suggest about reading and its possible consequences? What do you think: agree or disagree? Why?
187. Reinvent your reading life: experiment. Explain.
188. Imagine that: Books and reading help those readers who help themselves. Explain the statement's meaning. Is it true for you? Why or why not?
189. Each child finds his or her own way in reading and reading life. Explain.
190. Think about it: Reading is all about feeling. Agree? Disagree? Why?
191. Words grow the young child. "Translate" the statement into your own words. What does it mean and suggest? How did words affect you when you were very young?
192. Big picture books are mothers and fathers to very young children. What does the statement mean and suggest? How powerful were picture books when you were growing up? Why? Explain your answer.
193. Reading rechargers: mind and imagination. Explain.
194. Reading means unlimited thinking and thoughtfulness. Explain the statement's meaning. What do you think: agree or disagree? Why?
195. Reading and books help you understand a constantly changing world. Explain.
196. Books do furnish a mind. Explain the statement's meaning and consequences.
197. Lifelong reading means you never stop searching. Explain the statement's meaning or what suggests. What would you be searching for? Why?
198. The more you read, the more you see,
     The more you read, the more you feel,
     The more you read, the more you think,
     The more you read, the more you discover,
     The more you read, the more you understand.

     What does the statement mean or suggest? Do you agree or disagree with it? Why?
199. A book in the hand is worth two on the shelf. What does it mean or suggest? What do you think about it? Why?
200. Besides thinking skills, readers also need listening skills. Explain.
201. Reading and books can make everyday life seem too serious. Explain. Do you agree? Why or why not?

202. Get into this: Reading and books help you express the unexpressed, silent worlds that exist inside you. What does the statement mean? Is it true in your reading life? Would it be important in other readers' lives? Explain your answers.

203. Reading: Tune in and drop in, in, in. . . . What is a key to reading according to the statement? Do you agree? Why or why not?

204. Be true, faithful, and loyal to your reading life and it will be true, faithful, and loyal to you. What does the statement mean and suggest? Do you agree? Why or why not? (*Hint*: How are you "true, faithful, and loyal" to your reading life?)

205. A good reading life is simple: read. Explain. Do you agree? Why or why not?

206. Do you think kids don't read enough or have trouble reading because they:

   a. were not shown how
   b. just don't care
   c. would rather play video games or use the Internet
   d. want to watch TV and listen to music
   e. have problems
   f. all of the above

   Pick one or more answers and give a reason for each one.

207. Think about this: Your reading life is one never-ending ride through the mind and imagination. Explain the statement's meaning. What do you think? Why?

208. Reading and books show you there are always newer worlds to discover. Explain. Is this true for you? Do you believe it? Why or why not?

209. To read or not to read—that is the question. And what is your answer, please? Why?

Reading Process

(APQs in this category are numbers: 213, 215, 216, 217, 218, 219, 221, 223, 224, 230, 232, 233, 234, 235, 245, 246, 247, 248, 250, 251, 253, 254, 256, 257, 258, and 259.)

210. Do you ever feel that many things are coming at you at the same time when you read? Explain your answer by giving an example from your reading life.

211. Describe your "thinking life" when you read. Give an example.

212. What conversations go on inside your head when you read? Who is talking? What is being said? Is it connected to your reading or something else? Explain.

213. What are you listening to when you read? Who or what does the listening? Describe this "silent communication" that goes on during reading. Why is it important to the reading process? Explain.

214. Beauty is in the mind's eye of the reader. What does the statement mean? Is it true for you? If it is, explain by giving an example from your reading life.

215. Imagine that: Reading "televises" your mind to you. Explain.

216. Caution: Readers read read read in the zoom zoom zoom fast-image lane . . . zip zip zip. . . . What does the statement mean? What does it suggest about readers and the reading process? Explain your answers.

217. Reading is a "window" to your heart (feelings). What does the statement mean? What is meant by "window"? Reflect on the statement. Give an example of it from your reading life.

218. Reading lets you leave your world and enter an author's world to view his/her idea of reality. Give an example of getting into a writer's world, one foreign to you and the way you see things. Describe this "new world." Compare it to yours: similarities and differences.

219. Read, breathe, read, breathe, read, breathe, read, breathe. . . . Why is the statement connecting reading to breathing? Is there any connection? Explain your answer.

220. How can your reading world become like the "twilight zone" or an absurd, strange world? How does this happen? Give an example.

221. What is the connection between tension and alertness in reading?

222. Slowing down, decelerating, delaying—and relaxing—can help make Johnny a better reader. What does the statement mean and suggest? What do you think about it? Explain by giving an example from your reading life.

223. How fast do you travel through your imagination when reading? Are you moving at fast or slow speeds while you read and imagine? Give examples.

224. How is your mind like a "vacuum cleaner" when you read?

225. How intense can your reading get? Give an example.

226. How is a novel like a movie?

227. Think about it: Is reading a separate reality apart from the real world? Explain.

228. Analyze this: What is exchanged between readers and writers of books? (*Hint*: Look up "exchange" in a thesaurus for synonyms before answering.)

229. The last movie show performed in my mind's magic reading theater was . . .

230. Analyze this: You are both an observer and a participant when you read fiction (novels, short stories, fables, and fairy tales). Explain what the

statement means. How can you play two roles at the same time while reading without getting messed up?

231. Do you feel, at times, like you're in a "bubble" when you read? Explain.
232. Why is reading a novel like acting in a play? (*Optional*: Describe a "performance" from a novel you read.)
233. Analyze this: A reader's solitude gets hectic when critical thinking, creative thinking, and personal thoughts meet each other in the mind.

   - What does the statement suggest?
   - What does it say about reading, solitude, and thinking?
   - How can you read with so much thinking going on?
   - How do you keep your concentration and stay focused on reading?

234. Reflection time: Do you have to be a good listener to be a good reader? Why?
235. Why is observation important in your reading and reading life? Give an example. (*Hint*: Look up "observation" in a dictionary or thesaurus for definition and synonyms before answering.)
236. Do you ever feel like you're in a trance when you read? Explain your answer. (*Hint*: Look up "trance" in a dictionary or thesaurus for definitions and synonyms before answering.)
237. What is the connection between reading and personal thoughts? Do they ever interrupt each other? Are they friends or foes? Explain your answers.
238. Imagine that: Reading invades your private space—your self—and takes over completely. How can that happen?
239. Think about it: Can you forget about yourself when reading? Why or why not? If you can and do forget about your self, how does that affect your reading? Explain.
240. Thinking makes reading sane, clear, true, real, and "whole." Can thinking do all these things for reading? Why or why not?
241. Do you like reading that slows down your pace and makes you think a lot? Why or why not? Give an example from your reading life.
242. What kinds of questions come to mind after you finish a novel? Give examples of questions triggered by a novel you read. Why do novels trigger questions?
243. Can you leave yourself behind and become a character in a novel you're reading? Why or why not? If you can, what is your method? Does it help your reading? Explain your answers.
244. How is reading books like playing sports?
245. Analyze this: Reading books is outside inside outside inside outside inside outside. . . . Explain the statement's meaning. What is it saying about reading books and the reading process? Which part is more important: the "outside" or "inside"? Why?

246. Reading = self-expression. Explain.
247. Picture this: A book is an imaginary skyscraper built up, up, up, up, up, up, up in a reader's mind. "Translate" the statement into your own words and explain its meaning. What would you expect to find on the different floors of the building? What helps build it straight up in the reader's mind? (*Hint*: Visualize this scene by picture-storming images and/or brainstorming ideas.)
248. What makes a book (fiction or nonfiction) seem more real than reality itself? How does that happen? Has it happened to you? Explain your answers. Give an example from your reading life.
249. Can a poem seem more real than the reality it portrays? Why? Give an example.
250. How does a novel "live" inside you?
251. How does a poem "live" inside you?
252. How do words "live" inside you?
253. How can you make reading into a slow-motion movie in your mind? What would you do while you read? How would this affect your reading and reading life? Explain your answers.
254. Can reading and reading life ever become an MTV world? Why or why not?
255. What is the connection between reading and analyzing things?
256. Reading magnifies both your inside and outside worlds. Explain the statement's meaning. How does reading "magnify things"? Is it true for you? Why or why not? (*Hint*: Look up "magnify" in a dictionary or thesaurus for definitions and synonyms before answering.)
257. Imagine that: Reading and books make "big things" out of "little things." What does the statement mean or suggest? Do you agree? Why or why not? Does it help or hurt readers? Explain your answers.
258. Think about this: Developing the mind's eye ability to see inside impacts how you see or view the outside world with your real eyes. Are there any connections between your mind's eye and your real eyes? Explain your answer.
259. Think about this: What are the connections between the reading process and movement? Give examples.

Words and Word Activities

Note: Most questions in this category are considered APQs because of the multiple skills needed to respond to them, such as creative and critical thinking. Also, their crossover nature, that is, combining several question categories, makes them more difficult.

260. Dissed: Where does this word take you?
261. Cool: Contemplate the word for one minute and describe whatever comes up in your mind.

262. Tiny words = jumbo jets. Explain.
263. "Bite me! I'm a word." What does the line suggest to you, the reader, about words? Explain.
264. Contemplate the word "sunset" for sixty seconds. Describe the pictures, feelings, thoughts, ideas, and/or memories triggered by the contemplation.
265. Did you ever read a word that triggered a memory? What word? What memory? What happened?
266. Did someone ever say a word in a conversation that triggered a memory? What word? What memory? What happened?
267. Have you ever heard a word on TV that triggered a memory? What word? What memory? What happened?
268. Where does the word "kite" take you? (*Hint*: Word-storm words, brainstorm ideas, or picture-storm images to find answers.)
269. Give an example of a word—read, spoken, heard, written, or imagined— that took you on an adventure ride in your imagination. What happened on the ride?
270. Infinity: What are you? Where are you? _____
271. Hit, smack, punch, blow, strike, whack, slug, sock, wallop, clobber:

   • Read the list silently and orally.
   • Name three feelings the list brings up.
   • Connect three thoughts to the words.
   • Draw quick pencil-sketches of the mind-pictures triggered by the words.
   • How powerful are these words?

272. Laugh, smile, grin, crack-up, giggle, howl, roar: Where do these words take you? What "places"? Describe them.
273. Expand the word "miracle" in your mind: What do you see? (*Hint*: Try picture-storming images, brainstorming ideas, or word-storming words to find answers.)
274. Where does the word "break" take you?
275. Find a word—noun, adjective, or verb—that you think is silly, ridiculous, dumb, or funny. Contemplate it for a minute. Pencil-sketch one mind-picture triggered by the contemplated word. When you finish the sketch, write about what you see.
276. Reflect on the word "favorite" for thirty seconds. Turn it over in your mind and see what happens. Just let it go and then write about your experience.
277. What "lives" in most words? Search for a word—noun, verb, or adjective— and describe its "life" in twenty-five words.
278. Confusion: _____
279. Pretend you're a movie director setting up different scenes for: babies meet puppies. What shots do you visualize with your mind's eye as you zoom around "babies meeting puppies"? Describe three scenes you'll

use in your movie. (*Hint*: The movie can be realistic—a comedy—or
a fantasy.)

280. Visualize the word "butterfly." Picture one in your mind. Now picture
another one and more and more until they completely fill your mind.
Stop: Look at the mind-picture you created. Describe what you see and
then draw the image.

281. Contemplate the phrase "autumn leaves" for sixty seconds. What does
your contemplation conjure up: images, feelings, and thoughts? Draw
one image you visualized during the contemplation. (*Hint*: Use markers
or crayons for your drawing.)

282. *Relax*:

- What happens if you read, hear, imagine, or reflect on the word "relax"?
- Word-storm, brainstorm, and picture-storm the word mentally (no writing).
- Write a twenty-five- to fifty-word description and definition of "relax."
- Describe new insights or understanding you found about "relax."

283. *Think*:

- What happens if you read, hear, imagine, or reflect on the word "think"?
- Word-storm, brainstorm, and picture-storm the word mentally (no writing).
- Write a twenty-five- to fifty-word description and definition of "think."
- Describe new insights or understanding you found about "think."

284. *Try*:

- What happens if you read, hear, imagine, or reflect on the word "try"?
- Word-storm, brainstorm, and picture-storm the word mentally (no writing).
- Write a twenty-five- to fifty-word description and definition of "try."
- Describe new insights and understanding you found about "try."

285. *Create*:

- What happens if you read, hear, imagine, or reflect on the word "create"?
- Word-storm, brainstorm, and picture-storm the word mentally (no writing).
- Write a twenty-five- to fifty-word description and definition of "create."
- Describe new insights and understanding you found about "create."

286. What would happen if "balloons" and "bubbles" met each other?

- Close your eyes and visualize a mind-picture of the scene.
- Look carefully at the image and fill in the details of your impression.

- Pencil-sketch a picture of the meeting of "balloons and bubbles."
- What comes to mind when you finish the drawing?

Optional: Use colored markers or crayons for the illustrations.

287. What would happen if the words "black" and "white" met? What images do you see in your mind? Write two thoughts you get into as you view the images. What did you realize as your inner eye observed the meeting of "black" and "white"?

288. Read the word "blood" silently and out loud:

- What feelings does it trigger?
- What pictures pop up immediately?
- What are you thinking now?
- Where else does the word take you: dreams, nightmares, past experiences?
- Describe the trip with "blood" in twenty-five to fifty words and read it over.
- How far or deep did you go? Were there any surprises? Explain your answers.

Optional: Use storming to help jumpstart your trip—if necessary.

289. Read the word "lucky" silently and out loud:

- What do you see with your mind's eye?
- What thoughts and feelings are triggered by the images?
- Describe any memories, dreams, fantasies, or daydreams that come up.
- Where else does this word take you?
- Write about your travels with "lucky" in twenty-five to fifty words and read it over.
- What did you think about the trip? Why?
- Did you learn anything new? Explain.

Optional: Use storming to jumpstart your travelogue—if necessary.

290. Read the word "party" silently and out loud:

- Observe the word as it moves inside your imagination.
- What tracks does it leave: sights, sounds, vibes, memories, and experiences?
- Trace your ride in twenty-five to fifty words and reflect on what you wrote.
- Was your little voyage fun and pleasant? Explain.

Optional: Use storming to help you complete your voyage—if necessary.

291. Read the word "school" silently and out loud:

- What is your first thought, feeling, and image?
- Reflect on each of the above: What else comes up?

- Write about your encounter with "school" in fifty words and read it over.
- Does your encounter match your actual experience of "school"? Explain.

Optional: Use storming to jumpstart your encounter.

292. Choose one of the following words and trace its path from beginning to end: ghosts, winter, crazy, cry, reject, heart, drugs, kickball, rules, liar, justice, joke, excuses, depressed, reward, disappear, refuse. Use the upcoming guide questions to help write a twenty-five- to fifty-word story, narrative, anecdote, or essay of your selected word:

  - What is the word's first stop in your mind and imagination?
  - Where does it lead or take you afterward?
  - What mind-picture(s) really stand out?
  - What thoughts and ideas come up?
  - What is the word's power and impact?

Hint: Use storming to jumpstart your "story."
Word choice: _____
"Story": _____

293. How practical, useful, and helpful are words? For example, can a word resolve a conflict between you and a friend? Why or why not? Give an example of a word that helped you or a friend.

294. Describe the "notes" these words "strike on the keyboard of your imagination":

  - pillow
  - attic
  - music
  - silence

295. Words contain information, knowledge, insights, and secrets if you try to reflect on them. Describe the potential wisdom you can discover in each of these words:

  - imagination
  - awareness
  - motivation
  - change
  - ignorance

296. Just for the fun of it, try to discover the potential wisdom in one or more of these words: communicate, control, beauty, mystery, wonder, discover, exercise, myths, poetry, explore, solitude, sensitivity, dream, anger, mistake.

297. Picture this: Whenever I read or hear the word "parakeet" I remember Peppy and Skippy. I can easily visualize their blues, blacks, greens, yellows; little beaks; tiny black-dot eyes popping out of little pinheads;

powerful pink feet gripping wooden perches; beaks cracking open seeds; Peppy splashing in his plastic bird bath; poor Peppy all drenched in the cage; listening to Peppy's happy words, "Hello Peppy," "Pretty birdy"; and then I see Skippy bouncing back and forth in his cage, keeping me company at a time when I really needed it. . . . The pictures never seem to end. The word "parakeet," for me, becomes a "word-show."

What words create a "word-show" in your mind? Think of a word that changes your mind into a magic reading theater where your inner eye views the show. Do you have a word yet? What "show" does the word put on in front of your inner eye? What images are you watching? Describe as many pictures as you can visualize and remember in twenty-five to fifty words.

298. Think about this: "Ragin' words." Angry, mean, growling words that snarl inside you at times, words that can blow you away before you know it, words that seem like heavy metal rock or rap music once you hear, read, speak, or imagine them. What are these "words of wrath" (anger) for you?

- List two words and give a reason for each of your choices.
- Pick one word and contemplate it for sixty seconds.
- Write a story or describe a memory connected to the word in fifty words.
- Sketch a mind-picture from your story or memory.

Hint: Word-storm, picture-storm, and/or brainstorm to jumpstart your story.

299. Imagine that: A dream word instantly gets you into a dream world. It ignites the imagination and your inner eye views an amazing panoramic dream spectacle.

- Visualize an imaginary meadow where different dream words rest.
- What words do you see? Pick one for your "dream word."
- Contemplate it for sixty seconds and let it ignite a dream world.
- What mind-pictures are triggered? What do you see?
- Use the images to start your dream world story of fifty words or more.

Hint: Use storming techniques to begin the story.

300. Imagine that: Did you ever feel that a word spoke directly to you?

- Think of three words that "speak directly" to you.
- Pick one and contemplate it for sixty seconds.
- What is communicated between the word and you? What do you experience?
- Write a fifty-word story or description of your contemplation and communication.

Hint: Use storming techniques to begin your story.

301. Picture this: Little boy Paul had his share of bad days. When they came, he went to his retreat called WORDSAREME, where he kept "words of interest." Paul looked at them one-by-one in his mind and then contemplated each for thirty seconds. He went through his "word sanctuary" until he felt he could return to a bad day in a good way.

   • What words do you think Paul stored in his mind?
   • List five "words of interest" he kept ready for bad days.
   • Contemplate one "word of interest" to see how it works for sixty seconds.
   • Write about how the word works in twenty-five to fifty words.

   Hint: Word-storm, brainstorm, and/or picture-storm the "word of interest."

302. What would happen if "something" met "nothing"?

   • Visualize the meeting and draw a cartoon of it.
   • Imagine a conversation between the two: What would they say to each other?
   • Create a short, silly dialogue for them as if you were writing a play.

   Hint: Use storming techniques for "something" and "nothing" to jump-start your play dialogue.

303. Think about this: Nighttime can be funny, where funny means strange, weird, mysterious, eerie. For example, words can flash through your mind like rockets and leave a trail of thoughts that instantly activate your mind and imagination.

   • Recall or imagine a night when you saw words racing fast through your mind.
   • Give examples of these "flashing words." What thoughts did they trigger?
   • Contemplate one of those thoughts for a few seconds. What comes to mind?

304. Exaggerate the word "power" in your mind. Stretch, magnify, distort, expand, and intensify it. Take "power" to extremes: In twenty-five words or more, describe what you see with your inner eye.

305. What words create powerful pop-out pictures in your mind?

   • Find five to ten extremely powerful words (nouns, adjectives, and/or verbs).
   • Put the words in a column and read them silently and orally to yourself.
   • Reflect on the words for sixty seconds or more and visualize them in your mind.
   • Describe two "pop-out pictures" triggered by the words and pencil-sketch the images.
   • Were there any surprises in your visualizations? Explain your answer.

306. Scary story times: After the hurricane and floods, you look down the road, that once was a road, and see another road, where multitudes of words slowly make their way to the mountains. You watch words walking in pairs, bunches, or posses, while some plod alone. After the storm the world has changed for you: You see it all reflected in "The March of Words" along this ugly muddy road.

- What words do you visualize on the new roadway?
- Make up a list of ten "marching words": Read them silently and orally to yourself.
- Give a reason each "marching word" is walking down the road to the mountains.
- Do your "marching words" tell the story of the disaster? Why or why not?
- Did "The March of Words" express what and how you felt? Why or why not?
- What thoughts and ideas does your story trigger? Describe them briefly.

Ratings and Quotations

(APQs in this category are numbers: 310, 311, 312, 313, 314, 315, 316, 317, 318, 319, and 320.)

307. "Books had instant replay long before televised sports" (Bert Williams). What is "instant replay" in sports? What would be "instant replay" in reading? Why is it so important to reading?

308. Your memory—how much you can recall—is one key to successful reading. How good is your memory when reading? Rate it on a scale from 0 to 10, where 0 = poor or no memory, and 10 = excellent memory (recalling 100 percent or almost all of what you read). Give reasons for your rating.

309. What is reading about according to this quote: "It is better to read a little and ponder a lot than to read a lot and ponder a little" (Denis Parsons Burkitt). Do you agree? Is the quote realistic for your reading life? Explain your answers.

310. "The real purpose of books is to trap the mind into doing its own thinking" (Christopher Morley). What does the quote mean? Rewrite it in your own words. Is the quote true for you? Do books "trap your mind to do its own thinking"? Explain your answer.

311. "Uttering a word is like striking a note on the keyboard of the imagination" (Ludwig Wittgenstein). What does the quote mean? What words "strike notes on the keyboard of your imagination"? Give three examples. Pick one word and describe its "striking power."

312. "Each time we reread a book we get more out of it because we put more into it: A different person is reading it, and therefore it is a different book" (Muriel Clark). Rewrite the quote in your own words. What does it suggest about rereading and the reader? Do you agree or disagree? Why?

313. "I am part of everything I read" (John Kieran). What does the quote mean? Are you "part of everything you read"? How? What is this connection? Explain your answer.

314. Explain how rereading a book can become more enjoyable using the following quote: "I'm rereading it with a slow deliberate carelessness" (T. E. Lawrence, English soldier).

315. "A word after a word after a word is power" (Margaret Atwood). Explain the quote's meaning: How does "a word after word after a word" become power? What creates this "power"?

316. "When I read a book I seem to read it with my eyes only, but now and then I come across a passage, perhaps only a phrase, which has meaning for me, and it becomes part of me" (William Somerset Maugham). What does it mean if a passage or phrase "becomes part of you"? What phrase, passage, or line from a book, story, or a poem has "become part of you"? Why?

317. Explain what the following quote suggests about books: "Books do furnish a room" (Anthony Powell). What does "furnish" mean in the quote? (*Hint*: Look up "furnish" in a dictionary or thesaurus for definitions and synonyms before answering.)

318. "Knowledge speaks, but wisdom listens" (Jimi Hendrix). What meaning does the quote have for you, the reader? What connection is there to the reading process?

319. "Gentle words, quiet words, are after all the most powerful words. They are more convincing, more compelling, more prevailing" (W. Gladden). Give examples of three gentle, quiet words from your world. Pick one and describe its gentleness and quietness. Explain its "power." (*Hint*: Look up "compelling" and "prevailing" in a dictionary for definitions before answering.)

320. What does the quote say about reading, readers, and the senses: "Why all this insistence on the senses? Because in order to convince your reader that he is THERE, you must assault each of his senses, in turn, with color, sound, taste, and texture. If your reader feels the sun on his flesh, the wind fluttering his shirt sleeves, half your fight is won. The most improbable tales can be made believable, if your reader, through his senses, feels certain that he stands at the middle of events. He cannot refuse, then, to participate. The logic of events always gives way to the logic of the senses" (Ray Bradbury).

Do you agree or disagree with the quote? Why? If you agree, prove his statement by showing how a paragraph or a sentence affects your senses and makes you a participant in what you're reading. Find and copy a sentence(s) or short paragraph, and then describe how it affects your senses.

321. "You've really got to start hitting the books because it's no joke out there" (Spike Lee). What is the author's message? How serious is he? Why? Do you take him and his message "seriously"? Why or why not?

Reading Reflections: Book Recalls, Nonfiction, and Poetry

(APQs in this category are numbers: 322, 323, 326, 327, 330, and 331.)

322. The last book to bring me peace was _____.
Why?

323. What book has become "part of you?" Why?

324. What book demanded a lot from your imagination? Did you see more things as a result? Was your imagination changed, expanded, or improved afterward? Explain your answers.

325. What book or reading surprised you by how good it was? What were the surprises?

326. Describe a poem you have read or heard that triggered different feelings. List two feelings you experienced at the time. What pictures did you see? What thoughts came up? Did any memories return? Write about whatever you can recall from this "emotional" poem.

327. Think about this: A line from a poem can create its own world. Recall a line from a poem that does this. What "world" does it create? Draw what you experience when you read or hear the line. (*Hint*: Read the line several times and visualize it. Say it silently and orally.)

328. Do you think that reading poetry helps you with reading novels? Why or why not?

329. You lose track of time when you read, experience, and enjoy a poem. What does the statement mean? Do you think it's true? Explain. Give an example from a poem you read. Why did you "lose track of time"?

330. Reflection time: Have you ever met your "twin" or "double" in a book (fiction or nonfiction)? If you have, or at least found a character close or similar to yourself, explain how it affected your real life and/or your reading life. (*Hint*: If you never met a "double" or character similar to you, imagine how it would affect your real and reading life.)

331. Recall a book character (novels) or a real-life person (biographies/memoirs) who did not reflect on, question, or look at his life, who led an unexamined life. How did this person's life turn out? Did it get better or worse? Explain your answer.

332. Recall a book or story (fiction or nonfiction) that portrayed life as an "experiment." Describe what "life as an experiment" means according to

the book or story. What were the results? Was anything solved? Was a decision made or conflict resolved by the character(s)? Can such a reading help you in your everyday life? Explain your answers.

HOW TO USE BOOK 4

One Suggested Sample Survey Approach for Presenting Questions with Notes

Review the upcoming survey approach for Book 4; examine the questions closely to see their degree of difficulty—the creative and critical-thinking skills needed to respond—and why some are considered APQs.

Begin Book 4 with opener or introductory questions. Check out the questions to find an eclectic range. Pump them up for this concluding round of questions. *Examples*:

- Do you ever feel that many things are coming at you at the same time when you read? Explain your answer by giving an example from your reading life.
- Visualize and then draw a dream image of a mother reading with her child. What thoughts and feelings does your drawing trigger?
- Describe your "thinking life" when you read. Give an example.
- When does reading totally absorb you? Describe what happens.

Choose five openers and ask them on consecutive days to begin Book 4.

A second approach for starting Book 4 is use one-line statement AP questions:

- Reading means freedom: Explain the statement's meaning. Give an example from your reading life.
- Imagine that: Wherever you read, there you are. Explain the statement's meaning.
- Reading is also contemplation. Explain. What do you think? (*Hint*: Look up "contemplation" in a thesaurus or dictionary for synonyms and definitions before answering.)

Select ten one-liners and mix them up with your other questions; or, try a two-question-a-day approach (for three consecutive days): one question in class followed up by one at home.

A primary goal of *Motivating Teen and Preteen Readers* is to delve into and expand adolescent thinking about the reading process: What is the mind's magic reading theater? What really happens inside of it? What kind of show or entertainment is it for the reader? How much of the picture show can readers see?

Review the following reading process questions and ask yourself: Which ones are advanced placement questions (APQs)?

- How fast do you travel through your imagination when reading? Are you moving at fast or slow speeds while you read and imagine? Give examples.
- Think about it: Is reading a separate reality apart from the real world? Explain.
- How is your mind like a "vacuum cleaner" when you read? Explain.
- How is a novel like a movie?

Pick ten reading process questions and divide them up in your questioning.

The word questions in Book 4 take kids further into the creative, fun, humorous, and playful aspects of words—and some are brain-frying questions. They become key motivators for the reading and writing processes. Word questions take teens and preteens to the imaginative world of the reading process, and put them on stage inside the mind's magic reading theater.

Examples of AP word questions are:

- What lives in most words? Search for a word—noun, verb, or adjective— and describe its "life" in twenty-five words.
- Read the word "lucky" silently and out loud:

  a. What do you see with the mind's eye?
  b. What thoughts and feelings are triggered by the images?
  c. Describe any memories, dreams, fantasies, or daydreams that come up.
  d. Where else does this word take you?
  e. Write about your travels with "lucky" in twenty-five to fifty words and read it over.
  f. What did you think about the trip? Why?
  g. Did you learn anything new? Explain.

Optional: Use "storming" to jumpstart your travelogue if necessary.

Choose five to ten questions on "words" and blend them in with other questions.

Reinforce word questions with word activity questions, where students contemplate or reflect on words or phrases. Activity questions take kids deeper into the experience of words through serious, self-entertaining creativity. *Examples* (consider this first question AP):

- Hit, smack, punch, blow, strike, whack, slug, sock, wallop, clobber:

  a. Read the list silently and orally.
  b. Name three feelings the list brings up.
  c. Connect three thoughts to the words.
  d. Draw quick pencil-sketches of the mind-pictures triggered by the words.
  e. How powerful are these words? Why?

- Contemplate the phrase "autumn leaves" for sixty seconds. What does your contemplation conjure up: images, feelings, and thoughts? Draw one image you visualized during the contemplation. (*Hint*: Use markers or crayons for drawing.)

Select three to five word activity questions: intersperse among your other questions.

After one-line statement, reading process, and word/word activity questions, the absurd, surreal writing questions flow naturally out of them. Check out the sample writing questions to see the connections and why they're advanced placement questions:

- What word is a good story starter?

  a. List ten potential words to start a story.
  b. The words can be nouns, adverbs, adjectives, verbs, prepositions, or pronouns.
  c. Review each one until you find a story starter: the first word of your story.
  d. Let it take you to the end of your short story of fifty words or more.
  e. Let the word go wherever it wants to go and see what happens.
  f. Use storming techniques to help trigger your story.

- Imaginary tales: They say that words are already inside you when you are born. These special words reveal your life and destiny. Picture this happening to you. Can you think of any words that might have been planted in you at birth? What word(s)?

  a. Search for a word you might have been born with.
  b. Contemplate it for sixty seconds. What comes to mind?
  c. Why this word? How does it affect you—your life? Why?
  d. Write about a one-hundred-word dream you had titled "My Birth-Word of Destiny."
  e. Use storming techniques to jumpstart your story.

Optional: You can also write a fable, myth, tall tale, or fairy tale about the word.

Can you follow the progression of questions that lead up to, and connect with, these sample writing questions? There is a degree of difficulty in each question that requires different skills and techniques to respond to the questions. The term "advanced placement" should be understood and appreciated before asking these questions. Pick three to five writing questions and mix them up in your questioning: Ask one long writing question in class or with a child (one-to-one) every other week (time/schedule permitting). Longer writing questions can be closers for the books of questions.

Book 4's drawing questions become creative cruises in the mind's magic reading theater. Check out the cerebral, visual, emotional, surrealistic features of the following APQs:

- Visualize an imaginary "book zoo." Draw a cartoon picture of it and add a caption. What books would be in the cages for people to see? (*Hint*: Brainstorm different books, book titles, or ideas, and then picture-storm images.)
- WORDS: breakfast of reading champs. Picture-storm cartoon images for the statement. Visualize and sketch your favorite one. Explain the statement's meaning.

Select three to five drawing questions and mix them up with your other questions.

There are new drawing questions in Book 4 that ask kids to create abstract illustrations of reading and reading life: Call them "abstract drawing questions." Instead of representational art, they use lines, shapes, forms, colors, and designs to complete or draw their answers. This APQ taps into deeper creative-thinking. *Examples*:

- Draw an abstract picture—lines, shapes, forms, colors, and designs—of you struggling with your concentration while reading. Look at your finished drawing and record your thoughts and feelings.
- A book you're reading fires you up. Draw an abstract picture—lines, shapes, forms, colors, and designs only—of this experience. What does a "fired-up mind" look like as an abstract drawing? Explain.

The students' *abstracts* and their responses about how they came up with the drawings make great discussions, plus a modern art exhibit. Mix in abstracts with your other drawing questions: Intersperse all drawing questions throughout the other questions.

Book 4's hypothetical reading situation questions bring out key motivational ideas about reading through real and unreal circumstances. Read these sample AP questions to find the critical and creative-thinking needed for responding:

- "You can communicate with a book? You gotta be kiddin' me! It's only a book; I can't hear it because it don't talk." What doesn't the person understand about books and reading? How would you explain "communicating with a book"? What would you say?
- Think about this: Mary was confused about reading: Some days she liked it, and other days she disliked it. How would you, as the reading guidance counselor, help Mary to end her confusion and finally make a decision about reading? What would be your rap to her? Why?

- Think about it: One day, while looking into a mirror, you see yourself as the author of an autobiography you're reading. You feel good because you think you know who you are. Everything about you and your life come together in the mirror's reflection. The world makes sense now. . . .

    a. What does this suggest about reading and self-knowledge or knowing yourself?
    b. How could this experience affect your everyday life?
    c. Would it help or hurt? Why?

These examples are mental-emotional workouts and are answerable. Choose five hypothetical questions.

Opinion questions compel students to reflect on and search their reading lives to find via patient inner-eye scanning objective, honest, genuine answers—and to avoid snap judgments. Some are more challenging than those in earlier books. *Examples*:

- I read, therefore I feel. Explain. Do you agree? Why or why not?
- The life in a book comes from the life in you. "Translate" the statement into your own words. Explain its meaning. What do you think about it: agree or disagree? Why?
- Read to live, but don't live to read. What does the statement suggest about reading and its possible consequences? What do you think: agree or disagree? Why?

Keep prompting kids in teacher/parent raps to take a second before writing, especially with opinion questions that ask if they "agree," "disagree," or "what do you think?" The questions are more cerebral than those in Books 1, 2, and 3, and like the hypothetical reading situation questions, opinions wrap up important aspects of and attitudes toward reading and reading life. Pick five opinion questions.

Some book recall questions, in comparison to Books 1, 2, and 3, don't ask about characters and themes directly. The "recalls" ask students to think creatively and critically about reading by dropping them into areas of the reading process and reading life they may not be aware of or have taken for granted. *Sample questions*:

- What book has become "part of you"? Why?
- What book demanded and expected a lot from your imagination? Did you "see" more things as a result? Was your imagination changed, expanded, or improved? Explain your answers.

Can you see the differences in these "book recalls" and why some are called APQs? Pick three to five book recall questions.

Conclude Book 4's questioning with quotations: They combine important facets of adolescent reading life and address the purposes and goals of *Motivat-*

ing Teen and Preteen Readers. The nature of quotations, fusing many past and present reading experiences, makes them APQs because of the need for deeper thinking and reflection skills to write strong answers in this question category. Check out these quotes to see the work involved:

- "Uttering a word is like striking a note on the keyboard of the imagination" (Ludwig Wittgenstein). What does the quote mean? What words "strike notes on the keyboard of your imagination"? Give three examples. Pick one word and describe its "striking power."
- "A word after a word after a word is power" (Margaret Atwood). Explain the quote's meaning: How does "a word after a word after a word become power"? What creates this "power"?

The quotations are not easy to decipher. They fit into AP status; however, if you developed an appreciation for and understanding of the creativity in words, you will see that students have been prepared to handle the potentially difficult closing questions. What do *you* think? Choose three or more quotes to finish Book 4 or Round 4.

KEY INFORMATION AND PROCEDURES FOR ASKING AND ANSWERING QUESTION CATEGORIES

Book 4 gets kids to rethink reading and reading life. It calls for greater exploration and probing of the reading experience: What happens? What affects, effects, and aftereffects do readers experience? "Rethink" means to consider again with a view to reevaluating and changing. Book 4 or Round 4 completes the reading journeys started in Books 1, 2, and 3 or Rounds 1, 2, and 3. It develops, improves, and advances adolescents' connections to reading, or their responses to literature by getting them hooked on feelings.

Start Book 4 with a rap: "This book is a test with no grades that examines your involvement and progress in *Motivating Teen and Preteen Readers*. It's a self-evaluation of your growth over the entire year of responding to many questions on reading and reading life. Expect the questions to be a little tougher than the others. Many are 'advanced placement' questions, which means you're going to have to concentrate more when thinking about and writing your responses. There are other questions called 'good for dudes,' which I think you'll really like because they're fun, challenging questions."

Check out these sample *APQ multiple-skills/combination and crossover questions* to see their toughness:

- Read, breathe, read, breathe, read, breathe, read, breathe. . . . Why is the statement connecting reading to the breathing? Is there a connection? Explain your answer. (*Question categories*: one-line statement, common,

everyday reading experiences, past reading experiences, reading process. *Multiple skills* needed to respond: recall, thinking, reflection, visualization.)
• Think about this: The silent communicator—a book. What comes to mind when you reflect on this statement? (*Question categories*: one-line statement; common, everyday reading experiences; book recalls; past reading experiences; reading process. *Multiple skills* to needed to respond: recall, reflection, creative thinking, thinking, visualization.)

How would the second question be answered? *Author's sample response*:

"When I reflect on the statement, I see myself with the book I'm reading now. The book is in my hands and I'm looking at it and reading: It communicates without saying a word or anything, even though there's a whole lot of noise—thoughts, feelings, pictures, experiences, and ideas—going on inside my head. That's funny, you know, a silent communicating book that triggers a lot of sound in my mind. It's amazing when you think about it: A book's silence sparks action in my imagination. Yeah, everything is really quiet, I mean the book's not speaking, yet my mind's hearing and listening to all sorts of things from the story read by my inner reading voice. I can hear characters in the novel talking to each other: I eavesdrop on their thoughts and thinking, maybe feel what they're feeling. That's the silent communicator, my book, cranking up the noise of dialogue, thoughts, feelings, actions, behavior, and images and connecting with me, my mind, imagination, and heart."

How will kids respond? Expect the class/child to begin to realize this magical process of a "silent thing making noise and communicating." The beauty of the discussion following is getting a variety of answers showing the paradox of a book as a "silent communicator" creating sounds in a reader's head. For any APQ, make sure they understand it first before letting them write answers.

Take a look at this *word question* to discover if it has AP status:
Confusion: _____

After asking various word and word activity questions, the students have been prepped and should be ready to fill in the blank lines without prompts. What will they say to "confusion"? What would *you* say to the word? What strategies would help to respond to the question?

Try: word-storming words—trigger one word after another—for "confusion"; brainstorming ideas—trigger one idea after another; picture-storming images—trigger one image after another (visualize different pictures of "confusion"); and recalling—do an inner-eye scan—of different past memories and experiences when experiencing "confusion."

APQs push adolescents to find and use different techniques, creative strategies, and creative/critical thinking to come up with responses. *Stress* their application in raps/discussions: "What thinking processes do you use to create an answer? What are your methods?" Let students model how they think: Also, model your response and describe how to come up with it, the same way the author did here.

Meta-cognition, thinking about thinking, is an important concept because it's about reflection, cerebration, and deliberation, all keys to motivating reading and changing attitudes toward reading life.

Try this sample *poetry reading life APQ*:

Visualize and then briefly describe mind-pictures from an imaginary poem titled "Blue Fog." Picture-storm or create images in your mind connected to the poem's title. What feelings and thoughts are triggered by each of your images?

The question gives a title, "Blue Fog," and asks kids to create images in the mind connected to it. Call this advanced visualization because they have to generate imaginative mind-pictures from a title. Picture-storm images: imagine, yeah, imagine. . . . *Author's response*:

"I see a soft blue fog: (a) rolling in from the ocean onto the shore; (b) circling around towering green mountains; (c) drifting over a still lake early in the morning; (d) sucking me up until I disappear inside it; and (e) hovering over the skyscrapers of New York City's skyline."

There was a whole lot of picture-storming, visualizing, and creative thinking going on, so it took a few minutes to conjure up the images.

What feelings and thoughts do the images create?

Feelings triggered by images are: peaceful, happy, harmony, relaxed, calm, scary, fear, panic, confusion, power, rapture, ecstasy.

Thoughts triggered by images are (connected feelings in parentheses): (a) The ocean with a blue fog calms me down and I feel good about myself (*peaceful, happy, relaxed, calm, harmony*); (b) Mountains seem more majestic and mysterious when they are encircled by blue fog (*rapture, ecstasy, power*); (c) The world stops as I sit on the shore watching the blue fog over a still lake; everything seems so quiet, you feel the solitude of this place (*peaceful, relaxed, calm, harmony, happy*); (d) It's like a frightening science fiction movie to be sucked up by a blue fog and vanishing inside it (*scary, fear, panic, confusion*); (e) The sight of the New York skyline with a huge blue fog over it and with me in it is awesome and makes me stop, look, see, and contemplate: *Who am I?* (*rapture, ecstasy, power, calm*).

Look at the skills needed to find the mind-pictures of "Blue Fog": picture-storming; recalling and visualizing memories and experiences; creative thinking and creative visualization to conjure up original images; and reflection and contemplation (continued thinking about real and/or imagined images). Call it an APQ: This one is tough and requires lots of creativity. . . .

Discussion leaders: Keep probing, expanding, and enriching the mind-pictures kids see to get them to the "promised land" of a three-dimensional, holographic, virtual reality of the "blue fog" scene. By questioning them about what they visualize, feel, and think, you are attempting to make those images pop out of the imaginary TV screen in the mind: Create a dramatic effect similar, ideally, to the images of a 3-D movie. Enhance the imagery with more details, color, and form; at the same time, have them explore the connected feelings and thoughts to the mind-picture. Show them how to trigger a virtual reality from the mind-picture through expansive questioning. Let them create an image that seems real or life-like, approaching what they see with their real eyes in the outside world.

Try this little experiment: Have the class/child close their eyes. Ask them to search with the inner eye to find a picture of themselves, a friend, or family member. The kids can look for a photograph, a "good shot," or even a portrait they have in their mind. When they have an image, prompt them to imagine the person popping out of the rectangular, two-dimensional mind-picture: The person's face should come right out of the frame and become a virtual reality (almost real). *Prompt* them to keep visualizing and looking at the image. *Discussion leaders: Ask more questions*: "What are you seeing in this 3-D, virtual image? What's different about this mind-picture? What details do you see? Can you describe what you're visualizing, feeling, and thinking? How does this imaginary 3-D reality affect you? How does it impact your inside world? Does it take greater concentration to see the image? Is the image more exciting in any way?" *Continue and say*: "Zoom in closer with the inner eye." (You want them to create an inner, virtual reality that would make it seem as if they were looking at the person with their real eyes open.) *Explain*: "You can do the same things with the words you read from a novel, poem, or a history book. This experiment gives you an idea of how to create and find those images."

Note for teachers: Keep in mind when asking APQs that there is a whole class or smaller groups providing a variety of responses, which will trigger additional on-the-spot, spontaneous answers, and that's great, so let the kids go if they come up with more 3-D images. Impromptu oral responses will go a long way to help students answer the questions. This organic, student-centered approach motivates reading and reading life from the *inside* and *empowers* adolescents.

Try this APQ question yourself to see the different skills needed to answer it: Analyze this: Reading is outside inside outside inside outside inside outside. . . . Explain the statement's meaning. What is it saying about reading and the reading process? Which part is more important: the outside or inside? Why?

The back-and-forth movement of reading, from the *outside* (reading words from a page), to thinking about and visualizing words on the *inside*, requires strong concentration to keep the reader balanced between the two worlds without getting messed up and lost in a crowd of words, thoughts, feelings, and images. The APQ gives kids a *framework* to understand what they're doing in the act of reading, something that may not be so obvious to many of them. Teachers and parents should not be surprised when they come through with some creative responses to ignite a discussion, and also work as models for others who are struggling. (*Multiple skills* needed to respond to this question are: recall, critical thinking, analyzing, synthesizing, reflection, and visualization.)

Another new term is the *"Good-for-Dudes" question* (GFDQ). These challenging, entertaining questions promise to fry kids' brains a bit:

- She started to read a novel and just took off on the first flight in her imagination. *Where* did she go? Why? (*Hint*: Imagine, yeah, imagine. . . .)
- How is reading like playing sports?
- Which gets you more inside a character's mind: books or movies? Explain.
- Reflection time: Have you ever met your "twin" or "double" in a book (fiction or nonfiction)? If you have, or at least found a character close or similar to yourself, explain how it affected your real life and/or your reading life. (*Hint*: If you never met a "double" or character similar to you, imagine how it would affect your real and reading life.)

Here are the fun, challenging elements to each GFDQ, respectively:

This *open-ended* hypothetical reading situation begs for extraordinary responses. Students have a blank slate to describe wherever the girl's flight in her imagination takes her. *Where* did she go? It's the element of openness—almost anything can fill in the blank—which challenges them to create an imaginary sequence or a real experience. Call this an entertaining problem-solving situation, requiring creative thinking, critical thinking, visualization, recalling, reflection, contemplation, and/or storming techniques.

Most adolescents would not think about comparing reading to playing sports. They will enjoy themselves thinking creatively and critically to come up with comparisons. It falls into the category of having fun frying your brains. But what are the comparisons? For both reading and playing sports you need to: concentrate; think fast; stay alert or awake; be motivated; practice to get better; be patient; work hard; demand a lot from yourself; be determined to succeed; never give up; and treat your successes and failures the same by never getting too high or low about your abilities. This is a great discussion question and an eye-opener for kids.

The catch word in this GFDQ is "movies": a medium most adolescents favor over reading. If students read a book and watch the movie of it, they would have plenty to say about how they imagined the book character versus seeing the character in a movie, how they were similar, different, or the same. GFDQs precipitate many questions for discussion: Did they get into the book character more using the imagination? Did they *see* or understand the character better on the movie screen? Can they describe their visualization of the book character? How does the visualization compare to the character viewed on the movie screen? Which medium created greater emotion: the book or movie? Which character moved them more? Which character did they like more? Did seeing the character on the screen show them more than the book? Was there a big difference? Was the movie character portrayed realistically? Was the movie character loyal to the book character?

Books and movies are different worlds: one a three-dimensional virtual reality, the other, a two-dimensional, flat-screen reality (although 3-D movies are a current rage). While there's great intensity of feeling in movies, it's compressed and short-lived in comparison to books, where emotions are drawn out and experienced over a longer period of time, and also where things move slower or according to the reader. And look at the skills needed to get inside the character's head when reading the book: visualization, creative thinking, critical thinking, reflection, analyzing, synthesizing, and contemplation. If watching the same character in a movie, how much time is there to use these skills? And how many of the same skills could and would be used to watch the movie?

Do kids ever see themselves in characters from novels: Someone who reminded them of who they are? Have you ever gotten up close and personal with yourself in a book or short story? Did you suddenly imagine or see yourself as a person in a poem? It can be surreal, almost eerie, but something teens and preteens may want to write about: *confidential tales* they wouldn't normally disclose, except when a reflection time GFDQ comes out of nowhere to stir them up.

Looking into the *mirror* of a book and seeing the *reflection* affects a student's real life by: validating who she is ("There are people like me"); making her feel good to see her twin resolve a conflict ("I can do it"); or helping to create self-belief by showing her other kids like herself who survived to tell their tales ("I will survive"). This GFDQ connects with adolescent angst about identity and freedom and provides an edgy comparison to the *real* image they see in a *real* mirror before their *real* eyes. The question connects reading life with real life and brings up a long-range goal of *Motivating Teen and Preteen Readers*: to choose reading and literature as a road to self-discovery, self-understanding, self-awareness, and self-knowledge.

Some questions are "experiments" and should be treated as such by discussion leaders. Various surreal, absurd-word, word-activity, and drawing questions were made up to see how students would respond to more expansive creativity. What would happen? How would they handle new voyages in the mind's magic reading theater?
Examples:

(a) Imaginary word encounter #3: Imagine what would happen if sleepwalkers met shadows. What do you see with your mind's eye? Picture-storm images and pencil-sketch one.

(b) Try this experiment: Draw an abstract design for the word confidence. Visualize the word using shapes, lines, forms, colors, and designs. Pencil-sketch your drawing. Does the word connect with your abstract drawing? Explain. (*Hint*: If you have trouble with your abstract, word-storm confidence to find connected words and then continue drawing.)

(c) Pretend you're a movie director setting up different scenes for: "babies meet puppies." What shots do you visualize with your mind's eye as you zoom around babies meeting puppies? Describe three scenes you'll use in your movie. (*Hint*: The movie can be realistic—a comedy—or a fantasy.)

(d) Think about this: A line from a poem can create its own world. Recall a line from a poem that does this. What world does it create? Draw what you experience when you read or hear the line. (*Hint*: Read the line several times and visualize it. Say it silently and orally.)

How would you, as discussion leader, respond to these APQs? Each requires mostly creative-thinking to find answers. And then the question becomes: How do you go creative?

For question a, follow the instructions: picture-storm images. What is seen, created, and visualized as the words "sleepwalkers" and "shadows" are dropped inside the imagination?

Sample author response:

"I'm looking at a bunch of walkers with their eyes closed and arms extended in front of them as they wander around a dark room dimly lit by a streetlamp. They bump into each other while their shadows walk along the room's white walls, creating a huge traffic jam of real people and unreal shadows getting in each other's way."

Figure 4, the author's pencil-sketch, no masterpiece by any means, reflects the description of sleepwalkers colliding with each other and the commotion created

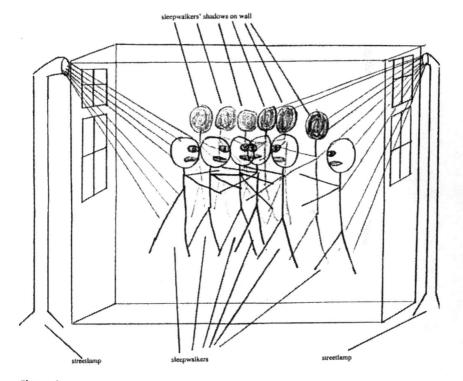

Figure 4.

by their shadows on the room's white walls. The question gives kids a chance to play with the creative possibilities of words, so teachers and parents should keep an open mind to the myriad of drawings presented in discussions. The pencil-sketch will hopefully show a child's creativity, as well as conveying a conceptual understanding of the imaginary word-encounter.

Discussion leaders: Help kids create a three-dimensional reality in their imagination with the word and word activity questions. The scary, weird, twilight zone effects/affects will come from within, from the holographic, virtual reality formed as kids push the inner or mind's eye to see more and more. To practice creating these inner virtual realities, have the students/child try the "little experiments" like the previous example of visualizing a photograph, portrait, or picture of themselves or someone else.

For question b, take the hint and word-storm "confidence." Use the list to create an abstract. *Author examples of stormed words are*: strong, tough, ready, believer, positive, sharp, alert, self-reliance, brave, fearless, courage, bold, hopeful, secure. Using the words, draw the "designs": lines, shapes, forms, and colors to create an abstract drawing with no people, things, and places. What would the abstract look like using the descriptive words for "confidence"? Make a design with bold shapes, lines, forms, and colors using pencil or pen and ink that exudes "confidence." The picture should leap out at the viewer, like the author's attempt (see figure 5).

Expect some whacky abstracts. Finish the mini-lesson with an art exhibit and students/child explaining how they conjured up the drawings. Consider it a combination APQ and GFDQ, where hesitating before responding, that is, thinking, visualizing, and reflecting, will go a long way to triggering a good response.

For question c, use the hint and start off with picture-storming (creative thinking) to find funny, fantasy, or imaginative scenes for "babies meeting puppies." The mind-pictures came quickly to the author:

- Babies riding the doggies like cow-babies.
- Puppies licking the baby faces.
- Babies racing the puppies across the floor.
- Babies tickling the bellies of laughing, smiling puppies.
- Babies and puppies barking together.
- Babies and puppies sharing a pizza pie as they walk all over it.

Stress picture-storming to create images for the make-believe encounter. Explain that they would have to take their *camera*, the inner eye, closer by zooming in on the fictitious scenes to get descriptions. As an example, for "babies riding the doggies like cow-babies," the author's close-up visualization shows the babies with cowboy hats riding the puppies as if they were wild horses bucking away, and their hands flailing in the air as they try to hold on to the poor little creatures. *Emphasize*: "Enjoy yourself in thought while 'babies meet puppies' in the mind's magic reading theater."

Figure 5.

For question d, a student haiku by Erika Perez was used to respond:

A crow so blind
taps at the window
of a haunted house.

A haiku is a one-line poem broken up into three lines, consisting of no more than seventeen syllables, whose imagery tells a story or describes a moment in time. This writer followed the hint and read the haiku several times, visualized the image it created in his imagination, and pencil-sketched it from this written description (see figure 6).

"I see a crow, in all its blackness, desperately tapping at an old corroded window of a dilapidated, broken-down house. The house gives off an eerie feeling while lying in a field of giant weeds. It seems like years since anyone has lived in this abandoned house. But the crow wants to make contact with whatever

Figure 6.

remains inside, so it keeps tapping away at the window to get a response. I hear the tap, tap, tapping rebounding in my ears, and because the house is haunted, those sounds get louder and stranger as the crow continues to hit the panes."

This drawing's description reflects the author's visualization of a crow tapping away at the decrepit window of a haunted house expecting to get some answers to its coded message. Surrounding the house are huge weeds, which makes the scene weirder. The haiku "creates its own world" through emotion, thought, and imagery. A scary, empty, sad feeling resounds inside me as the tapping echoes throughout the haunted house. It makes readers think: Why doesn't the crow stop tapping at the window? Doesn't it realize it's futile to keep knocking at a *door that isn't going to open*? Maybe the haiku says something about the poet's and our experience: Why keep knocking at a door that will not open for us? Why not move on and find a door that will welcome us? Don't we all want to go where we're wanted? The haiku ultimately draws you inside *your* mind as well as the poet's. (Go to figures 1, 2, and 3 for more information on mind-pictures triggering thoughts and feelings.)

There are lots of stories in a haiku or a single line of poetry. *Emphasize*: "Take a line and drop it inside your imagination and picture-storm images, brainstorm ideas, and/or word-storm words to see where your creative and critical thinking go. Play with words and see what happens. Put a little fun into the lives of words. *Ask yourself questions*: 'Am I visualizing the haiku imagery like I'm really there with the crow tapping away at the window? How close am I to the crow and its strange experience? Has the poem become a virtual reality or almost real to me? What am I experiencing?'" Discussion leaders should push the envelope with questions to help kids see more. However, on the other hand, you want them to do the same thing, that is, to ask questions of themselves in order to re-create the reality portrayed in the haiku.

The *longer writing questions* are logical and illogical culminations to Books 1, 2, 3, and 4. Many of the question categories naturally lead to the writing closers. Before asking these questions (considered APQs and GFDQs), prepare the kids developmentally via word, word-activity, and shorter writing questions of twenty-five to fifty words. The age-appropriate questions, connecting adolescents to their writing and reading lives, are timely, organic fun because of their absurdity, imaginativeness, and goofiness, adding up to creative, critical, innovative, and dynamic thinking; *for example*:

Imagine: "Mrs. Words."

- Who is she? What does she do? What does she look like?
- What are her connections to words? What do words mean to her?
- What words does she use? How does she use them?
- How do they affect her life and other people's lives around her?
- Where do the words take her? What places? What worlds?
- Visualize Mrs. Words and contemplate this imaginary word-being's life.
- Write a fable, fairy tale, fantasy, myth, or tall tale of one hundred words on her life.
- Draw a picture of her and add a caption.

Hints: Use the questions as guides; you don't have to answer each one. Use storming techniques to get your story started.

Can you see how it qualifies for an APQ/GFDQ? It's very involved, but, students enjoy creating a response to farcical, yet meaningful, questions.

How do kids respond to "Mrs. Words"? What strategies can be applied to answer the question? Students can try the following: (1) Picture-storm images of what Mrs. Words looks like by triggering silly mind-pictures of her. (2) When a desired image is found, they review the above guide questions and connect them to Mrs. Words' imaginary life. This is an absurd tale or story, which can be silly or serious, whatever works best. (3) Once they finish thinking about the guide questions (kids can write short notes and descriptions), the image and ideas are combined by contemplating Mrs. Words' surreal, extraordinary life and seeing where it takes them.

Notes: Students pencil-sketch Mrs. Words following picture-storming her, if that helps to jumpstart their stories. This is a suggested approach: There are other creative strategies that would answer the question. Instead of using the guide questions, they brainstorm ideas for her imaginary life of words and write stories from their brainstorms. *Stress*: "Respond to the question in a manner that works for you. You may use your own creative style to write a story; however, the key is to think creatively, visually, and critically before writing."

Discussion leaders: A key to developing a story for "Mrs. Words" would be shaping a virtual image of her inside the mind and imagination. If your students/ child can gradually build this imaginary figure up in their head, piece by piece, detail by detail, they will slowly see their creation come to life and truly enjoy themselves in thought before writing the story. The guide questions give kids ideas about how to see her and write the piece, yet the actual mental image of Mrs. Words remains wide open for them to have fun with and create.

There are many longer writing questions to add variety to your choices. Here are two approaches to use with these questions:

Small-group approach: After explaining the questions and instructions, break up the class into small groups of four to six and monitor each to make sure things run smoothly. Here are some things teachers should keep in mind: (a) Assign group leaders to run discussions, where kids read aloud and talk about their written responses and show their illustrations. (b) Use different longer writing questions for each group. (c) Have a follow-up whole-class discussion to present samples of work from each group. The time frame for small group activity would be twenty-five minutes to finish the written responses. Add another ten minutes for small-group talks, plus another ten minutes for a follow-up whole-class discussion (time/schedule permitting).

Remember that longer writing lessons require longer time frames. If class time is limited—for middle and high school—kids can finish writing/sketches at home. Whole-class discussions should follow the next day. Refer to the *book club approach* in the upcoming section called "Implementing Workable Schedules/ Strategies for Presenting Questions in Book 4" for further details and procedures.

Whole-class approach: Work with the entire class. Students respond to one longer writing question that is followed by a discussion. (Give them a choice of two or three writing questions in whole class lessons.) Allow thirty minutes for responding, plus fifteen minutes for discussion. Discussions for whole-class and group activities follow the next day. Collect work and look at it before dialoguing with students. Use raps to discuss their work if extra time is needed. The writing questions work best with grades 4 to 10 and should come toward the end of the school year, where teachers and students have more time and are under less pressure to appreciate them. *Parents* can follow the same procedures for their longer lessons plus the follow-up one-to-one discussion with their child.

To measure the kids' connections to and involvement with words, writing, drawing, and creativity, ask them to make up their own writing questions similar to those they responded to in class or at home. Students can also create word and word-activity questions. The question-making activity should not be restricted to the above categories; they can make up questions for any category: hypothetical reading situations; poetry reading life; common, everyday reading experiences; and so on. Refer to *create your own questions* and *question triggers question* in "Implementing Workable Schedules/Strategies for Presenting Questions" in Books 3 and 4, respectively, for more details and procedures for these approaches.

Discussion leaders can wind up Book 4/Round 4 using quotation questions:

"The real purpose of books is to trap the mind into doing its own thinking" (Christopher Morley). What does the quote mean? Rewrite it in your own words. Is the quote true for you? Do books "trap your mind to do its own thinking"? Explain your answer.

The closer question reinforces the idea that reading books is about thinking: "trapping" or getting readers to think on their own. *Motivating Teen and Preteen Readers* wants adolescents to realize at its conclusion that reading means thinking: readers evaluate, think about, and reflect on what is read through their own thought processes (analysis and synthesis), and don't accept automatically an author's words, thinking, beliefs, attitudes, perspectives, and ideas as truth.

This is an APQ because they first have to decipher the quote, which is not that easy. A key to answering the question is the word "trap": How will students define or interpret it? Although not hinted at in the question, they're allowed to go to the dictionary or thesaurus for meanings and synonyms of "trap" to help them respond (synonyms for "trap" are lure, entice, tempt, and snare). Second, they can reflect on the reading process and visualize what happens in it; and third, recall books; past reading experiences; and common, everyday reading experiences via inner-eye scans to see if the quote is true for them.

Two-a-day questions, one in-class and one for homework, can start in Book 1 or 2; however, this strategy will work better later on in the school year (Books 3 and 4) after they answered many questions and know more about responding and the energy that goes into it. The basic idea is similar to a class lesson in math followed up by homework examples for reinforcement. Do the same thing here: Follow up an AP word question in class with AP word question to do at home. (*Parents* follow this procedure in a one-to-one situation.)

Class question: *Where* does the word "break" take you?

Homework question: What lives in most words? Search for a word—noun, verb, or adjective—and describe its "life" in twenty-five words.

Responses to the class question are wide open. They can take "break" any-where by storming (give them a hint before they respond): word-storm words for "break"; brainstorm ideas that come to mind when they think of "break"; and/or picture-storm images, memories, and experiences when they drop "break" in the imagination. Put the word "break" inside the mind's magic reading theater and see what happens. . . .

The homework question follows up the open-ended class question by asking kids to describe the "life" of a word, be it a noun, verb, or an adjective. Is there a connection to the class question? To answer, they: search for and choose a word; examine it carefully by visualizing and contemplating it; use the concept of reading and visualizing (words creating pictures, feelings, and thoughts); and/or apply storming techniques such as brainstorming ideas, word-storming words, and picture-storming images for the chosen word. Students have several strategies to help them find answers to this and other homework questions.

Look for connections between the following in-class and homework questions:

Class question: If you were given a year off from school with the condition that you read books two hours every day, what would you read and why? Brainstorm a list of books or whatever reading you might do. What would be your daily reading schedule? Could you read two hours a day in everyday life? Why or why not?

Homework question: What steps would you take to change your present reading life? List three steps.

Refer to "Implementing Workable Schedules/Strategies for Presenting Questions" in Books 1, 3, and 4 for more information on assigning homework questions and giving two-question mini-lessons.

Instead of asking quotations and longer writing questions to end Book 4/Round 4, try these wrapper-uppers about reading and reading life:

- An unmotivated reader is _____.
- The more you read, the more you see,

  The more you read, the more you feel,
  The more you read, the more you think,
  The more you read, the more you discover.
  The more you read, the more you understand.
  What does the statement mean or suggest? Do you agree or disagree with it? Why?

- Can reading and books shut down your world? Explain your answer.
- A good reading life is simple: Read. Explain. Do you agree? Why or why not?
- Is reading real life or is it something else? Explain your answer.

Most closers require students to search their written responses and experiences in *Motivating Teen and Preteen Readers*, and also, to ask themselves questions about their own reading lives, via deliberate, patient, and objective inner-eye scans, for attitudinal and motivational changes in reading. Can the closers challenge the status quo in adolescent reading life? Would kids appreciate the potential solutions to their reading woes suggested by the questions? Can they fill-in-the-blank of the "unmotivated reader"? Will they really see connections between reading life and everyday life?

Try this as a *grand finale project for Book 4/Round 4* if it fits in with the year's worth of questions:

Write a funny tale about bunnies for kindergarten children (age five):

- Word-storm ten words or more about bunnies.
- Brainstorm ideas and picture-storm images from the words.
- Use the words, images, and ideas to write and illustrate your silly tale.
- Write short captions for each illustration.
- Read your story silently and orally while checking out the drawings.
- Critique your story: What are the pluses and minuses? Give reasons.
- Describe the entire writing experience from beginning to end in twenty-five to fifty words. *Hint*: For illustrations, use markers, crayons, paints, pastels, or colored pencils. *Optional*: Read your story to a kindergarten class to see how they respond. For example, did your tale make them laugh? Ask what they liked and disliked about it.

This tough APQ/GFDQ project encompasses many experiences—questions, answers, raps, discussions, and evaluations—from the books of questions. Look at the skills necessary to respond: word-storming, brainstorming, picture-storming, visualizing, inner-eye scanning and searching, creative and critical thinking, contemplating, critiquing, analyzing, synthesizing, reflecting, describing, drawing, and oral/silent reading. The combination/crossover question includes the following *categories*: writing, everyday reading experiences, book recalls, past reading experiences, reading process, word/word activity, drawing, creative thinking, and rating.

This final one to two week project at the end of *Motivating Teen and Preteen Readers* becomes nostalgic, sentimental, emotional, psychological, and brain-frying: a blast from the past that asks students to write a fun and funny story with the idea that it will hopefully bring passion to reading via the writing-reading connection. The task puts kids through the gamut of creative and critical-thinking skills and processes in writing and reading.

Go over the instructions carefully for such a complex assignment. Let the class/child write "storming notes" and draw pencil-sketches for the book illustrations. Descriptions of the writing experience might go beyond fifty words, and that's okay, especially if they show details of the creative imagination and experience. Don't let them simply list things like: "First I brainstormed ideas; second, I made pictures; and third, I wrote captions for the pictures." Encourage them to get into their experience of story writing and meta-cognition to inspire reading through writing. This is an ideal, long-range goal of the books of questions. Parts of this project can definitely be done at home.

Final Notes on Book 4/Round 4:

- Go back over all four books for questions you missed and/or passed up. Post extra credit, bonus box questions on the class/section website.
- *Emphasize* how to answer the questions in raps/discussions: Students should be knowledgeable regarding the creative strategies and capable of applying them when responding to the diverse questions. Review the entire repertoire of creative and critical approaches for answering the questions. Constantly model and reinforce them until techniques become second nature.
- It is the kids who make *Motivating Teen and Preteen Readers* work: Their responses fire up raps and discussions in a student-centered approach. Students' ideas will cross-fertilize and boost each other's motivation to read and write. Probing their experiences and modeling how to answer the questions will provide channels for adolescents to get deeper into reading and reading life, as well as writing and writing life, and will revitalize these phenomenal worlds.

IMPLEMENTING WORKABLE SCHEDULES/STRATEGIES FOR PRESENTING QUESTIONS IN BOOK 4

- Extend time limits for more complicated questions such as writing, word, word activity, and drawing. Allow forty-five minutes for the more involved writing/drawing questions plus the discussion (thirty minutes for completing responses and fifteen minutes for discussion). Kids may pencil-sketch their illustrations for expediency and simplicity. Also, drawings can be completed at home.
- Assign homework questions to compliment, reinforce, and advance class questions. For example, word or word activity questions can be supplemented by homework questions in the same category (as previously shown).
- Use an extended mini-lesson to ask advanced placement combination questions or quotation questions: Allow ten to fifteen minutes for responding and finish it with a ten- to fifteen-minute talk (the same or next day, that is, if discussion leaders have time and want to review the written answers).
- Asking writing questions is up to the teacher's discretion. If time, scheduling, and instructional programs in writing become detracting factors, teachers can omit this category area. Parents, who don't have the same time constraints or restrictions as classroom teachers, are advised to try some longer writing questions because they have more time for lessons in this vital area.
- All teachers should keep in mind that by Book 4 they are into the latter part of the year, a time when most test-prepping and standardized and competency testing are over, giving them the luxury of extending time limits for mini-lessons, raps, and discussions. The number and types of questions

asked can also be increased and varied, respectively. This becomes a *go-for-it* situation if the discussion leader has the inclination and the kids have been inspired throughout the first three books of questions.

- Continue the bonus box: Use an assortment of questions from all four books. Or, use the strongest questions that kids will miss and throw them into the bonus box. Again, post bonus box questions on the class/section website. Present the bonus box as a *challenge*. Create a chart listing the students' names on a piece of oak-tag and give credit (checks, pluses, or stars) every time a bonus question is answered that shows effort and thought. Teachers check their notebooks from time to time to review responses and give extra credit. When kids see the results, they can get really competitive and jealous, too, and work harder on the bonus questions. So much for intrinsic motivation. . . .
- Keep working with the "exchange programs" for selected mini-lessons, and also, when notebooks are shared following student and teacher evaluations.

Check out a bunch of new strategies and approaches for asking kids questions:

- Try another question-and-answer strategy in Book 4: Select five different questions to use in an extended-time lesson. Give one question to six students, a second to another six, a third to another six, until each student in the class has a question to answer. Each "nongroup" will answer their question. The question-category areas can be varied or kept the same, but teachers should refrain from asking the longer questions. For the follow-up whole-class discussion, have several students who responded to the different questions read their answers out loud and briefly talk about them. Allow five to ten minutes (max) for writing answers, and twenty minutes for a class dialogue. Let the kids question classmates about their responses and expand on them. Teacher discussion leaders can chime in, too, with questions and comments to further develop what has been expressed and exchanged amongst the students.
- Once again, because Book 4 comes at the school year's end, classroom teachers have some extra time to work in "undeveloped" areas such as motivating reading. Try a new approach: Set up small groups like *book clubs* to answer additional questions. Assign competent student discussion leaders to run groups of four to six kids. The adolescent as discussion leader is not an easy one. If there aren't responsible leaders in the class to control the groups, skip the book club approach. In this writer's opinion, middle to high school students would do best with the book club concept if the emotional intelligence quotient is high.
- In the *book club strategy*, student discussion leaders assign questions and explain them to make sure all group members understand what they're asking. The kids then write responses, which are followed up by a small group

discussion similar to a whole class lesson. Students read their responses and the leader and other group members ask the writer questions to expand on what has been said to get greater insight into reading and reading life (total time for writing and discussion is twenty to thirty minutes). While kids work on and discuss their responses, teachers move from group to group checking on the interchanges and help out only if necessary.

- As a follow-up to "creating your own questions" in Book 3, the *question-triggers-question strategy* has kids creating/brainstorming a question from a question given by the teacher/parent. The new question can be similar to the original or totally different. The aim is to work off the first question to get kids thinking about and seeing other possibilities, issues, ideas, and experiences in reading and reading life. After they respond with the triggered questions, students hand them in for evaluation and potential use in the bonus box or a class/small-group mini-lesson. Allow five minutes to create another question and ten minutes to read aloud. Briefly discuss the stronger responses. *Ask:* "Why are these good questions?" This activity can also be posted on the class/section website as a homework assignment. (Recommended for grades 4 through 10.)

- In *double answers*, kids first write responses to a given question in a mini-lesson. After completing their answers, they stop for a minute and take a short detour to conjure up another response that is as good, or better, than the first one. The aim is to demonstrate that open-ended questions can have more than one answer, and that there are many possibilities when thinking about and discussing reading and reading-life experiences. If adolescents give extra effort to their second responses via more reflection time, they might discover new ideas in reading they hadn't realized. Let the class or one-to-one student-parent discussion sort out the results: How does the second response compare to the first: better, worse, or about the same? Allow ten minutes for the "double answers" and another ten minutes for talking about the comparisons. This technique may also be used for a homework assignment and posted on the class/section website. (Recommended for grades 4 through 10.)

- For the *read-aloud-marathon*, each student takes either an original question he or she created, or a question from *Motivating Teen and Preteen Readers* handed out by the teacher, answers it, and then reads aloud the response to the entire class. Students read for about fifteen minutes in the reading marathon. The purpose of the follow-up ten-minute discussion is to see what they learned and realized about reading/reading life experiences. This "wrapper-upper" activity comes at the end of Book 3 or the school year (Book 4). The strategy gives kids chances to reveal their reading lives in a friendly, open-ended, open-minded discussion. (Recommended for grades 4 through 10.)

Important notes about concluding the four books of questions:

- Refer to "Evaluation Questions for Book 4" and "Not-for-Parents-Only Guide to *Motivating Teen and Preteen Readers*" for more information on presenting and scheduling student questionnaire 4 and student-teacher/parent chat 4. The final chats become more doable for middle and high school teachers because these evaluations come late in the school year.
- Add extra time for the final three class discussion lessons, which include wrap-up questions, reflection, writing, and drawing. Time limits for the three discussion lessons are approximately twenty minutes each, while the same lessons for one-to-one, student-parent discussion lessons are about fifteen minutes per. Refer to "Final Three Discussions and Conclusion to the Books of Questions" for further information and procedures for implementing these lessons.
- Complete *Motivating Teen and Preteen Readers* by adding three to five days of brainstorming sessions using original, innovative, challenging prompts about reading/reading life, creativity/imagination, and writing from the epilogue. Parent discussion leaders working in one-to-one situations should also follow through with oral and/or written brainstorming sessions with their child. Refer to the "Epilogue to *Motivating Teen and Preteen Readers*," "Not-for-Parents-Only Guide to *Motivating Teen and Preteen Readers*," and "Why Won't Michael Read? One Solution . . ." for further information and procedures for implementing these lessons.

Notes for middle and high school teachers:

Again, all extended-time lessons are applicable for grades 6 through 10 because they fit into the time schedules. APQs are good for preteens to teens, whether they are below or above average students. However, if these challenging questions prove to be too time-consuming and/or difficult, teachers may omit them.

- Continue using the new questions-and-answers strategy described in Book 3, where several questions are presented to the class in a lesson. The approach fits into most forty-five-minute middle/high school schedules. It's another way of introducing additional questions that will not be seen or answered by students during their one-year journey through *Motivating Teen and Preteen Readers*. Refer to "Implementing Workable Schedules/Strategies for Presenting Questions in Book 3" for more information about this approach.
- The new "book club" approach is a good closer for the last month of the school year. Students can assert their desire for autonomy and determine their reading life destinies as readers, discussion leaders, and group members, who cooperate, collaborate, and communicate their ideas and experiences in reading.

- Student questionnaire 4, a self-evaluation of progress made in *Motivating Teen and Preteen Readers*, should not be skipped because it gives kids a chance to reread, review, and reflect on their written responses from the entire year. They see for themselves where they started and how they ended in regard to attitude, passion, and ability in reading.
- On the other hand, student-teacher chat 4 remains optional (although not for parent discussion leaders). Teacher discussion leaders might want to interview certain kids who have trouble motivating themselves to read (and they don't have to be struggling or "bad" readers because many good readers don't bother reading outside school for pleasure). It could become an awe-inspiring moment if teachers talked with the problem readers at this point in time so they could be sent off to the wonderland of summer thinking about their reading lives. . . .
- The final three discussion lessons, which follow the evaluation questions, realistically should be toned down to three shorter, fifteen-minute, mini-lessons. Or, another practical way would be to have one forty-five-minute final class dialogue, which combines all three discussion lessons and completes the one-year journey through the books of questions. (See the "Final Three Discussions" in a later section.)
- The brainstorming sessions from the forthcoming epilogue help to put the year's work into perspective, while at the same time assess the students' growth and development in reading/reading life, creativity/imagination, and writing. If discussion leaders can get in three ten- to fifteen-minute sessions in the final week, that would be great. Brainstorming epilogue prompts may come at the beginning or end of the period. Reducing the time limits is fine, as long as teachers make sure they present the prompts for storming. Students and teachers and parents alike will appreciate what comes out of these expansive brainstorming sessions. (Go to the epilogue for more information and procedures for using the various prompts.)

EVALUATION QUESTIONS FOR BOOK 4

Evaluation Procedures: Student Questionnaire 4 and Student-Teacher/Parent Chat 4

The evaluation processes and procedures differ from Books/Rounds 1, 2, and 3:

- Student questionnaire 4 comes after completing thirty to seventy-five questions from Book 4 or from questions randomly chosen from all four books (Round 4).
- Class/child rereads all responses from Books 4, 3, 2, and 1 (in that order) or from all four rounds.

- Students/child answer(s) one essay question out of five choices in thirty to forty-five minutes.
- Teacher/parent reads, comments, and talks about essays in discussions/raps.

Optional student-teacher chat 4 follows student questionnaire 4:

- Teacher skims and reviews student notebooks with written responses.
- Teacher talks informally with kids about oral responses to: *Why do you read?*
- Students respond freely to the final question, with questions asked by the teacher.

Note: See "Evaluation Questions for Book 1" and "Not-for-Parents-Only Guide to *Motivating Teen and Preteen Readers*" for further information on the procedures used in student questionnaire 4 and student-teacher/parent chat 4.

INSTRUCTIONS FOR STUDENT QUESTIONNAIRE 4

Instructions given by discussion leaders for student questionnaire 4:

- "The fourth and final questionnaire is different from the first three. Student questionnaire 4 has one essay question to answer out of five choices. Read each question carefully to see which one you can answer best."
- "Think, reflect, concentrate, recall, visualize, or contemplate before responding. The final question needs more time, deliberation, energy, and patience."
- "Use brainstorming, word-storming, and picture-storming to respond to the essay question. Write some quick notes to help make up an answer of one hundred words or more. Take thirty to forty-five minutes to write your essay answer."
- You spent a year working on the books of questions. You have been thinking and writing about, as well as discussing your reading and reading life, and your classmates' experiences to discover more about these worlds. Review the many feelings, thoughts, reflections, ideas, mind-pictures, and memories that you have had. Show the insights into reading and reading life resulting from your progress and the questions' impact on you. Essays will be reviewed, analyzed, and commented on before discussing them."

Notes: Before responding to student questionnaire 4, kids reread their answers from Books 4, 3, 2, and 1 or Rounds 4, 3, 2, and 1. They review their written responses at home or in school. Parents can follow the same basic procedures/ instructions in a one-to-one situation (of course, minus the exchange of classmates' reading experiences).

SUGGESTED ESSAY QUESTIONS FOR STUDENT QUESTIONNAIRE 4

Choose one of the following five essay questions to answer:

What is the reading life? Write an essay of one hundred words or more describing your reading life. Write notes; brainstorm ideas; picture-storm images; or, word-storm words before responding to the question.

List ten items that are part of your reading life and write an essay about one. Use brainstorming, word-storming, picture-storming, or your own methods to create your reading life list. Pick one item and write an essay of one hundred words or more describing its importance in your reading and reading life.

What have you learned about reading and reading life by answering the questions? Write an essay of one hundred words or more describing your knowledge, insight, and awareness gained by answering many questions. Outline ideas, write notes, recall, reflect, think, visualize, or brainstorm before responding to the question.

Describe your journey through the books of questions. Write an essay of one hundred words or more describing your one-year tour through *Motivating Teen and Preteen Readers*. Write a quick outline, take notes, recall, reflect, think, visualize, picture-storm images, or brainstorm ideas before responding to the question.

Contemplate the expression "reading life" for five minutes. Think about, visualize, and reflect on the phrase before writing anything: What feelings, thoughts, ideas, pictures, experiences, memories, and dreams come to mind? Write an essay of one hundred words or more to describe your contemplation. Outline a list of all things you thought about during the contemplation (and what you remember) and then write your response.

SUGGESTED FINAL QUESTION WITH PROCEDURES
FOR STUDENT-TEACHER/PARENT CHAT 4

- The suggested final question for each student is: *Why do you read?*
- Give students/child five to ten minutes (max) of "think time" to write a short outline, take notes, or use storming techniques before responding orally.
- Allow students/child to respond freely to the question, even in a stream of thoughts, about why they read. Encourage them to convey whatever thoughts, ideas, feelings, and experiences come up. As they answer, and hit important points, *stop* them with a question to expand on what was said.
- If students have trouble responding, *prompt* them with the following questions:

  1. What are your reasons for reading: fun, knowledge, or because you *have to*?
  2. Do you read because you're curious and wonder about things?
  3. Do you read to find out information?
  4. Do you read to learn about yourself, others, and the world?

   5. Do you read to get smarter and for success?

   6. Do you read to escape?

- Expand sketchy responses. For example, a fictitious, sketchy answer may be: "I like reading because it's fun." Follow-up interview questions could be:

   1. How is reading fun for you?

   2. What do you read for fun?

   3. How much fun is it?

   4. What is a fun book you have read?

   5. Describe the fun in reading a book.

   6. What other reasons are there to read?

- Have their reading lives grown after a year of answering diverse questions and discussions? During the meetings or in your final discussions ask kids about their growth as readers. Extend the interview (time permitting) with other connected questions such as:

   1. Does *Motivating Teen and Preteen Readers* make sense to you now?

   2. What new discoveries have you made about reading and reading life?

   3. Has reading become a stronger habit for you?

   4. Has your attitude toward reading changed since the books of questions began?

   5. Where do you think your reading and reading life will take you in the future?

By the last meeting, discussion leaders will know students well enough to ask the questions that will influence, impact, and inspire their reading and reading lives.

Final Three Discussions and Conclusion to the Books of Questions

In three windup discussion lessons, after the completion of 120 or more questions, student questionnaires, and student-teacher/parent chats, pose questions to your class/child about readers, reading, and reading life.

Suggested questions for discussion lesson 1:

- What are your secrets to reading?
- What are the pluses and minuses of reading for you?
- What have you achieved from the round-trip through your reading worlds?
- Do you think you have changed as a "reader"?
- Has your motivation to read changed after finishing your journey?

Suggested question for discussion lesson 2:

- What are the cool, strange, hypnotic, magical, mysterious, and miraculous delights of your secret, hush-hush reading life?

Discussion leaders can handle this question in one of two ways: (1) Class brainstorms responses orally in a discussion, which includes questions by the teacher and students to clarify, develop, and expand what was expressed; or (2) Class writes responses of one hundred words or more in their notebooks.

Teacher reviews their essays and writes comments. A class discussion of fifteen minutes on their answers follows the written part. Both teacher and students ask questions about the written responses to increase their knowledge of and pleasure in reading and reading life.

Note: Parents should follow the same procedures as teachers.

Suggested drawing question for discussion lesson 3:

For the grand finale to the books of questions, have students create drawings, sketches, diagrams, paintings, and even abstract designs expressing their connections to, realizations about, and insight to reading and reading life. Display their illustrated reading lives and worlds around the room. Students explain their work and why they chose to wrap up their involvement and evolvement in *Motivating Teen and Preteen Readers* with a particular drawing. End the show with this question: *Have you pumped up your reading and reading life?*

Epilogue

DESCRIPTION AND PURPOSE OF THE EPILOGUE

The epilogue consummates the questions, answers, discussions, evaluations, experiences, and knowledge from the books of questions. There are three types of prompts or sparks: reading/reading life, creativity/imagination, and writing. Each section contains various questions, quotations, one-line original statements, poems, aphorisms, theorems, thoughts, ideas, definitions, equivalences, hints, fragments, advertisements, absurdities, innovations, hypothetical situations, experiences, and reflections.

And it is the last word—*reflections*—that is the key to the resolution to *Motivating Teen and Preteen Readers*. The upcoming *prompts* review, summarize, and expand the diverse aspects of reading, reading life, creativity, imagination, and writing that teachers, parents, and kids encountered during the school year. These areas become interconnected through the plethora of questions answered and discussed in the mini-lessons.

Many concepts presented in the epilogue via the different strategies should sound familiar (and some unfamiliar) because they add up to the purposes of the books of questions. The epilogue reinforces topics from the questions in Books 1 to 4.

The books of questions target adolescents' motivation to read, and revitalize attitudes and understanding held by educators, parents, and other concerned people in a time of high-stakes testing. The epilogue's provocative material is yet another assessment of the year's work. It will bring discussion leaders and kids back to the heart of reading and reading life, the one building block that is fuel for launching the reading rocket into outer and inner space: *motivation.*

Let this concluding compilation return everyone involved with literacy in and out of the classroom to one major ideal which has been missing in recent years in the school: to have a little passionate fun with reading, and also, to have a respite, to take a holiday and get some space away from test instruction.

Maybe, if the questions do anything, it will keep the eyes of educators, administrators, policy makers, politicians, teachers, parents, and students—readers all—on the real prize: that reading and writing are peaceful journeys, which hopefully still have meaning today.

HOW TO SELECT PROMPTS

Enjoy *skimming* the prompts or sparks. Scan the epilogue randomly to see what pops out. Check the ones you like and that cover the questions asked in the mini-lessons. Then, reread your selections in groups of three to five prompts by *stopping, thinking, and brainstorming responses mentally* (similar to skimming the four books for questions).

Discussion leader: What answers are triggered while brainstorming the chosen prompts? Notice any connections demonstrated between reading and writing. Also, look over prompts on creativity and imagination that are main ingredients in the one-year long project, areas most likely covered in questions on reading and reading life, and that can be applied during the final month.

Review the prompts before reading Book 4's questions to have an idea of where the book is going, and then search for accessible, practical ones good for classroom/home use. Let your kids rule the court with their responses; after all, a student-centered approach features kids as the major players who will determine their reading destinies—of course, with a little help from their friends, teachers, and parents.

Note: Do not try to read all the prompts at once because it's too much to absorb.

APPLYING PROMPTS IN RAPS AND MINI-LESSONS

Think about it: You might want to throw out some sparks in your raps as *quickie questions* to see how they would respond and get a dialogue going. In this approach, the prompts become *catalysts* to synthesize many experiences from the books of questions. Read a prompt and let the kids brainstorm responses to it (whatever comes to mind). Wait for different answers and then go on to another prompt. Keep the brainstorming rap going at a fast pace: try to get in a few prompts in one session. If one prompt has an overwhelming response from students/child, stick with it for the duration of the rap, and elaborate on it with expansive discussion questions.

Use prompts as additional questions—an alternative approach—in class mini-lessons. Your *throw-outs* can be brainstormed collaboratively by a class and in a one-to-one student-parent situation. Instead of writing responses to the given mini-lesson question, kids brainstorm responses orally to the ideas triggered by the prompts. This provides a welcome change from writing done throughout the year. Teacher/parent raps and discussions should prove quite interesting at the end of a long road of questioning.

VISUALIZING BRAINSTORMING SESSIONS

Simply read a prompt and let students/child respond with their conjured-up thoughts, ideas, feelings, images, reflections, memories, and experiences. Present the following sparks to your class/child in a fictional brainstorming session and visualize what might happen. Imagine the possible responses to the prompts: imagine, yeah, imagine. . . .

* Read for power.
* The life of a word goes on and on. . . .
* Wake up and read, wake up and read. . . .
* "What is reading but silent communication."
* "There is creative reading as well as creative writing."
* Peaceful reading . . .

Stop . . . for a moment of reflection: Where would the prompts take the kids? Where do they take *you*?
Check out more sparks and see where they might go with them:

* Read to feel, to be, to release, to see, to understand.
* Reading is the mother of invention.
* My early reading life, my early reading self . . .
* Reading in the zone: hypnotic concentration
* The real motivation to read comes from inside—*you*.

The epilogue balloons into a massive reflection about the questions asked and answered. Cranking out epilogue prompts should inspire everyone: teachers, parents, and students alike. Things will make more sense at the end after composing an ode to reading life. These sparks, according to the author's experiences, will *motivate kids to motivate themselves to read*, to find a passion for reading and writing through their interconnections. It works if you believe, and, as New York Mets pitcher Tug McGraw said years ago to all the sinking hearts of New York Met fans during a tight pennant race: "You gotta believe."

SAMPLE BRAINSTORMING SESSION

The brainstorming sessions, whether it's for a whole class, small group, or an individual (one-to-one child-parent situation), are rapid-fire fifteen-minute lessons where you basically keep *throwing out* prompts or sparks. Ask students/child to respond orally with answers connected to the given reading/reading life prompts (or creativity/imagination and writing prompts). The discussion leader calls out the spark and kids respond with answers. Use several prompts per session to activate the *kids'* accumulated knowledge and wisdom acquired *by* responding to the questions. (*Note*: Discussion leader = DL, and the different students = S1, S2, S3, etc.)

DL: (prompt) *Peaceful reading . . .*

S1: Reading in the library

S2: Reading sitting under a shady tree

S3: Just feeling good reading a good book

S4: Reading relaxes me before I go to sleep.

DL: (prompt) *Books = connections*

S5: What are books connections to?

DL: Yes, that's the question. . . .

DL: Can you figure out what are the connections?

S5: The world

S6: History of the world

S7: Myself, my life, my everyday life

S8: Feelings

S9: Thoughts and ideas

S10: Experiences, dreams, memories

S11: Nature, flowers, trees, animals

S12: Outer space, the planets, and dinosaurs

S13: To everything . . .

DL: (prompt) *Reading is a see cruise. . . . Won't you take yourself on a see cruise?*

S15: What is a "see cruise"?

DL: Can anyone describe a "see cruise" in reading?

S17: You see things when you read.

S18: Yeah, you visualize things, worlds, people, and scenes.

DL: So what do you see on a reading "see cruise"? What have you seen lately?

S14: I see wolves running together in a pack.

S20: I see beautiful countries outside the U.S.

S24: I see how to draw people.

S26: I see players in a sports book playing a game of basketball.

DL: (prompt) *Word explosions . . .*

S5: What's that?

S6: When a word blows up. . . .

S7: A word just goes off or pops in your mind.

DL: What word blows up or erupts if you put it in your mind?

S12: Pizza . . . I just see all that cheese and tomato sauce dripping down in my mouth.

S13: A ham sandwich . . .

S27: Homework. It's like a chain that keeps me strapped to my desk all afternoon.

S29: Snow makes me sing and pray there'll be no school the next day. I see winter wonderland.

If a prompt doesn't connect with the students/child, that is, if the brainstorming is just not coming, either skip it, or let a student/child explain it (or *you* give a quickie explanation) and then let them respond orally. Keep at least ten prompts with you in the final week of the project. If you should use the prompts as a quickie rap, make sure you have three to five on hand.

Parents, in a one-to-one with a child, can let her brainstorm responses alone. However, if responding stops, you can brainstorm another response of your own to keep the session going. Again, like a classroom teacher, "prompt" the child with questions so she will understand what the prompt means and can continue brainstorming answers.

READING AND READING LIFE PROMPTS

Reading is all about the action in the mind's magic reading theater.

Read for power.

The solitude created by reading is your sanctuary from everyday life.

Thinking about what you read is what makes you a reader, a *real* reader.

The best things in life are free—and so is reading and reading life.

The life of a word goes on and on and on. . . .

Words, words, words, I got nothing but words in and on my mind.

Books = teachers, counselors, poets, parents, brothers, sisters, friends, and pets

Where are you when you read? Are you in your mind, body, heart, brain, or the book? *Where* are you really?

Do you become an *imaginary being* when you read a book? *Who* are you when you read?

Is it possible that you *leave your body* when reading a great novel?

Why don't kids reflect when they read?

Reading is reflection and you must force yourself to look back at the words.

Wake up and read, wake up and read. . . .

"Words are the voice of the heart." (Confucius)

Words = thoughts

Reading jumpstarts life, passion, beauty, and infinity.

"We read to know that we are not alone." (C. S. Lewis)

Reading will find you your place under the sun. . . .

"I have never known any distress that an hour's reading did not relieve." (Montesquieu)

Did you ever put a magnifying glass to a word?

"You'll never be alone with a poet in your pocket." (John Adams)

Words are power.

"To learn to read is to light a fire; every syllable that is spelled out is a spark." (Victor Hugo, *Les Misérables*)

"What is reading but silent communication." (Walter Savage Landor)

Has a word ever hypnotized you?

"We shouldn't teach great books, we should teach a love of reading." (B. F. Skinner)

Read and never be lonely. . . .

"There is creative reading as well as creative writing." (Ralph Waldo Emerson)

"There is an art of reading, as well as an art of thinking, and an art of writing." (Issac D'Israeli)

What *stuff* lies below the words you write, read, speak, and imagine?

My reading list of books is i-n-f-i-n-i-t-e. . . .

"It is well to read everything of something, and something of everything." (Lord Henry P. Brougham)

Peaceful reading . . .

Reading does for *you*, what *you* do for it. . . .

Read to feel, to release, to see, to understand.

Reading is not just reading. . . .

My books, my self, and my reading selves . . .

Your words are you.

Reading brings awareness.

It's not what your reading can do for *you*, but what *you* can do for your reading.

Reading and writing go together wherever they go. . . .

Ahh, the good reading life . . . how sweet it is. . . .

Open a book, open a mind.

Go ahead, read and drive yourself crazy, I dare you. . . .

Do you read and believe?

Readers just want to have fun.

Reading and the reflection connection . . . go on and on and on. . . .

He's got word power, look at him go, go, go. . . .

What was the last word that blew out the lights in your mind?

"A real book is not the one we read, but the one that reads us." (W. H. Auden)

Readers and words: You can't have one without the other.

"Fair words gladden so many a heart." (Henry Wadsworth Longfellow)

Reading is a mystery defined by *magic*.

Reading balances the real and the unreal.

A good book to read at bedtime fills in the blanks of the day.

Books are celebrations of the self and humankind.

"Books are not men yet they stay alive." (Steven Vincent Benet)

Readers are not born, they grow themselves.

He surrounded himself with thousands of books and this is what he saw:

Paradise lost: reading

Can a word *beat you up*?

Did you ever *get lost in a word*?

The bookworm climbs a ladder that spirals round and round a monolithic book case in search of a life to live.

"To read and drive the night away." (Geoffrey Chaucer)

To read and drive myself away . . .

"One kind word can warm three winter months." (Chinese proverb)

Do words *fight* in your mind?

Words sweet as honey . . .

A word that lasts forever . . .

"Winged words." (Homer, "Smyrns of Chios," *The Iliad*)

Action words: Can you visualize them in your mind?

Are you aware of the words that come out of your mouth?

Reading = meaning

Reading: freedom for the open mind

Reading as a window to the heart . . .

Reading is the mother of invention.

Reading = solitude

Silent reading = prayer

Reading = contemplation

Reading is the freedom-to-BE.

Visualization is the art and science of reading.

> "A word is dead,
> When it is said,
> Some say.
> I say it just begins
> To live that day."
>
> —Emily Dickinson

Words are free to take you anywhere you want to go. . . .

Reading = intensity

Reading = peace

"Some books leave us free and some books make us free." (Ralph Waldo Emerson)

Reading's solitude surrounds a noisy self.

"It is not true that we have only one life to live; if we can read, we can live as many more lives and as many kinds of lives as we wish." (S. I. Hayakawa)

Become a reader and never go home again. . . .

It's a wonderful life: books.

What are your *magic words*?

Read and write before you lose it. . . .

"I cannot live without books." (Thomas Jefferson)

"Many a book is like a key to unknown chambers within the castle of one's own self." (Franz Kafka)

Do you have book friends? Yes, I have book friends.

"I am part of everything I read." (John Kieran)

"To acquire the habit of reading is to construct for yourself a refuge from almost all the miseries of life." (W. Somerset Maugham)

"When you sell a man a book, you don't sell him 12 ounces of paper and ink and glue — you sell him a whole new life." (Christopher Morley)

"The books which help you most are those which make you think the most." (Theodore Parker)

Which words *wake you up*?

Which word(s) would you like to possess?

Which word(s) possess you?

Go back to the books you read when you first started reading and think about why you liked them. Return to and visualize yourself at age five, six, or seven and recall your reading life. . . . My early reading life, my early reading self . . .

"If we look beyond ourselves, past our bodies and minds, we would see millions of words, an infinite landscape of words, because we are words that never stop, because we say, read, imagine, see and think them and dream them, our lives are our words, our lives, our words, we are words, we are living, breathing words: Imagine a kid growing up nowadays thinking such thoughts, these fancies, this expansion of what we really are, and now, imagine the same child looking at a book. What would she see?" (Jeffrey Pflaum)

Books = connections

"Every word we speak is million-faced or convertible to an indefinite number of applications. If it were not so we could read no book. Your remark would only fit your case, not mine." (Ralph Waldo Emerson)

Reading = cheap thrills

Reading = reflection = meaning = meta-cognition: thinking about thinking

Reading creates space and time in solitude.

How do you see mind-pictures while reading?

What does the inner or mind's eye look like? What is this imaginary concept?

"Thinking in pictures precedes thinking in words." (Immanuel Kant)

Reading in the zone: hypnotic concentration

Reading in the *bubble* of yourself . . .

The reading self: Is it real or unreal?

Your reading world is a virtual reality in the mind's magic reading theater.

Between readers and writers: a cross-fertilization of ideas.

Reading is about emotional intelligence: self-efficacy, self-reliance, self-motivation, self-discipline, self-control, self-guidance, self-understanding, self-knowledge, self-awareness.

Reading is personal: intrapersonal and interpersonal.

Listen to the words you read. . . .

The kingdom of reading lies within. . . .

The real motivation to read comes from inside—you.

Reading leads to questions, and if it doesn't, what are you doing?

Reading leads to never-ending questions about everything.

Reading is a virtual reality: you're living in a parallel universe, an imaginary landscape called the mind's magic reading theater when you change words into pictures.

Find the love you lost in reading. . . .

Parents, teach your children well: Read to them.

Readers re-create the created and uncreated worlds of writers: They reinvent what was invented, making reading a creative act or process.

Reading is not all about speed: It's about *"stopping by woods on a snowy evening."*

Reflect on words and create a deeper reality to reading life and real life—the poets do. . . .

All we are saying is give reading a chance. . . .

The pace of reading creates lifelong readers.

The peace of reading _____.

Read before you go to sleep: pleasant dreams. . . .

Good readers who don't read: Why?

Bad readers who hate to read: Why?

Illiteracy = fear of failure or fear of success: Why? Why?

Reading is demanding: sorry. . . .

Get engaged: read!

For adolescents only: Fight for your reading freedom, independence, and identity.

Find out who you are: Read.

Have you ever gotten the feeling that your words never land anywhere?

Can you be a serious and a happy reader at the same time?

Reading is a *see cruise*. . . . Won't you take yourself on a *see cruise*?

My travels with books _____.

Grow a reading life like you grow a garden. . . .

What are the "right" words?

What are the "wrong" words?

Do words mean anything to you?

Is there reading without learning?

Rereading = re-creation

The loneliest pleasure of reading _____.

"Poetry can be wittier and funnier than any kind of writing; it can tell us
about the world through words we can't forget. . . ." (Gerald D. McDonald,
anthologist)

"I remember the special quiet of rainy days when I felt I could enter the pages
of my picture books." (Jan Brett, author)

If you believe in books, do you believe in magic?

Did this ever *happen* to you? "Books began to happen to me, and I began to believe in nothing but books and the world in books. . . ." (Langston Hughes)

Picture this: The perfect reading life . . .

Read, reread, read, reread, read, reread, read, reread, read, reread. . . .

Why that poor little girl almost lost herself in a book: It's wonderful, wonderful, oh so wonderful, my child. . . .

Reading is *drawing* in the mind. . . .

Go to your heart to find the *good* words.

Words that make you grumble . . .

"A good book has no ending." (R. D. Cumming, author)

I walk into a tunnel and all I have to say is Pinocchiiiiiiiiiiiii-
ooooooooooooooooooooooooooo. . . .

Ah, to read, to leave myself behind, that my friend, is what I call dreaming . . .
dream, dream, dream, dream. . . .

The words you speak, read, write, think, imagine, dream, remember, experience, and feel create your history, your real life story.

"Words are things; and a small drop of ink,
Falling like dew upon a thought, produces
That which makes thousands, perhaps millions, think."

　　　　　　　　　　　　　　—Lord Byron

"By words the mind is winged." (Aristophanes)

Everything you read becomes *yours*. . . .

A book is something you hold on to, and if you read it right, it will hold on to
you. . . .

"Everyone is full of words waiting to sing as a forest full of birds before sun-
rise." (Harry Behn)

Poetry in motion: words living inside words . . .

"Words, when well chosen, have so great a force in them that a description
often gives us more lively ideas than the sight of things themselves." (Joseph
Addison)

"What can a poem do? Just about anything." (Eve Merriam)

A love of reading _____.

Reading = possibilities

Books are not only words and words and more words on pages and pages and
more pages, but collages, impressions, abstractions, paintings, driftwood,
and symphonies. . . .

Reading = renaissance

Reading takes you beyond the *now*. . . .

How do you read a sentence? That is the question of reading.

"I think we should read only the kind of books that wound and stab us." (Franz Kafka)

I put myself in a trance the second I pick up a book to read: Why does that happen?

Reading = self-hypnosis

Did a page from a book you were reading ever become luminous?

Reading should, at times, take you out of your *comfort zone*. . . .

Take it easy when you read. . . .

Taking *side trips* while you read can be pleasurable and challenging off-road reflections.

Speedo-reader just suffered his ninety-ninth manic-reading breakdown.

"Words! Mere words! How terrible they were! How clear, and vivid and cruel! One could not escape from them. And yet what a subtle magic there was in them! They seemed to be able to give a plastic form to formless things, and to have a music of their own as sweet as that of the viol or lute. Mere words! Was there anything so real as words?" (Oscar Wilde, *The Picture of Dorian Gray*)

When I read, I live in books; and when I live, I live in life.

"All my life I have been trying to learn to read, to see and hear, and to write." (Carl Sandburg)

"Books are lighthouses erected in the great sea of time." (E. P. Whipple)

Read to feel yourself. . . .

Read to see if you're *there*. . . .

Reading is about the silence inside you and what you hear. . . .

What is a reader's paradise?

Hey, don't bother me when I'm inside my reading cloud floating along in the jet streams of my imagination.

Word winds

Tornado words

Word tornadoes

A cyclone of words

Words as cyclones

It's raining words. . . .

Words falling through the sky like little baby lullabies . . .

Drumming words

Ricocheting words

Boomerang words

Word flurries

Word storms

Word-storming

Word explosions
Luminous words
Flurries of sparkling words . . .
One bad word can freeze the heart.
Imagine all the solitude that goes into writing books. . . . That same solitude
    finds the reader.
Charley the talking parrot kept eating words instead of seeds until he morphed
    into a dictionary. . . . No thesaurus for you tonight, kiddo. . . .
Read intensely.
Read and reflect,
    read and reflect,
    read and reflect,
    read and reflect. . . .
Listen to the words inside you because they have something to say and express.
Words = nuclei of thoughts
"Words have no wings but they can fly many thousands of miles." (Korean
    proverb)
"Every spoken word is a covering for the inner self. A little curtain-flick no
    wider than a slice of roast meat can reveal hundreds of exploding suns."
    (Rumi, "The Night Air")
Reread = renew, refresh, rejuvenate, revive, revitalize, reactivate, rekindle
"By words the mind is excited and the spirit elated." (Aristophanes)
"Books let us into their souls and lay open to us the secrets of our own." (Wil-
    liam Hazlitt)
"In reading, a lonely quiet concert is given to our minds, all our mental facul-
    ties will be present in this symphonic exaltation." (Stephane Mallarme)
Books are quiet: I live inside their peaceful solitude where no one and no-thing
    can interfere.
Reading gets you in touch with the mysteries of your own solitude and inner
    peace.
Reading connects you with the mysteries of the real and the unreal.
Read through the night and through your fears . . .
What book puts you in a good mood?
Books = wonderlands
A closed mind catches no ideas.
Books = re-creation of reality as a virtual reality
Reading is p-a-n-o-r-a-m-i-c.
Watch the show inside the mind's magic reading theater using a wide-angle
    camera lens: your inner eye.
"For me, the novel is experience illumined by imagination." (Ellen Glasgow)
"A book—a well-composed book—is a magic carpet on which we are wafted
    to a world we cannot enter in any other way." (Caroline Gordon)

Reading enriches, accompanies, augments, complements, and enhances you, the reader.

When you speak, you create a story in the mind's magic writing theater, like a writer writing.

What does a *bad* book steal from you?

"The end of reading is not more books but more life." (Holbrook Jackson)

"If you believe everything you read, better not read." (Japanese proverb)

How can the private worlds of writers ever change *your* life?

"Reading furnishes the mind only with knowledge; it is thinking that makes what we read ours." (John Locke)

"Outside of a dog, a book is probably a man's best friend, and inside a dog, it's too dark to read." (Groucho Marx)

"I find television very educational. Every time someone switches it on I go into another room and read a good book." (Groucho Marx)

Reading = refuge

Books = quiet harbors

Books = daily spas for the mind and imagination

Books = home away from home

Read a book and *return to yourself.* . . .

Reading = prayer

Can a reader go crazy reading a book? Or, can a book go crazy reading a reader? Which is it?

"A teacher walked by my room and observed my class reading silently and said he thought he was in a religious school where the kids were praying—one of the greatest compliments I received about my teaching." (Jeffrey Pflaum)

What is a good book?

What book changed your life? Can you please answer the question, please?

Libraries = the last frontier of peace, love, and happiness in reading

What does the landscape of a passionate reader's mind look like?

Reading is the fastest transportation, carrier, vehicle, channel, agent, medium to anywhere, somewhere, and sometimes, nowhere. . . .

What kind of *mind-map* does reading books create in you?

This is my book that sits on my night table and waits quietly and patiently for me at the end of the day, any kind of day—it doesn't matter. . . .

Do you remember anything you read, or do you forget everything?

If you read a book and stop to stare out the window, are you reflecting, daydreaming, spacing out, or looking at your reflection in the glass?

Picture this: a little kid reading and looking at the illustrations in a big picture book and smiling while his mother massages his head so he can take off into his cool dream worlds. . . .

"Words are really atoms zooming and circulating in your mind at supersonic speeds so you can't see all their meanings and their *lives*, there's just too much for you to watch, and the sight of multitudes of universes all at once would blow out the lights in your head and home." (Jeffrey Pflaum)

Reading and contemplating . . .

Reading and rolling down the river . . .

Reading under the sun . . .

CREATIVITY AND IMAGINATION PROMPTS

An open mind leads to a creative imagination. . . .

Creativity means taking risky trips to unknown places.

Creativity = no fear

To be creative is to keep moving on and changing: to empower.

Creative imagination means *"staying alive, staying alive, staying alive. . . ."*

See the creativity in words and discover new virtual worlds: Reinvent your reading life and everyday life.

Absurd ideas live in the imagination, so why not use them to start your story?

Experimenting = the creative life

I create, therefore I grow.

Reading is a hip-hop concert when the mind's magic reading theater rocks in three dimensions.

Reading is the re-creation of a parallel universe imagined by a writer.

If reading is creative, then the more you read, the more you create, and the more you practice reading, the more creative you'll become.

Creating is simple: Just make up things and have fun with your thoughts.

Creating means letting go . . .

Change, change, change . . . break a string in my heart, heart, heart. . . .

The power of creativity. . . .

Think in mental pictures and you will see all the *pretty horses.* . . .

Did you ever see *golden apples* in your mind? *Now you have.* . . .

Creativity is all detours. . . .

I imagine my heart: I see hearts, hearts, hearts. . . .

Reading opens the doors of perception and the windows of imagination.

How far can a little imagination go in reading? *Answer*: A long way. . . .

Curious, George? Go creative. . . .

Put an idea in your imagination. Wait for a picture to appear: So where are you and how do you feel?

Put butter on your corn, add some salt, and chomp away, baby: *How good was that?*

Look up and watch the clouds float by so you can imagine all day long. . . .

Imagination *rules* reading life and real life.

Make things happen: imagine and create. . . .

Where do your ideas come from?

"Imagination is the living power and prime agent of all human perception." (Samuel Taylor Coleridge)

"No one travels so high as he who knows not where he is going." (Oliver Cromwell)

Lost? Dial 1-800-IMAGINE.

Creative-thinking = EMPOWERMENT

"Imagination is more important than knowledge. For while knowledge defines all we currently know and understand, imagination points to all we might yet discover and create." (Albert Einstein)

Imagine the feeling of peace . . . and world peace. . . . *How does it feel?*

Do you lose track of time when you're deep in your imagination?

To live in reality you need an imagination.

The first step to change is imagining it . . . and the second step is creating it. . . .

The courage to create . . . is the courage to be. . . .

"The human mind once stretched by a new idea never goes back to its original dimensions" (Oliver Wendell Holmes)

The truth of your real life lies inside your imagination.

Look with your imagination and see the world new every day and everywhere.

"Everything you can imagine is real." (Pablo Picasso)

"We are what we imagine ourselves to be." (Kurt Vonnegut)

Creative thinking leads to critical thinking.

The best way to get a lot of ideas is to brainstorm . . . and then take your best shot. . . .

Here's a brush: Now paint a picture in your imagination and describe it . . . so????

Open up your mind and imagination and live the good reading and writing life. . . .

"Imagination is the beginning of creation." (George Bernard Shaw)

Your imagination lives in the past, present, and future: Where is yours right now? Prove it. . . .

Creation means meditation.

If imagination has no boundaries, how would it affect your reading and reading life?

"To think creatively, we must be able to look afresh at what we normally take for granted." (George Kneller)

Imagine that you're a *genius.* . . .

Imagine living in an upside-down world: Where would your head be at?

"What lies behind us and what lies before us are tiny matters compared to what lies in us." (Ralph Waldo Emerson)

Once you expand your imagination, you can go *anywhere.* . . .

Imagining = hanging *l o o s e r* and *l o o s e r* and *l o o s e r.* . . .

Dreaming inside my imagination . . .

Drop a *dove* inside your imagination and see where it flies. . . .

Connect the quote to the imagination: "You cannot step twice into the same river; for other waters are continually flowing in." (Heraclitus)

Words become music, a concert, in the mind's magic reading theater.

Creativity makes the imagination go round. . . .

To create means to take a trip in the dark and grab some light wherever you can find it before you get to the end of the tunnel. . . .

Reading creates dream worlds.

Creativity is a roll of the dice. . . .

Where does your heart fit into your creativity and imagination?

The beauty of imagination is _____.

"My eyes make pictures when they are shut." (Samuel T. Coleridge)

Let your imagination go and see what happens: Who knows? You could wind up in paradise. . . .

Creative power leads to self-motivation, self-education, and passionate readers.

Read and imagine . . . and imagine . . . and imagine. . . .

What's so difficult about creativity? You create your life every day. . . .

When I look inside my imagination, *all I see is black*. . . . Why?

Creativity: *making something from nothing.*

Creativity = self-entertainment

To create, to imagine, to dream, to be at peace with yourself . . .

The creative imagination makes the real world a surreal world in the mind's magic reading and writing theaters.

Imagination is always going somewhere; even in sleep, it moves inside your dreams. . . .

Imagination = devil or angel?

"Creativity is a type of learning process where the teacher and pupil are located in the same individual." (Arthur Koestler)

"The writer's creative imagination lies in the kingdom of writing, the mind's magic writing theater, where images are not just images, but 3-D virtual realities, with the writer holding the control stick via his inner eye." (Jeffrey Pflaum)

"The possible's slow fuse is lit by the imagination." (Emily Dickinson)

Reading = re-creation

"If you intend to see the phenomenal holographic realities of the mind's magic reading theater, better stayed tuned and don't hit the remote switch too quickly, or you'll be lost in space, inner space. . . ." (Jeffrey Pflaum)

Creativity, like reading, is magical.

Creativity = mind magic

Creativity = magic shows

How do you get a good imagination? Practice, practice, practice. . . .

What's the longest trip you ever took in your imagination?

Which is scarier: the pictures you see in your imagination or a horror movie?
"Creativity = coming together of energy, concentration, reflection, visualiza-
tion, thinking, feeling, perception, freedom, peace, inner and outer space,
love, contemplation, passion, motivation, humor, sensation, intuition, bore-
dom, anxiety, fear, anger, and anything else you can add . . . *that's some
recipe.*" (Jeffrey Pflaum)
Creativity = *search me*?
Clear your mind before you create—meditate. . . .
Don't worry, be happy: create. . . .
I imagine, therefore I see. . . .
Imagine, yeah, imagine. . . .
Imagination = creation: the roots of reading and writing
Is the imagination connected to the heart, or are they separate worlds?
Is your imagination real?
Can you visualize the *tree* I'm imagining right now?
"Imagination . . . its limits are only those of the mind itself." (Rod Serling)
Imagination is the unreal life that makes your life *real.*
Are *you* your imagination?
What sees further: your inner eye or your real, outer eyes?
Imagining is self-empowering.
Imagine, dream, and be. . . .
Imagination = inner space magic shows
Imagination works fast, but what if you made it go real slow? What would
you see?
Are there boundaries to the imagination? Answer: Think about *outer space.* . . .
You can travel as far as your imagination takes you. . . .
Go fly a kite in your imagination and see where it takes you: So *where* did
you go?
Imagination = revival, rebirth, resurgence
What happens if you mix reality with imagination?
Did you ever feel like you were an *imaginary being*?
"The gift of fantasy has meant more to me than my talent for absorbing posi-
tive knowledge." (Albert Einstein)
"Logic will get you from A to B. Imagination will take you everywhere."
(Albert Einstein)
Nonsense makes sense to your imagination.
"He who has imagination without learning has wings but no feet." (Joseph
Joubert)
"The most beautiful thing we can experience is the mysterious. It is the source
of true art and science. He to whom the emotion is a stranger, who can no
longer pause and stand wrapped in awe, is as good as dead; his eyes are
closed." (Albert Einstein)

WRITING PROMPTS

Writing takes you to unknown places, and that's a good thing, but a little scary.
. . .

Writing means living different *lives* in your imagination at one time.

Writing: dream on, dream on, dream on. . . .

Write to wonder. . . .

Write to connect. . . .

Writing is about connecting to words.

Write soft and tender words to sing lullabies in your imagination.

Write to see the world through your reflections. . . .

Write from your dreams. . . .

Write if you care or you don't: Just feel the vibe running down your arm to your fingers.

Writing = self-efficacy

Writing means listening to your *inner writing voice.*

Write, write, write = right, right, right

"Writing only leads to more writing." (Colette)

Writing is a *lonely pleasure* like reading.

Writing is man's escape *from* and *to* himself.

Write to collect your thoughts. . . .

Write to *see* better. . . .

Write to open the doors of perception.

Write to change your thoughts and feelings.

Write to celebrate yourself.

Writing, like reading, is magical and mysterious.

Writing = healing

Your writing, your self . . . your writing selves . . .

Write to know yourself.

Writing from the dark side of your mind *lightens you up.*

Have you ever felt you had to write or else your insides would explode?

Is writing painful?

Is there such a thing as "painless" writing?

Write P-L-A-I-N-L-Y so everyone can *see* what you have to say.

Everyone has something important to say: *So write your heart out, baby.* . . .

"Turn those bad feelings into words, more and more words, and the more you write, the more you'll change the vibes, that is what words and writing can do for you." (Jeffrey Pflaum)

Write: *get into it, and get it out.* . . .

Keep on writing until you hit a vein of black gold and watch the words gush up.

Lose yourself to the words on the paper when you write.

"What release to write so that one forgets oneself, forgets one's companion, forgets where one is or what one is going to do next to be drenched in sleep or in the sea. Pencils and pads and curling blue sheets alive with letters heap up on the desk." (Anne Morrow Lindbergh)

Writing is about remembering.

Write to discover yourself *hidden* in all the words.

Writing, like reading, can be a process of self-discovery.

If you read to escape, why not write to escape to your private, little world?

Write about something in order to forget it.

"Got something on your mind, but don't know what it is, write it out on paper, yes, that's right, keep on writing until it all comes out." (Jeffrey Pflaum)

"You're kidding, you got nothing to say? Start looking at your day, at what happened: Focus closely, look in and reflect. Did you find something? *I knew you would.*" (Jeffrey Pflaum)

To write means to step inside your imagination and listen to what you have to say.

"Write about what you know. But I don't know nothing. So write about yourself. But I don't know myself. So write about what you don't know—about yourself." (Jeffrey Pflaum)

Got nothing to do? Write. Find out what's on your mind. . . .

Are you *dead* or *alive*? What? You don't know? So write, right away. . . .

Let your imagination go to work for you the moment your pen touches the paper. . . .

Writing is about solitude and silence like reading.

Read what you write, again and again, until it makes sense to you, and says what you mean.

Write until you get it right. Right?

"When you write, say it in your *voice*: What? You don't know *your voice*? Keep writing and it will come crying out and you'll hear it, loud and clear, sooner or later." (Jeffrey Pflaum)

Writers and readers = communicators

Writers and readers = artists

Writers read a lot.

Writers are daydreamers. . . .

Writers = mirrors and reflectors

Do you ever feel like you're in a *bubble* while writing?

"I want to write but more than that I want to bring out all kinds of things that lie buried deep in my heart." (Anne Frank)

Writing = releasing

Writing = EMPOWERMENT

Writing and reading = re-creations

Writing = thinking

Writing = visualization

Writing = reflection

Writing = sensation

Writing = self-education

I write, therefore I am. . . .

Writing = dreaming in the mind's magic writing theater

Write to make something beautiful.

Write for fun.

Write with love and peace in your heart.

Write to put a little love back in your heart. . . .

"Fill your paper with the breathings of the heart." (William Wadsworth)

Writing means showing yourself, who you really are.

Writers are not spaced out, they're *spaced in.* . . .

A writer's mind and imagination never stop running. . . .

Writing brings peace—or war? What do you think?

"Let your *real eyes* filter in life, living, and nature to the *inner eye.* Let it view
the images or stories in the mind's magic writing theater. Mix the events
with other realities, real or unreal, to transform experience into words, sentences, paragraphs, pages, into writing." (Jeffrey Pflaum)

"There are stories in everything. I've got some of my best yarns from park
benches, lampposts, and newspaper stands." (O. Henry)

"Writing is like polishing your shoes: You've got to keep rubbing to get that
shine out of the words." (Jeffrey Pflaum)

When you write, write from your heart, so you can feel it.

Write from your heart to make your readers feel what you feel.

Write for yourself, to express yourself, because you've got a lot to say.

Writing, like reading, is tuning in, in, in. . . .

Writing is feeling, just like reading.

Writing is a three-dimensional, virtual, holographic reality like reading.

"My task which I am trying to achieve is, by the power of the written word to
make you hear, make you feel—it is, after all, to make you see. That—and
no more, and it is everything." (Joseph Conrad)

The more you like to read, the more you'll like to write.

Writing will put wings on your thoughts and let you take off to worlds beyond
yourself.

Writing means the freedom to be *you.* . . .

Build your world: find yourself—write.

Writing will make you feel things like you never felt before. . . .

Writing tastes good if you write about food.

"Writing means constant change from moment to moment, so feel the force
and power of the winds blowing inside your mind and imagination." (Jeffrey Pflaum)

Slow down, focus, now focus more carefully, concentrate, contemplate, then
write. . . .

Write about what you know, or just make things up from your imagination.

Write how you speak.

"Writing means looking at the empty page in front of you and seeing something there: *Hey, I just saw my niece's cats Peanut and Valentine. . . .*" (Jeffrey Pflaum).

Read out loud what you write and see how it sounds. . . .

"My aim is to put down on paper what I see and what I feel in the best and simplest way." (Ernest Hemingway)

"Put it before them briefly so they will read it, clearly so they will appreciate it, picturesquely so they will remember it, and above all, accurately so they will be guided by its light." (Joseph Pulitzer)

"All the fun is how you say a thing." (Robert Frost)

Writing makes you forget about time.

Write, write, write: imagine, imagine, imagine. . . .

Write in the self-amusement park of your imagination.

Writing = self-abandonment

Writing and reading = self-communication

Writing = self-help

Writing = self-mastery

Writing is user-friendly.

Bibliography

Adler, Mortimer J. 1972. *How to Read a Book: The Classic Guide to Intelligent Reading.* New York: Simon & Schuster.

Ashton-Warner, Sylvia. 1963. *Teacher.* London: Virago.

Bettemann, Otto L. 1987. *The Delights of Reading: Quotes, Notes & Anecdotes.* Boston: David R. Godine.

Boggiano, A. K., A. Shields, M. Barrett, T. Kellam, E. Thompson, J. Simons, and P. Katz. 1992. "Helplessness Deficits in Children: The Role of Motivational Orientation." *Motivation and Emotion* 16:271–96.

Buchwald, Emilie, and Michael Dorris, eds. 1997. *The Most Wonderful Books.* Minneapolis: Milkweed Editions.

Cameron, J., and W. D. Pierce. 1994. "Reinforcement, Reward, and Intrinsic Motivation: A Meta-Analysis." *Review of Educational Research* 64:363–23.

Canfield, Jack, and Gay Hendricks. 2006. *You've Got to Read This Book! 55 People Tell the Story of the Book That Changed Their Life.* New York: HarperCollins.

Chabon, Michael. 2011. "On 'The Phantom Tollbooth.'" *New York Review of Books* 58, no. 10: 33.

Coady, Roxanne J., and Joy Johannessen, eds. 2006. *The Book That Changed My Life: 71 Remarkable Writers Celebrate the Books That Matter Most to Them.* New York: Penguin.

deBono, Edward. 1967. *The Use of Lateral Thinking.* London: Cape.

———. 1970. *Lateral Thinking: Creativity Step by Step.* New York: Harper & Row.

———. 1971. *Practical Thinking: 4 Ways to Be Right; 5 Ways to Be Wrong; 5 Ways to Understand.* London: Cape.

Deci, E. L., and R. M. Ryan. 1985. *Intrinsic Motivation and Self-Determination in Human Behavior.* New York: Plenum.

Dirda, Michael. 2000. *Readings: Essays and Literary Entertainments.* Bloomington: Indiana University Press.

———. 2004. *An Open Book: Chapters from a Reader's Life.* New York: Norton.

———. 2005. *Book by Book: Notes on Reading and Life.* New York: Henry Holt.

Eco, Umberto. 2005. *The Mysterious Flame of Queen Loana.* Orlando, FL: Harcourt.

Frey, N., and D. Fisher. 2006. "'You Got More of These?' Re-engaging Adolescent Readers and Writers with Meaningful Texts." *RHI* 1:7–12.

Gilbar, Steven. 1999. *The Reader's Quotation Book: A Literary Companion.* New York: Barnes & Noble.

Jackson, Holbrook. 2001. *The Anatomy of Bibliomania.* Chicago: University of Illinois Press.

———. 2001. *The Reading of Books.* Chicago: University of Illinois Press.

Koch, Kenneth. 1973. *Rose, Where Did You Get That Red?* New York: Random House.

———. 1974. *Wishes, Lies, and Dreams: Teaching Children to Write Poetry.* New York: Chelsea House.

Lux, Thomas. 1997. "The Voice You Hear When You Read Silently." *New and Selected Poems, 1975–1995 by Thomas Lux.* New York: Houghton Mifflin Harcourt.

Manguel, Alberto. 1997. *A History of Reading.* New York: Penguin.

———. 2004. *A Reading Diary: A Passionate Reader's Reflections on a Year of Books.* New York: Farrar, Straus and Giroux.

Pamuk, Orham. 1998. *The New Life.* New York: Vintage International.

Pearl, Nancy. 2003. *Book Lust: Recommended Reading for Every Mood, Moment, and Reason.* Seattle: Sasquatch Books.

Pflaum, Jeffrey. 1992. "Contemplation Writing." *Teachers & Writers Magazine* 23 (5): 6–12.

Quindlen, Anna. 1998. *How Reading Changed My Life.* New York: Ballantine.

Scarry, Elaine. 1999. *Dreaming by the Book.* New York: Farrar, Straus, Giroux.

Schwartz, Lynn Sharon. 1996. *Ruined by Reading: A Life in Books.* Boston: Beacon.

Spufford, Francis. 2002. *The Child That Books Built: A Life in Reading.* New York: Henry Holt.

Zafon, Carlos Ruiz. 2004. *The Shadow of the Wind.* New York: Penguin.

About the Author

Jeffrey Pflaum has created original curricula in reading, writing, thinking, poetry, creativity, vocabulary, concentration, and emotional intelligence since the late 1960s to the present. His students' poetry has been published across the United States in college, secondary, children's, and writers' literary journals, as well as in newspapers, magazines, and by major book publishers.

Made in the USA
Lexington, KY
17 November 2013